MACHINE LEARNING IN TRANSLATION

Machine Learning in Translation introduces machine learning (ML) theories and technologies that are most relevant to translation processes, approaching the topic from a human perspective and emphasizing that ML and ML-driven technologies are tools for humans.

Providing an exploration of the common ground between human and machine learning and of the nature of translation that leverages this new dimension, this book helps linguists, translators, and localizers better find their added value in a ML-driven translation environment. Part 1 explores how humans and machines approach the problem of translation in their own particular ways, in terms of word embeddings, chunking of larger meaning units, and prediction in translation based upon the broader context. Part 2 introduces key tasks, including machine translation, translation quality assessment and quality estimation, and other Natural Language Processing (NLP) tasks in translation. Part 3 focuses on the role of data in both human and machine learning processes. It proposes that a translator's unique value lies in the capability to create, manage, and leverage language data in different ML tasks in the translation process. It outlines new knowledge and skills that need to be incorporated into traditional translation education in the machine learning era. The book concludes with a discussion of *human-centered machine learning in translation*, stressing the need to empower translators with ML knowledge, through communication with ML users, developers, and programmers, and with opportunities for continuous learning.

This accessible guide is designed for current and future users of ML technologies in localization workflows, including students on courses in translation and localization, language technology, and related areas. It supports the professional development of translation practitioners so that they can fully utilize ML technologies and design their own human-centered ML-driven translation workflows and NLP tasks.

Peng Wang is a freelance conference interpreter with the Translation Bureau, Public Works and Government Services Canada, a part-time professor in the School of Translation and Interpretation, University of Ottawa and Course designer and instructor for Think NLP and Machine Translation Masterclass at the Localization Institute. She has published two books in Chinese, including *Harry Potter and Its Chinese Translation*.

David B. Sawyer is Director of Language Testing at the U.S. State Department's Foreign Service Institute and a Senior Lecturer at the University of Maryland, USA. He is the author of *Foundations of Interpreter Education: Curriculum and Assessment* and co-editor of *The Evolving Curriculum in Interpreter and Translator Education: Stakeholder Perspectives and Voices* (both John Benjamins).

MACHINE LEARNING IN TRANSLATION

Peng Wang and David B. Sawyer

Routledge
Taylor & Francis Group

LONDON AND NEW YORK

Designed cover image: Getty Images | ipopba

First published 2023
by Routledge
4 Park Square, Milton Park, Abingdon, Oxon OX14 4RN

and by Routledge
605 Third Avenue, New York, NY 10158

Routledge is an imprint of the Taylor & Francis Group, an informa business

© 2023 Peng Wang and David B. Sawyer

The right of Peng Wang and David B. Sawyer to be identified as authors of this work has been asserted in accordance with sections 77 and 78 of the Copyright, Designs and Patents Act 1988.

British Library Cataloguing-in-Publication Data
A catalogue record for this book is available from the British Library

Library of Congress Cataloging-in-Publication Data
Names: Wang, Peng, 1975- editor. | Sawyer, David B., editor.
Title: Machine learning in translation / edited by Peng Wang,
    David Sawyer.
Description: Abingdon, Oxon ; New York, NY : Routledge, 2023. |
    Includes bibliographical references and index.
Identifiers: LCCN 2022041174 | ISBN 9781032343228 (hardback) |
    ISBN 9781032323800 (paperback) | ISBN 9781003321538 (ebook)
Subjects: LCSH: Translating and interpreting—Technological innovations. |
    Translating and interpreting—Data processing. | Machine learning. |
    LCGFT: Essays.
Classification: LCC P306.97.T73 M33 2023 | DDC 418/.020285631—
    dc23/eng/20221110
LC record available at https://lccn.loc.gov/2022041174

ISBN: 978-1-032-34322-8 (hbk)
ISBN: 978-1-032-32380-0 (pbk)
ISBN: 978-1-003-32153-8 (ebk)

DOI: 10.4324/9781003321538

Typeset in Bembo
by Apex CoVantage, LLC

CONTENTS

FIGURES

TABLES

INTRODUCTION

Machine learning in translation – a new perspective

Machine learning (ML) enables digital computer systems to automatically learn from a set of training data and make decisions based on the resulting model with a minimum level of human intervention. From a methodology perspective, machine learning is a form of statistical learning that uses computational algorithms to find patterns in empirical data, rather than symbolic rules developed through the analysis and intuitive reflection of humans. Neural machine translation (NMT) is driven by machine learning, which is applied to a neural network language model[1] so as to predict what word comes next in a sequence of translated text. There are many more language tasks where ML can be leveraged in a translation process.

In theory and practice, machine learning and translation do not have to be seen as separate undertakings. After all, there are clear links between human approaches to translation and a machine's processing of data, which also result in representations of thought and reality. While human approaches to translation follow long-established methods of theorization, machine approaches, originating by the way in the minds of computer scientists and software developers, utilize computer programs to automate part of the translation process.

Take an encoder-decoder ML architecture for example. In this model, machine learning converts a real-life translation task into a mathematical formula (encoding), and then after a series of arithmetic operations, it converts the mathematical formula into a translation solution (decoding). In this sense, ML can be considered at least a methodological and theoretical translation framework, although it may be premature to call it a paradigm equivalent to other translation theories such as equivalence, functionalism, descriptive translation studies (DTS), cultural or sociological 'turns' of translation studies, localization, or audiovisual translation theories, to name but several based primarily upon human analysis and reflection.

DOI: 10.4324/9781003321538-1

Let us use an analogy of a mirror to illustrate how different views come into play when perceiving translation. A mirror offers a perspective on reality, which from an objectivist viewpoint is a form of 'truth'. However, each individual stands in a slightly different place when looking into a mirror (Christie, 1987, pp. 53–54). If there exists a comprehensive 'truth' in translation, it would require the examination of the object of translation from different perspectives, allowing a 'truth' to be constructed through observation from multiple angles and stances. What individuals perceive in the mirror of 'truth' may vary, but all these reflections must have something in common, if they all – one might argue – are intended to represent some aspect of the same or at least a similar 'truth'.

This book introduces ML theories and technologies that are most relevant to translation processes by drawing parallels between these two areas. Following the analogy of a mirror offering multiple perspectives of the same object, we explore Machine Learning in Translation (MLinTrans) as a continuation of linguistic, communicative, and cognitive approaches to translation, rather than a separate discipline approached from the angle of computer programming and engineering. The following discussion is devoted to defining fundamental ML concepts and the scope of ML and translation for the purposes of this book.

Defining fundamental concepts

Machine learning is closely related to artificial intelligence (AI) and natural language processing (NLP). Following the mirror analogy discussed earlier, these related fields can be seen from various angles, with each one providing unique value.

Artificial intelligence: laying the groundwork

In the proposal for the Dartmouth Summer Research Project on Artificial Intelligence, McCarthy et al. (1955) coined the term itself and delineated the fundamental project task:

> The study is to proceed on the basis of the conjecture that every aspect of learning or any other feature of intelligence, can in principle be so precisely described that a machine can be made to simulate it. An attempt will be made to find how to make machines use language, form abstractions and concepts, solve kinds of problems now reserved for humans, and improve themselves.
>
> *(p. 12)*

In McCarthy's (2007) terms, AI is "the science and engineering of making intelligent machines, especially intelligent computer programs" (p. 2). Until now, AI has been used as an umbrella term covering a broad field of science encompassing not only computer science but also psychology, philosophy, linguistics, and other areas. Understandably, computer science is a reasonable starting point from which to approach AI. For example, Simon (1995) points out that "AI deals with some of the phenomena surrounding computers, hence is a part of computer science" (p. 95). However, computer scientists have not yet characterized in general what kinds of computational procedures can be called intelligent. Thus, definitions of intelligence typically depend on relating it to human intelligence (McCarthy, 2007, pp. 2–3).

Consequently, other areas of study contribute to the understanding of the concept of 'intelligence'. Many scholars define intelligence by what it does; for example, Nilson (2009) stated that "intelligence is that quality that enables an entity to function appropriately and with foresight in its environment" (pp. xiii–xvi).

Gardner (2003) incorporates cultural elements in his definition: "an intelligence is the ability to solve problems, or to create products, that are valued within one or more cultural settings" (p. xxviii). Some experiments were proposed to define the concept of intelligence from empirical, cognitive, and philosophical perspectives. For example, the Turing Test (Turing, 1950) posited that if a machine were perceived as human by a knowledgeable observer, then the machine could be considered intelligent. In the Chinese Room Argument, however, Searle (1980) argues that the Turing Test is inadequate. In this experiment, Searle imagines himself alone in a room following the steps of a computer program designed to provide responses to Chinese characters that are slipped under the door. Searle does not understand Chinese, and yet by following the computer program's steps for manipulating Chinese symbols and numerals, based simply upon their shape, he sends appropriate strings of Chinese characters back out under the door. His responses lead those outside to mistakenly assume that there is a Chinese speaker in the room, even though Searle does not understand the meaning of any of the Chinese characters. This analogy implies that programming a digital computer to follow Chinese syntax may make the computer appear to understand the meaning or semantics of Chinese, even though that is not the case (Cole, 2020).

The above definitions do not limit intelligence to humans. McCarthy (2007) stated that "varying kinds and degrees of intelligence occur in people, many animals and some machines" (p. 2). It follows that intelligence is not the only capacity that distinguishes humans from animals and machines, and intelligence does not account for every human mental activity. According to Martínez-Freire (1998), the mind is a collection of various classes of mental processes, and intelligence is only one of them. There are different approaches to describing relationships between the mind, intelligence, and spirit, depending on the field of study, scope of concept, and research purpose. No matter how advanced it may become, AI does not represent human capacity in its entirety.

AI will have a significant impact on the development of humanity in the near future. There are ethical issues relating to fundamental questions, such as what we should do with AI systems, what AI systems themselves should do, what risks they involve, and how we can control them (Müller, 2020). Machine learning is situated in the context of AI and thus incorporates many aspects of AI, including its interdisciplinary nature, its intrinsic relationship with humans, and related ethical considerations.

Natural language processing and translation

An important and useful application area of AI is natural language processing (NLP), which is a field of study that encompasses translation and other linguistic tasks. According to Liddy (2001),

> Natural Language Processing is a theoretically motivated range of computational techniques for analyzing and representing naturally occurring texts at one or more levels of linguistic analysis for the purpose of achieving human-like language processing for a range of tasks or applications.
>
> *(p. 1)*

This definition is a good starting point for us to explore the essential aspects of NLP in translation in a new context, two decades after it was created, which is summarized in the following.

1   In the early days of NLP research, 'naturally occurring texts' are usually considered texts gathered from actual usage of human language(s), rather than specifically constructed for the purpose of the analysis (see Liddy, 2001, p. 1). However, the situation has become more complex after two decades of development, as researchers and engineers have begun to manufacture or synthesize language data, resulting in non-naturally occurring texts involved in NLP processes such as machine translation (MT) engine training or other ML tasks. What remains unchanged is the purpose of NLP, in that NLP techniques are applied to accomplish 'natural language' tasks, rather than 'artificial language' tasks.

2   NLP is deeply rooted in linguistics and the use of computer systems to simulate the linguistic levels of analysis that humans usually apply. Liddy (2001) pointed out that the notion of "levels of linguistic analysis" refers to the fact that there are multiple types of language processing thought to be at work when humans produce or comprehend language and that humans normally utilize all of these levels since each construes different types of meaning (p. 1). While Liddy (2001) seemed to aim for a comprehensive list of levels of language, this book intends to start with the most relevant concept and the foundation of linguistic structure in translation, which we discuss in Chapter 2.

3   The goal of NLP as stated in Liddy (2001)'s definition is "for the purpose of achieving human-like language processing for a range of tasks or applications" (p. 1). In addition, the range of computational techniques is "theoretically motivated" (p. 1). In this book, we will further elaborate human purposes, or intentionality, when using NLP techniques relevant to a translation process as a solution for real-life translation problems, such as MT, automatic post-editing,

and MT quality estimation, which a translator or other domain expert is more likely to guide and support than a computer scientist. From a philosophical perspective, machines do not possess intentionality, which is solely in the minds of humans. We discuss this further in Chapter 6.

4   The word 'processing' serves as a basis for sub fields of NLP such as natural language understanding (NLU), which refers to machine reading comprehension, and natural language generation (NLG), which can transform data into human words in communication. Though some frameworks consider NLU and NLG to be disciplines separate from NLP, this book considers them part of NLP, as only the purpose of processing natural language differentiates these tasks.

NLP research can be traced back to the late 1940s. Since its inception, NLP has evolved from rule-based (symbolic) to machine-learning (statistical) approaches. Symbolic approaches perform deep analysis of linguistic phenomena and are based on explicit representation of facts about language through well-understood knowledge representation schemes and associated algorithms. The description of the levels of language analysis, such as words, phrases, sentences, and paragraphs, is given from a symbolic perspective. Another example is rule-based MT. This approach relies on human analysis of language, with human linguistic and world knowledge tapped directly in the language engineering process.

In contrast to symbolic approaches, statistical approaches use observable data, usually in the form of large corpora, as the primary source of evidence. Roughly speaking, statistical NLP associates probabilities with the alternatives encountered in the course of analyzing an utterance or a text and accepts the most probable outcome as the correct one (Mitkov, 2003, p. xix). A typical model following this approach is statistical MT. The CANDIDE research project at IBM took a strictly non-linguistic, purely statistical approach to MT (Brown et al., 1990). The statistical approach to natural language processing includes both statistical analysis and inference methods, the latter being consistent with applied ML, as it generalizes the statistical analysis results from limited observations to the whole population.

One particular statistical method is based on connectionism, which is a movement in cognitive science that attempts to explain intellectual abilities using artificial neural networks (also known as 'neural networks' or 'neural nets') (Buckner & Garson, 2019). An artificial neural network (ANN) is composed of a large number of very simple components wired together (Barrow, 1996, p. 135). The origin of connectionism is closely related to the collaboration between neurophysiologists and mathematicians/logicians. In 1943, Warren McCulloch (a neurophysiologist) and Walter Pitts (a logician) proposed the first mathematical model of a neural network, which is based on the physical assumptions of the 'all-or-none' character of nervous activity (i.e., the activity of a neuron is either 'firing' or inactive) and that a certain fixed number of synapses must be excited within the period of latent addition in order to excite a neuron at any time (McCulloch & Pitts, 1943, pp. 115–133).

ANNs allow neurophysiological principles to be described by mathematical formulations. However, rather than modeling brain mechanisms, as much more research is needed in terms of how our brains work, neural network models were inspired by and resemble the anatomy and physiology of the nervous system, as Barrow (1996) points out. Key aspects of many neural network models are that they are able to learn and their behavior improves with training or experience (p. 135). In this sense, a connectionist approach entails machine learning that reflects certain characteristics of human cognition; we compare machine learning and human learning in Chapter 8.

Traditional statistical approaches also develop generalized models from examples of linguistic phenomena. What separates neural network models from other statistical methods is that neural network models combine statistical learning with various theories of representation, allowing transformation, inference, and manipulation of logic formulae (Liddy, 2001, p. 9). In connectionist systems, linguistic models are harder to observe due to the fact that connectionist architectures are less constrained by humans than traditional statistical ones, given the complexity and large numbers of simple components or neurons as well as connections between them. A typical example of this approach is neural machine translation (NMT), which Google, Microsoft, and Meta (formerly Facebook) started to commercialize in 2016. We discuss neural network language models in Chapter 3.

Since the first public demonstration of machine translation, the Georgetown–IBM experiment performed in 1954 (Hutchins, 2004, p. 1), many systems have been built in the attempt to deal with natural language input or output. Yet NLP tasks are very challenging; as Kornai (2008) points out, "[t]hese tasks are so hard that Turing (1950) could rightly make fluent conversation in natural language the centerpiece of his test for intelligence" (p. 248). This is not surprising, considering how much time and effort a child or an adult requires to learn a language. Ultimately, human–computer interaction (HCI) is needed to achieve a real-life communication effect, and the way translators interact with computer programs is through language data, which we discuss in Chapter 7.

The transition from symbolic to statistical approaches does not mean that symbolic approaches, which were widely used in early stages of NLP, are out-of-date. In reality, problems may be better tackled with one or the other approach, and in some cases, the tasks become so complex that it may be impossible to choose a single best approach. The solution depends on the purpose – how humans intend to use NLP computational techniques to accomplish specific tasks.

Furthermore, as Klavans and Resnik (1996, p. x) point out, every use of statistics is based upon a symbolic mode. No matter the application, statistics are based upon a probability model, and that model is, at its core, symbolic and algebraic, rather than continuous and quantitative. Regardless of the details of the model, the numerical probabilities are meaningless except in the context of the model's symbolic underpinnings. In this view, there is no such thing as a 'purely statistical' method. Conversely, symbolic underpinnings alone are not enough to capture the variability inherent in naturally occurring linguistic data and its resistance to inflexible, terse characterization. To sum up, statistical approaches and symbolic approaches are complementary. It is important to balance and combine these NLP approaches.

NLP is closely related to translation. The field of MT is one of the oldest non-numerical applications of the history of computers (Nirenburg & Wilks, 2000, pp. 159–188). In 1949, Warren Weaver published his memorandum on translation, which drew attention to the idea of MT and inspired many projects (Liddy, 2001; Hutchins, 2000). In January 1954, a joint project conducted by IBM and Georgetown University showcased a Russian-English MT system in New York. This was the first computer-based application related to natural language (Hutchins, 2004).

In addition to MT, translation activities include many other NLP tasks, such as translation-related text analysis, text summarization, text classification, multilingual information retrieval, and speech recognition. Translation is a special and important use case of natural language comprehension and generation. Thus, we propose a translation-driven conceptualization of NLP, defined as follows:

> *Translation is an important and useful area of NLP application. Through parsing, tagging and analyzing naturally occurring text/speech or other types of language data at various levels of linguistic analysis, computer programs can achieve a level of human-like language processing for tasks such as machine translation, automatic post-editing, and quality estimation, with the goal of functioning effectively in a translation process. NLP in translation is fueled by data, powered by a range of computational techniques, and driven by human purposes.*

Machine learning: the scope of discussion

In the field of AI, ML is considered to be a branch of AI (McCarthy, 2007). In NLP, ML is an important aspect of statistical and connectionist approaches. For example, artificial neural networks are closely related to artificial intelligence; and it is believed that intelligent behavior will emerge from sufficiently complex networks of large numbers of simple, interconnected units that are properly stimulated (Henderson, 2007, p. 171). Nevertheless, AI and NLP do not necessarily require machine learning. As we discussed earlier, symbolic approaches to NLP rely on human analysis of the data in order to form a theory or build a model. Computer systems developed with this approach, such as rule-based MT engines, demonstrate a certain level of 'intelligence' or 'human-like performance'. In contrast, ML systems following statistical approaches offer a higher degree of autonomy when building models upon the collected data. At the extreme end of the autonomous continuum, connectionist architectures based on artificial neural networks are less constrained by humans, and linguistic models built on human analysis and reflection are harder to observe.

To some degree, an artificial neural network language model is more like a separate, independent system of language processing than a simulation of the language-processing centers of the human brain. Such models are designed to optimize their own performance automatically without attempting to mimic the biological capacity of the human brain when processing language. They tackle tasks in their own way, looking into the mirror from their own place. This book is highly interested in the insights machines can generate and how humans can make use of them when they tackle the task of translation.

From the methodology perspective, ML, in essence, is a type of statistical learning, referring to a vast set of tools for understanding data (James et al., 2013). It uses computational algorithms to turn empirical data into usable models (Edgar & Manz, 2017, pp. 153–173). In terms of language comprehension and generation, tremendous increases in computing power enable computer programs to 'learn' on their own by using statistics to find patterns in massive amounts of data. The language model based on ML mechanisms is able to make statistical inferences without human intervention. Though ML modeling is, in many cases, an oversimplification of human mental and physical worlds, it does help approach the invisible aspects of human cognitive processes and produces results that are in many cases consistent with human linguistic and cognitive inferences. For example, neuroscientists find that the internal workings of next-word prediction neural language models resemble those of language-processing centers in the brain (Schrimpf et al., 2021).

As a matter of fact, the concept of ML originated before the term 'artificial intelligence' was coined, and it entails a philosophical question raised by Alan Turing in his article "Computing Machinery and Intelligence" (1950): "can machines think?" (p. 433–460), as 'learning' is an essential part of a 'thinking' process. Turing further clarified that by 'thinking machines', he refers to a particular kind of machine, usually called an 'electronic computer' or 'digital computer'. Turing emphasized that

> The reader must accept it as a fact that digital computers can be constructed, and indeed have been constructed, according to the principles we have described, and that they can in fact mimic the actions of a human computer very closely.
>
> *(p. 438)*

Turing used the phrase "a human computer" in this statement, implying that a person can be an instantiation of a computer program, similar to the subject in the "Chinese Room Argument" experiment (Searle, 1980). What differentiates humans and machines is not programming that follows specific instructions consciously or subconsciously, but rather human intentionality, which computer programs do not possess. Intentionality is solely in the minds of those who program computers and those who use them, those who enter the input and those who interpret the output. A computer and its programs are unintentional in nature. That is not their weakness; that is exactly the reason why we use them. They are applicable and potentially useful for any person who is willing to and able to bring them to life through the construction of intentionality in the mind. From this perspective, computers and their programs are merely tools for human beings – no more, no less – no matter whether they are a 'learning machine' or not.

We emphasize that machine learning and computer programs developed using ML technologies are tools for humans. We are interested in insights that machine learning can bring to humans and how people can leverage this tool by understanding its basic principles and developing a mindset facilitating its incorporation into conventional translation processes. ML provides a different perspective for a discussion on the nature of translation and has unique value in complementing human approaches to translation. For example, by processing large data sets and extracting patterns in a fraction of the time a human requires, ML can produce insights that would otherwise remain inaccessible.

When Searle (1980) introduced the concept of intentionality in machines, he divided the topic into contrasting categories: those who program machines and those who use them, those who enter the input and those who interpret the output. Most translators and linguists are not programmers. They are involved in system deployment by sending in the input and interpreting the output. In the system development stage, they function as domain experts offering subject-matter expertise. This book takes an inclusive perspective, with special attention to those downstream, for whom knowledge of ML is instrumental in planning their translation education and career in this new age of AI. This objective can only be achieved with the support of those who work upstream. Their understanding of the problem of translation from a human perspective and attention to those who use these systems, entering input and interpreting output, will help balance ML and human learning in translation.

Since ML was introduced, it has generated concern among translators and linguists, and there have been debates about whether ML technologies will replace humans. Indeed, the rise of neural language models (NLM) has increased speculation about whether ML will gradually take over some tasks that are conventionally done by humans. There are several questions to ask in this regard. Firstly, are these tasks really ideal for humans? Further, will there be other tasks – either already in existence or newly created – that will require humans? Making use of ML tools and leveraging their power is only the beginning. What is next? How can humans maximize their unique intentionality by customizing these tools? Are they aware of the weaknesses of these tools, and will they employ human intelligence to address them? Can they find the best scenarios to apply these tools and make wise decisions about the division of labor between humans and machines? Which tool best fits a given situation? In the age of ML AI, the combination of data and talent is the scarcest resource. To be more precise, it is human-touched data that makes the difference, as humans, not machines, create data. In the end, it is all about how humans materialize their thoughts with ML tools and the methodologies to meet specific human purposes. This new approach to thinking about ML is changing fundamentally how translators approach their task and the way translators plan and organize their activities.

Translation and the language industry

The concept of 'translation' requires clarification. Translation is examined in this book from a broad perspective, encompassing the theory and practice of written and spoken language mediation activities, as well as localization and other forms of technology-driven content alignment across languages and cultures. In this sense, 'translation' is not only a theoretical concept discussed in academic circles but also a professional practice in the language industry. When the concept incorporates industry practice, many other related activities are involved, for example, business operations and project management, which are often addressed under 'localization'. As Pym (2014, p. 119) points out, localization can involve a wide range of tasks; it usually concerns information technology and marketing, as well as language skills.

This broad conceptualization of translation involves stages beyond meaning conversion in the strict sense in both human and automated translation processes driven by machine learning. Although this definition unavoidably touches on specific areas such as project management, programming, and marketing, the priority is still on translation, which we consider a human-centered activity that uses machine learning to automate part of the process. In other words, the emphasis in this discussion is placed on the user side of ML translation applications. This allows the adoption of a bottom-up approach, starting from the ML frameworks and methodologies that are most relevant for translators and other domain experts in translation, rather than technical experts who are also drivers leveraging ML to scale human knowledge of translation.

Another significant characteristic of the concept of translation in the context of ML is that the widespread implementation of machine translation has gradually blurred the boundaries between 'translating' and 'editing'. The trend is toward replacing the grind of translation work with machines, and humans mostly performing editing tasks to ensure quality. In a typical machine translation post-editing (MTPE) scenario, for example, human translators start with MT output. In an interactive MT scenario, humans are editing what the system suggests, even though they may feel like that they are 'translating'. We discuss this in Chapter 4.

Similarly, the term 'translator' as a root concept encompasses various roles in translation and localization processes, including those of linguists, localization project managers, and other domain experts. In a typical translation process, the fundamental productivity lies in translating, from which other translation-related activities are derived. Although participants in other roles, such as linguistic analysts and project managers, do not necessarily translate, they add value to the translation product by managing human and linguistic assets, preparing and analyzing source texts, and editing target texts. They can also work with the translation product indirectly, e.g., by using parallel corpora to train their NMT engines to improve the quality of the product, rather than directly working with the results produced by human and machine translators. In this book, the term 'translator' is used in this broad sense.

The rise of ML has not only triggered a gold rush in areas such as data mining and machine training, but also disrupted the balance between humans and machines in the language industry. While many translation tools have been human-guided, assisting practitioners in their translation projects, ML aims for a minimum level of human intervention. MT is like a black box for most practitioners in translation and localization processes, aside from MT engine suppliers. To integrate MT better into existing workflows, we need to build a relationship of trust between these practitioners and those developing computer programs and MT systems. To this end, transparency and fairness are crucial. By building ML knowledge and expertise, translation practitioners can plan their own learning and future activities, and part of their work will be assisting machines to learn.

About this book

Objectives of the book

The book approaches Machine Learning in Translation (MLinTrans) from a human perspective and revisits the nature of translation with machine learning as a new dimension. It aims to address the challenges met by users of ML technologies, helping them develop their ML expertise. Rather than intimidating the uninitiated reader with technical concepts and formulae, the book aims to be accessible by focusing on the most relevant and applicable ML knowledge and skills that enable linguists, translators, and localizers to communicate with machines as well as other human actors, who vary in their ML knowledge, exposure, and attitudes.

By empowering translation practitioners with relevant ML knowledge, they can be more effective when communicating with machines and other human actors in a ML-driven translation process. Most importantly, the book aims to support the professional development of translation practitioners so that they can fully utilize a ML-driven translation environment.

This book also explores the implications of ML in traditional translator education. It proposes a fundamental equation for practitioners seeking to leverage ML: the human capacity to learn is augmented by that of machines. The digital revolution brought about a rapid increase in the electronic capturing and storage of human experience. When humans are accessing a much larger magnitude of information and resources, it is natural that they leverage ML to extract a more collective human perspective. On the one hand, human learning is augmented with data insights that computer programs can provide; on the other, potential risks arise due to automation processes that are less constrained by humans. Under such circumstances, the key to balancing opportunities and challenges is the human capacity to learn, to form dynamically internal models of the external world, and to adjust the parameters of their learning with the influx of ML applications. Human learning should be prioritized in this shared evolution of humans and machines.

Characteristics of the book

This book aims to help practitioners find their added value in a field increasingly shaped by translation technology. It is about humans, in particular translators, linguists, and other stakeholders who are proud and passionate about making translation their career. To this end, the authors approach the topic of machine learning from a human perspective, with the goal of providing the most relevant knowledge, skills, and best practices on MLinTrans. The book covers not only ML knowledge and skills in translation but also other relevant aspects of the entire localization ecosystem, including ML applications for translation document analysis, language data management (translation memory, terminology, and other tools for analyzing corpora), and translation-related NLP tasks (speech recognition, speech synthesis, and optical character recognition).

This book enables readers to draw on their previous translation and localization experience, in both theory and practice, and develop their own plan to implement ML frameworks and methodologies in their translation work. By identifying parallels between machine learning and translation, practitioners can draw on their knowledge and experience in translation theory and practice to understand the concept of ML and its application in translation processes.

The book provides a new, independent perspective on ML implementation and its impact on existing localization processes for both students and practitioners. It focuses on the principles behind ML frameworks and technologies that are generally applicable in a localization workflow, rather than specific business cases. The holistic view of this book benefits readers broadly, as they can apply relevant content to their own business scenarios, learning, and research.

In a practical sense, the book introduces key ML tasks in translation to expose readers to cutting-edge ML technologies and help them understand the benefits and challenges ML tools bring to translation processes. One of the greatest threats in the application of ML is the loss of balance between machine and human learning. In a ML-driven translation environment, a large amount of data is fed to the machine in order to train it, as this is how a 'learning machine' is created and developed. Under such circumstances, human interaction becomes only part of the ML environment, and the significance of human learning might be neglected if not intentionally planned.

Intended audience

This book adopts an inclusive approach, with special attention to those downstream and with the aim of winning the support of those upstream in systems development. The authors hope that the human-centered approach will make it especially appealing to users of ML technologies in localization workflows, including translation/localization practitioners with different levels of experience and students in the humanities who are familiar with linguistic and translation theories and wish to use ML technologies in their studies and practice. This book enables readers to make full use of their existing knowledge and skills in translation and understand their relevance to MLinTrans.

The book also offers insights for science and engineering students and STEM practitioners who want to understand the fundamentals of translation so that they can better design ML architecture to support translation processes. The book will help practitioners in the language industry to effectively integrate machine learning in their workflow, maximize the value of translation-driven language data, and learn from the data analysis that computer programs can provide to stakeholders, including:

- Buyers implementing MT
- Content Managers responsible for global content
- Decision-makers who must understand MT but don't want to become technical experts
- IT professionals implementing MT
- Project Managers implementing MT solutions
- Vendors leveraging MT to meet their clients' needs

Structure of the book

The book has three parts, each with three chapters.

Part I discusses *Human and machine approaches to translation*. Chapters 1 through 3 explore how humans and machines approach the problem of translation in their own particular ways, in terms of internal representations of meaning, chunking of larger meaning units, and prediction in translation based upon language models.

Chapter 1 introduces the human approach to translation and discusses its relevance to machine learning from the linguistic, communicative, and mathematical perspectives. By examining the representation of words as high dimensional, real value vectors – a defining feature of neural network language models – the reader can revisit the nature of translation with ML as a new dimension.

Chapter 2 approaches MLinTrans from the perspective of linguistic structure and levels of analysis. It compares how humans analyze text at different levels for translation purposes with how machines parse text and annotate segments in order to interact with humans in an automated translation process. It discusses how and why machine segmentation of large chunks of information relies on both mathematical calculations and human perception of language.

Chapter 3 focuses on the neural network language model and how it parallels the human faculty of prediction in translation and interpreting. It investigates links between human inference and generalization in machine learning used to predict output in translation tasks. It looks in particular at how meaning is represented numerically in a neural network language model.

Part II introduces *Machine learning tasks in translation*. Chapters 4 through 6 introduce key ML tasks, including MT, translation quality assessment and quality estimation, and other natural language processing (NLP) tasks in translation. These tasks and tools are examined in a broad translation environment, including not only MT but also other elements of a conventional computer-assisted translation (CAT) environment, thus illustrating the expansion of language technology in the translation/localization workflow. Intentionality is highlighted as the factor that differentiates humans and machines.

Chapter 4 adopts a holistic approach to MT, illustrating the expansion of language technology in the translation/localization workflow. It discusses different paradigms of machine translation, from linguistic rules to statistical models, and the basic principles behind these paradigms. It also covers some major considerations in MT deployment. Finally, the chapter proposes a framework for translation workflows in which MT is part of translation in a broad sense.

Chapter 5 introduces machine translation quality assessment (TQA), quality estimation, and other methodologies to help us manage risk in a ML-driven translation environment. This chapter also covers machine translation post-editing (MTPE) and other human–machine interaction in a MT-driven localization process.

Chapter 6 introduces other natural language processing technologies relevant to a continuous translation process, which a translator, linguist, or domain expert is more likely to guide and support than a computer scientist. These NLP tasks are based on specific purposes in an ML-driven translation process. From a philosophical perspective, machines do not possess intentionality, which is solely in the minds of humans.

Part III turns to *Data in human and machine learning*. Chapters 7 through 9 focus on the role of data in both human learning and ML processes. It proposes that a translator's unique value lies in the capability to create, manage, and leverage language data in different ML tasks in the translation process, including data from parallel and monolingual corpora, terminology, and data in other formats such as component content management system (CCMS). It discusses data relevancy, data annotation, data quality, data fairness, and data security when leveraging ML tools in translation. Maximizing the value of language data and supporting both human learning and ML requires data sharing among humans and computer platforms up front. Finally, the integration of ML in translation research and practice implies that new knowledge and skills need to be incorporated into traditional translation education.

Chapter 7 proposes the concept of *translation-driven language data*, whose main characteristic is comparability. The chapter draws distinctions between data, corpus, and information as concepts and between two fundamental uses of language data: human analysis and learning vs. machine analytics and learning. The chapter discusses translator–computer interaction (TCI) through language data from three perspectives: (1) data design and acquisition, (2) data annotation, and (3) language data use.

Chapter 8 adopts a definition of learning as forming a mental model and adjusting the parameters of the model. A significant characteristic of both human and machine learning is the capability to generalize new conclusions based on available observations. This chapter discusses the collective capability of ML technologies to facilitate personalized human learning and the importance of converting generic ML models to personalized tools that help humans acquire these technologies and translation-related knowledge and expertise. Examples include illustrating how ML can facilitate human learning by using vector space to visualize terminological schematic context (TSC), compiling source text-oriented comparable corpora, and building intelligent tutors.

Chapter 9 discusses how machine learning adds a new dimension to translator education. It describes the impact of machine learning and summarizes translator competences in this new context. It describes the educator's role in two approaches to structuring learning: bottom-up, learner-centered, and top-down, educator-guided environments. It discusses the value of educators when machine learning plays a significant role in translation and concludes with a discussion of new requirements for translation curriculum design in the ML era.

The book concludes with a discussion of *Human-centered machine learning in translation*, drawing attention to the need to empower translators with ML knowledge, through communication with ML users, developers, and programmers, and with opportunities for continuous learning.

Note

1   A neural language model is a neural network that learns to predict the next word from prior words (Jurafsky & Martin, 2020, p. 113).

Human and machine approaches to translation

1

CONVERGENCE OF TWO APPROACHES TO TRANSLATION

KEY CONCEPTS

- *The traditional human approach to translation is converging with machine learning from the linguistic, communicative, and mathematical perspectives.*
- *In machine learning and neural network language models, words are represented as real value vectors, which offer a new perspective on the nature of translation.*
- *Distributed representations in a neural network language model provide a feasible solution to describe sense-component relationships and can simulate the inner workings of meaning.*

1.1 Introduction

Translation, first and foremost, is a human activity. It originates out of the necessity of communication. When examining the history of translation, three characteristics stand out. The first is that translation practice is the foundation of *translation studies* as a discipline, which has a very short but lively history (Gentzler, 2014, p. 14; Holmes, 1972/2004). Although philosophical writing about translation stretches back to antiquity, the focus tends to be on practice, with for example Horace and Cicero, and other poets and philosophers in the Western tradition, discussing aspects of word-for-word and sense-for-sense translation in the first century BC (Ghanooni, 2012, p. 77). The second is the interdisciplinary nature of translation studies, widely recognized and discussed in the field. The third is that there are technology tools and computer applications associated with computational linguistics, computer engineering, and software engineering, among other areas, that have contributed to the maturation of translation as a practice and an autonomous discipline (see Ožbot, 2015).

DOI: 10.4324/9781003321538-3

These characteristics lay out foundational considerations about the nature of translation:

1   At its core, translation is a human practice, with the facilitation of communication as its basic function.
2   Humans are creative when using language and translating, and although many disciplines can contribute to the study of translation, none can address exclusively and entirely the problem of translation, making them individually unsuitable to address translation practice as a whole.
3   The study of language and the study of translation are inextricably linked – many epistemological translation constructs originate from the study of language and application of linguistic constructs to translation.
4   While technology tools and computer applications provide a means to do translations, they also offer a new dimension when thinking about the nature of translation; they are thus both a methodology and a theoretical framework.

These considerations lead us to think of a well-known, over 2,500 year-old quotation attributed to Confucius: *There are three methods to gaining wisdom. The first is reflection, which is the highest. The second is imitation, which is the easiest. The third is experience, which is the bitterest.* To some degree, these three methods describe aspects of translation practice over the centuries, except that with the rise of computer science in modern times, translators are now able to reflect on translation practice and gain translation experience not only by using their own minds but also electronic resources. These developments have led to more diverse participants becoming involved in translation-related activities, including technology experts who focus on developing computer applications and now feature prominently. These applications attempt to simulate human processes by using machines to practice translation. They are augmenting, magnifying, and scaling up human knowledge and capability in this area. The rise of technological power in translation leads us to rethink the traditional roles of translators and linguists. In this new collaborative relationship between humans and machines, translators are also domain experts and pioneers in new ways of practicing translation. They support the development of computer applications produced by technical experts, while simultaneously being empowered by these applications and, quite importantly, finding new opportunities to reflect on their translation experience.

The rise of this technology dimension allows us to identify two fundamental approaches to translation. One is linguistic and represents humans' intuitive and empirical reflection on translation practice from the interdisciplinary perspectives of translation studies. The other is mathematical and represents computer processing of linguistic information and translation data, which is fundamentally based on numbers, rather than texts. The focus of this book is on the relationship between machine learning and translation, which in theory and practice should not be seen as separate undertakings. Rather, there are clear links between a linguistic approach to translation that reflects humans' thinking processes and a mathematical approach that captures a machine's instantiations of thought and reality. In contrast to computer technology experts, however, for most translators, linguists, and other domain experts in translation, the linguistic approach is closer to existing patterns of thinking, and the mathematical approach is quite new. It may take some time to learn to follow a computer's logic. This chapter aims to compare and contrast both approaches as a means to revisit the nature of translation.

1.2 Language and translation – equivalence[1] in different systems of signs

Language is indispensable to us because it allows us to communicate human experience. By extracting linguistic forms from the mind, humans communicate with their inner self as well as other individuals in society. All language activities are deeply rooted in human cognition, and abstract thought is brought to the surface and manifested through language. Spoken communication begins with an idea. By turning an abstract concept into a concrete symbol, person A is able to express ideas and gain responses from B. Intangible thoughts in A's mind cannot be measured or described, whereas thought instantiated in linguistic form becomes specific and concrete. This difference in itself implies an inequivalent relationship, with speech uttered by A, resulting from focused attention, functioning as a set of stimuli that directs B's attention to a corresponding concept in the mind. In this process, what distinguishes humans from machines is not speech as oral communication, but the faculty of constructing meaning through language.

In the early 20th century, there was a shift of attention from historical linguistics to the exploration and description of the systemic structure of language, governed by rules and principles. In particular, Ferdinand de Saussure (1857–1913), who is widely acknowledged as one of the founders of modern linguistics and semiology, proposed that language is a system of signs that expresses ideas. According to Saussure (1966), a sign includes both the signifier and signified (or French, *signifiant* and *signifié*). The sign is arbitrary, meaning there is no inherent reason why a signifier is linked to the signified; in order to make sense of a sign, one can only examine how this sign relates to other signs in the same system (Saussure, 1966).

Specifically, to understand the word *cheese* in terms of its relationships, a person can resort to: (1) linguistic acquaintance with the meaning assigned to this word achieved by reflecting on its relations to other signs in the language system and (2) nonlinguistic acquaintance with *cheese* as a physical object. To understand a word, a person must have at least a linguistic acquaintance with it. In some instances, non-linguistic objects associated with the word do not exist at all. For those who have never consumed *ambrosia* and have only a linguistic acquaintance with the word as "the food of the gods," they can understand the word *ambrosia* and know in what context it may be used simply by depending on their linguistic acquaintance with it (Jakobson, 2021).

Although a word's relationship to nonlinguistic symbols is an important aspect of understanding, the language system in itself is a self-sustaining system, whose internal relationship endows a unique position to each sign. Suppose we convert the arbitrary language signs to numerical strings or numbers, and quantify the distance between each symbol in a collection of words to represent the relationship between these symbols. We would in effect simulate the language system in a mathematical way. While it may sound radical, it is not that difficult to understand if we observe how children learn to read or spell at an early age. Before the language signs start to make sense to them, children work hard to memorize the arbitrary signifiers and their internal relationships so that they can spell a word that provides a shared understanding in society. In theory, if the child were given numbers, rather than language signs, to learn the relations between them, they would be able to find meaning in a new set of numbers based on the pattern they had drawn on from the training samples. However, infants are exposed to of course the linguistic systems in their environment to begin their epistemological journey.

Let us now examine the concept of translation. According to Jakobson (2021), any interpretation of meaning involves translation: "no linguistic specimen may be interpreted by the science of language without a translation of its signs into other signs of the same system or into signs of another system" (p. 157). Jakobson distinguishes three ways of interpreting a verbal sign: (1) intralingual (within one language, i.e., rewording or paraphrase), (2) interlingual (between two languages), and (3) intersemiotic (between sign systems) (p. 157).

Among these three categories, this book will focus mainly on interlingual translation, including both spoken (interpreting) and written (translation), which involves equivalent messages in different language systems, aiming to achieve "[e] quivalence in difference" (Jakobson, 2021, p. 157). This goal, however, is not easy to achieve. Speakers of each language dissect nature and the universe in their own unique way. Hence the way different language systems are constructed is not the same, with each sign relating to other signs in its own particular way syntagmatically and paradigmatically. For example, the English word *ride* is related to such concepts as *ride a horse*, *ride a bicycle*, *ride metro*, or *ride a bus*. But if we use *qi* (骑), a sign in Chinese that seems to be an equivalent of *ride*, most Chinese speakers cannot understand why a person can *qi* (*sit in*) the metro or a bus, which their English-speaking counterparts have widely accepted. That is to say, in theory, no language system is exactly identical to any other, and thus no absolute equivalence can be found in interlingual translation.

1.3 A mathematical approach – machine learning in language and translation

Language is very unique compared with other human creations. Its meaning does not lie in its visual effect like a picture or a painting, although calligraphy and other artistic work that employs written language can have an aesthetic impact. In most cases, what makes a difference is the combination of linguistic units, which includes both the units themselves, such as letters or characters, and their order. Underlying such an ordered sequence there is meaning.

In mathematics, a sequence is an enumerated collection of objects in which order matters. All language occurrences are sequences of linguistic units. In other words, language in itself is mathematical, and mathematics can be a useful tool for people to reflect on the nature of language, because as a tool mathematics is generic and language-independent. Here the word *tool* does not have a derogative meaning. It is a tool because of its strong power of generalization, which is so strong that it can be seen as detached from reality. To many mathematicians, mathematics contains three great buildings, which are devoted to Geometry, Analysis, and Algebra: the study of space, the study of time, and the study of symbols and structures (Berlinski, 2011). Saussure's proposition of language as a system of signs with unique internal relationships maps perfectly onto the framework of Algebra, as well as that of Analysis when considering the concept of order in a sequence that entails the concept of time; that is, one thing happening before or after another. Finally, the concept of vectors is closely related to Geometry. In mathematics, a vector is a list of numbers. It has both magnitude (size) and direction. For example, in a 2D plane, a vector (x, y) represents the coordinate of a point. More generally, the vector represents a point in the n-dimensional[2] space.

With such a powerful thinking tool in hand, the next step is to put it to use by finding a domain to unlock its power in practice. In our case, that domain is translation, in which people use language to translate and communicate. Generally speaking, a domain expert such as a translator, a linguist, or a translation project manager is good at reflecting or learning from human-constructed systems, including multiple theories about language, such as linguistics, philology, and sociology, whereas a technical expert is proficient in using these mathematical frameworks to develop relevant computational techniques for natural language processing. Both domain and technical experts are the main drivers leveraging ML to magnify and scale up human knowledge of translation.

In reality, the task of translation is no easy matter. Unlike artificial languages that have been intentionally devised, usually by a single creator (see Okrent, 2019), natural languages are highly ambiguous, ever changing and evolving, leading to great challenges in applying computer techniques to process natural language, as Goldberg (2017) implies:

> People are great at producing language and understanding language, and are capable of expressing, perceiving, and interpreting very elaborate and nuanced meanings. At the same time, while we humans are great users of language, we are also very poor at formally understanding and describing the rules that govern language.
>
> *(p. 1)*

Here Goldberg touched upon two different concepts: one is language data that people produce, the other is the rules that govern language. When examining the nature of rules, there are two primary considerations: (1) rules are not superficial occurrences like data; rather, they are further processed, hidden patterns or representations based on data; (2) rules can be constructed by both humans and machines, and while humans infer the rules using their intuitive reflections, machines use mathematical methods to capture the patterns of data. When Goldberg aims to hard code linguistic rules into a computer program, he notices that many human-constructed rules may not necessarily be machine friendly.

These two types of rules, namely human-constructed linguistic rules and machine-generated rules, lead to two general approaches to using machines:

1   In traditional computer programming – the symbolic approach to NLP in our case – the system receives input training data as well as rules and returns answers.
2   In a ML-driven system – the statistical approach to NLP in our case – which includes both traditional statistical methods and artificial neural network models, one starts with input data and answers (training data), both of which are concrete and visible, and the results generated are patterns or rules that machines have summarized (see Figure 1.1).

The former is driven by rules that are dynamically discovered or summarized as a result of human learning, whereas the latter generates its own machine rules and avoids human intuitive explanations of natural language, which is inefficient in a two-digit computer system. As Samuel (1959) stated, "a computer can be programmed so that it will learn to play a better game of checkers than can be played by the person who wrote the program" (p. 535). He added that "programming computers to learn from experience should eventually eliminate the need for much of this detailed programming effort" (p. 535). From his line of argumentation, we can see that machine learning gives computers the ability to learn without being explicitly programmed. In other words, machine learning allows computer programs to develop their own capability to create and generate new output, rather than simply memorizing what has been fed to them through traditional programming.

The use of machines to generate patterns with or without a minimum level of human intervention led to a philosophical question: "Can machines think?", as Alan Turing (1950) asked in his article *Computing Machinery and Intelligence*. Turing supports the advantage of drawing a fairly sharp line between the physical and intellectual capacities of humans, proposing that machines can 'learn' similarly to how humans apply intellect by approaching what is visible. An important feature of a learning machine is that the rules get changed in the learning process, and its teacher will often be largely ignorant of what is going on inside, although still be able to some extent to predict the pupil's behavior. Turing also introduces the famous Turing Test, originally called the imitation game in the aforementioned

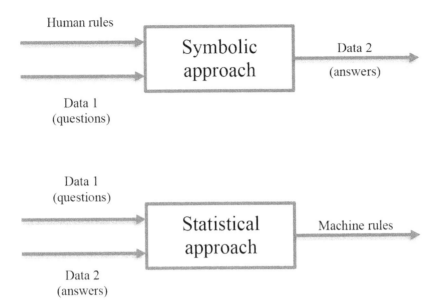

FIGURE 1.1   Two approaches to using machines

article, which aims to test a machine's ability to exhibit intelligent behavior equivalent to, or indistinguishable from, that of a human. Turing's work marks a new era of machine learning and artificial intelligence.

There is still much to explore in order to more fully understand aspects of how the human mind works in learning and inferencing processes. Yet apparently machine learning helps establish models to simulate a process generating results, and this simulation is concrete and visible to us. In the next section, we will explore how artificial neural networks simulate the representation of meaning.

1.4 Two approaches to meaning representation

As mentioned earlier, human language is a unique creation. A piece of naturally occurring text contains both multiple language units (e.g., words) and an order of these units. This is not a simple parts-to-whole problem, as underlying such a structured combination there is meaning, which is related to each unit but is more than the sum of the parts. Thus, meaning representation is a very complex activity for a computer program to simulate.

As discussed in the Introduction, artificial neural networks are able to combine statistical learning with various theories of representation. In particular, neural network language models, which are composed of large numbers of units (the analogs of neurons) together with weights that measure the strength of connections between the units (Buckner & Garson, 2019), can represent meaning in real value vectors. Specifically, in natural language processing, entities can be represented by activities of simple, neuron-like computing elements in an artificial neural network.

There are many representational schemes between a concept and its neuron(s), i.e., entities and computer elements. The most straightforward one uses one computing element (neuron) for each entity. This is called a local (or localist) representation. It entails a belief that there is a one-to-one correspondence between entities and hardware units. This representational scheme is easy to understand and implement because the structure of the physical hardware network mirrors the structure of the knowledge it contains (Hinton et al., 1986, p. 77), or rather, the surface structure of human knowledge.

In natural language processing, this one-to-one correspondence provides us with a gateway to start to understand language from what is tangible externally, from what we can see or hear in an actual piece of text or speech. By sampling real-life language occurrences and assembling a corpus, which is a large and principled collection of natural texts (Biber et al., 1998, p. 12), the researcher can observe specific linguistic forms at play. In terms of data type, textual data are categorical, rather than numerical, meaning they are discrete in nature, and arithmetic operations cannot be performed using these values. Just as with words on a piece of paper, each one is an entity unto itself – a separate kingdom – and mathematical operations using these linguistic forms is not possible.

This means that a machine cannot interpret the categorical data directly. They must be converted to numbers. For example, in order to study the language behavior of a small corpus that consists of two sentences – *He is a good learner. He gathers insights from a machine learner.* – we can label each unique word, or word type (Smith, 2019), with one unique decimal number. All unique words make up a vocabulary. In this case, if we ignore punctuation and capitalization, the length of the vocabulary or the total number of word types is 9, as shown in the first column of Table 1.1. In order to convert these word types to numbers, the simplest way is to assign a decimal number to each of them, as shown in the second column of Table 1.1. This is called label encoding (Chollet, 2017).

TABLE 1.1 Label encoding vs. one-hot encoding

Categorical textual data Unique word	Categorical decimal numbers Label encoding	Numerical data in a binary string One-hot encoding
He	1	100000000
Is	2	010000000
A	3	001000000
Good	4	000100000
Learner	5	000010000
Gathers	6	000001000
Insights	7	000000100
From	8	000000010
Machine	9	000000001

Label encoding is very straightforward, indicating a one-to-one correspondence between entities, i.e., word form and hardware processing units (neurons).
However, the numeric values can be misinterpreted by algorithms that are embedded with a hierarchy or order in them. This ordering issue is addressed in another
common alternative approach called "one-hot encoding" (Harris & Harris, 2012;
Chollet, 2017). This method is a binary representation of each word in a corpus, by
which we use a vector of 9 bits to represent the unique words in our vocabulary, by
simply making the 1st bit represent the word "He", the second bit the word "is",
etc. (see column 3 in Table 1.1).

However, this method has some disadvantages in terms of using computer elements to represent words:

1   One-hot encoding is a vector, that is, a list of numbers, and the
    size of the vector can be extremely large as the size of vocabulary
    increases. For example, if the vocabulary size of a corpus is 10,000,
    each word's numerical representation will be 10,000 digits.
2   Data are very sparse as vectors containing mostly 0s and only one 1
    (thus the name *one-hot*).
3   These vectors do not have information on the relationships between
    words or meanings derived from these relationships. For example, we
    would not know how the word *he* (100000000) is related to *learner*
    (000010000) just by reading the one-hot coding.

One-hot encoding treats words as discrete, atomic units, rather than continuous.
This is easy to understand when we consider a type of language in which one word
form – the signifier – corresponds to one computer element or neuron. Yet, when
considering the meaning of each word – the signified – this method is limited in
expressing complex connotations. Neither label nor one-hot encoding changes
the data type by simply assigning a number, decimal, or binary. They are still categorical, as adding or subtracting these numbers makes no sense. They are not real
numbers as shown in a vector space.

Localist models are very inefficient whenever the correspondence between concepts – the signified, or meaning of a sign – and neurons is not one-to-one. In this
case, the data have a componential structure. In our domain – language and translation – almost all data have componential structure: a word contains multiple sense
components, like the word *father* includes the meaning of *parent* and *male*.

Componential analysis, also known as feature analysis or contrast analysis, is
one of the cornerstones of semantics – the study of meaning (Leech, 1981; Love,
1983). Lyons (1995, pp. 106–108) points out that componential analysis is one
approach to lexical semantics. It involves the analysis of the component parts of a
lexeme. It has a long history of philosophical discussion and has been employed
extensively by linguists. An alternative term for componential analysis is lexical
decomposition. Here is an often used example: The words *man, woman, boy*, and
girl all denote human beings. We can therefore extract from the sense of each of

them the common factor *human*; that is, the sense of the English word *human*. Similarly, we can extract from *boy* and *man* the common factor *male*, and from *girl* and *woman* the common factor *female*. As for *man* and *woman*, they can be said to have as one of their factors the sense-component *adult*, in contrast with *boy* and *girl*, which contains the factor *non-adult*. The sense of each of the four words can thus be represented as the product of three factors:

1 *man*   = *human* x *male* x *adult*
2 *woman* = *human* x *female* x *adult*
3 *boy*   = *human* x *male* x *non-adult*
4 *girl* = *human* x *female* x *non-adult*

Another type of representation is called distributed representation, in which each entity is represented by a pattern of activity distributed over many computing elements, and each computing element is involved in representing many different entities. That is to say, distributed representation entails a many-to-many relationship between two types of representation (such as concepts and neurons). Each concept is represented by many neurons, and each neuron participates in the representation of many concepts. Suppose you see a *big, yellow, Volkswagen*. You will want to use a neuron, or a memory or processing unit to store this information; you create a *BYV* neuron. This seems efficient but consider all the different entities that humans can create in real life; for example, the large quantity of different types of cars. A computer will need an infinite number of these simple processing units to store information. One way to reduce the number of neurons is to extract features from these concepts. For example, for the concepts *yellow triangle* and *blue circle*, we can use two types of feature neurons – color and shape neurons – to represent them, by activating all constituent elements at the same time in a conjunction (*yellow* and *triangle*; *blue* and *circle*). If we have 5 options for color and 5 options for shape, yellow triangle and blue circle are represented in a 5 x 5 matrix by "1", as shown in Figure 1.2. This can also be done with the 23 possible combinations. If we further combine these conjunctions, say, we want to represent four entities at the same time (yellow triangle, blue circle, yellow circle and blue triangle) at the same time, the number of resulting entities will grow exponentially.

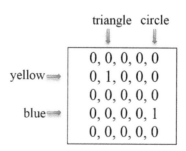

FIGURE 1.2   5 x 5 matrix

The strength of distributed representations does not lie in their notational convenience or ease of implementation in a conventional computer, but rather in the efficiency with which they make use of the processing abilities of networks of simple, neuron-like computing elements. Specifically, important features of distributed representations are (a) their essentially constructive character, (b) their ability to generalize automatically to novel situations, and (c) their tunability to changing environments (Hinton et al., 1986, pp. 77–87).

The pattern of activities involved in distributed representations aligns with human cognitive processing of language. People are very creative in their language use. They create new words and new combinations of words every day. However, no one could in effect store all these occurrences of language use in memory; rather, humans extract linguistic (or micro-) features to harness the power of human creativity. Grammatical categories (parts of speech, content words vs. grammatical words, tense) are a type of 'feature' that the human mind can extract from a massive amount of language data. Take the sentence *I do not like green eggs and ham* for example. We can reasonably imagine that for many people, the word *like* contains multiple subconcepts: it is a verb, a content word, and in the present tense. If a neuron or processing unit in the human brain is responsible for one sub-concept or micro-feature, the concept of 'like' is represented or processed by at least three elements or neurons. To some degree, each neuron represents some attribution of a person's understanding of the word 'like'. In other words, humans do extract features from raw language data.

Interestingly, when Lyons (1995) proposed the framework of componential analysis, he emphasized that he had "deliberately used the multiplication-sign to emphasize the fact that these are intended to be taken as mathematically precise equations, to which the terms 'product' and 'factor' apply exactly as they do in, say, $30 = 2 \times 3 \times 5$" (p. 108). In this example, *man* (30) = *human* (2) x *male* (3) x *adult* (5).[3] He also attempted to use algebraic expressions in his componential analysis and pointed out that

> To say that the sense of a lexeme (or one of its senses) is a compositional function of its sens-components is to imply that its value is fully determined by (i) the value of the components and (ii) the definition of the operations by means of which they are combined. To say that the sense of a lexeme is a set-theoretic function of its sense-components is to say that it is a compositional function of a particularly simple kind.
>
> *(Lyons, 1995, p. 112)*

Lyons realized that a simple sum like *father* = *parent* + *male* does not take account of the directionality of the relations and thus is inadequate. It does not make explicit the fact that fatherhood is a two-place (or two-term) relation or represent its directionality. He expanded the equation by adding variables in appropriate places. This type of analysis is found mainly in linguistics research, as there are many theoretical considerations in the process of quantifying sense-components and their relations. In addition, a word can have more than one meaning in different contexts, for example, *father* in *pray for me, father* has more sense-components than *parent* + *male*. The tangible benefits of constructing such rules in translation practice are not very high.

With the rise of neural network language model techniques such as word2vec, GloVe, and more context-sensitive architectures such as BERT, sense-component equations are empirically feasible. To achieve this goal, it is crucial to convert text to real value vectors at the very start, rather than using categorical numbers like label encoding. More importantly, in machine learning, the rules to extract features that machines figure out on their own are different from those of humans. In other words, many of the machine-extracted features cannot be mapped back to intuitive building blocks contributing to the word's meaning, which we will further discuss in Chapter 3. In this sense, machines do 'think' on their own, simulating the meaning representation process based on mathematical calculations, rather than the textual data that humans employ in their intuitive reflections.

1.5 A holistic view of translation

Now that we have a preliminary idea of the two different approaches to meaning representation – one from the human and the other from the machine – we return to the concept of translation and revisit its nature. As discussed in the first section, translation is primarily a human activity, which originates through practice, out of the necessity of communication. Even before Holmes (1972/2004) proposed translation studies as a separate discipline, it drew on theories from other fields, such as linguistics, psychology, and literary studies. Yet none of them was designed to address solely the problem of translation, and these theories tend to be descriptive of some translation phenomena, rather than a framework to address all use cases of translation. Furthermore, technology tools and computer applications not only provide methodologies to solve translation problems but also add a dimension of reflection on the nature of translation.

Undoubtedly, the study of language and translation are inextricably linked. In translation, the alignment between a linguistic sign in one language system and one in another relies on meaning. In terms of the meaning of a linguistic sign, Saussure (1966) argued that in order to make sense of it, one can only examine how this sign relates to other signs in the same system. Yet 'sign' is a complex concept. There is an inseparable union of a concept and its written or spoken linguistic form, and there is a gulf between a 'sign' as a whole in its own right and that same item playing a particular role within a contextual situation in human life.

Translation adds an extra layer to this complexity. As Vinay and Darbelnet (1995, p. 12) point out, when a word has an exact counterpart in another language in a given context, there is only one signified for two signifiers: *knife* and *couteau* in the context of *couteau de table* or *table knife*. But the signified of two signifiers, though normally considered interchangeable, may not coincide completely. This is the case with *bread* and *pain*. In English, *bread* has neither the same appearance nor the same importance as a food as *pain* in French.

To address this complexity, Saussure (1966) proposed a theoretical linguistic dichotomy: *langue* and *parole*. Specifically, *langue* encompasses the abstract, systematic rules and conventions of a signifying system; it is independent of language use. When we speak or write, these words belong to *parole*, the concrete instances of language use. This difference is important because most items of *langue* undergo a transformation when they are used in *parole*. In its turn, *langue* evolves according to usage in *parole*. "Parole precedes langue and the realizations of parole pass into the realm of langue" (Vinay & Darbelnet, 1995, p. 15).

This dichotomy also supports the line of argumentation proposed previously, that in pursuit of Jakobson's "equivalence in difference" (2021, p. 157), a translator cannot find absolute equivalence between items in separate sign systems, which vary both in terms of *langue* and *parole*. What is worth noticing is why a certain kind of equivalent relationship is construed in practice given the discrepancies between language systems. This might be due to the nature of communication as meaning-making. Humans want to make sense of contextual situations and attribute meaning to them. When the contextual situations are similar, the construed meaning will be as well. And to realize that meaning, there should be an internal connection between different signifiers across language systems. For example, when a translator aligns *bread* in English with *pain* in French, there must be a reason why they make such a decision. There must be a concept or meaning, representing part or the whole of the same *signifié* underlying both of them, and this common ground allows people speaking different languages to construe the same meaning. As meaning is dynamic, context-dependent, and subjective, a consensus on what a concept is composed of is difficult to achieve. Some studies on meaning (Leech, 1981; Love, 1983; Lyons, 1995; Griffiths, 2006) are instrumental to help us approach this problem through extracted linguistic features, yet these features and the mathematical equations of sense-components are not very applicable in language practice.

In contrast, distributed representations in a neural network language model provide a feasible solution to describe this flexibility and can more or less simulate the inner workings of meaning. In an artificial neural network language model, though each piece of knowledge that is encoded in a small, neuron-like processing unit is very simple, the connections between them are capable of supporting a large number of different patterns. By manipulating the weights (parameters) of the connections, which represent the strength of the connection between units, the system can control which neurons are to be fired and which to be put at rest, which units will be prioritized and how to optimize the pattern of activities based on human input. This type of knowledge representation is very flexible, and to some degree, language independent. It parallels human cognitive activity: people can recall items from partial descriptions of their contents (Norman & Bobrow, 1979), and they can do this even if some parts of the partial description are wrong (Hinton et al., 1986, p. 80). In one way or another, many human-constructed theories about different types of equivalence or other theories to explain translation, such as dynamic and formal equivalence, functional equivalence (Nida & Taber, 1969; Newmark, 1988), correspond to movement adjusted by weights of the connections and can be simulated or interpreted as various patterns or pattern categories of activities of neurons in a computer system.

In this sense, connectionism and artificial neural network language models provide an effective framework to revisit the concept of equivalence, based on parameters or weights of the connections in a network. Even with a limited number of neurons, there are many possibilities to construct patterns in a neural network as a whole. These options provide rich soil for a translator to see equivalence in a new light.

As Malmkjær (2011) points out, translation is an activity that strives to convey meaning or meanings of a given linguistic discourse from one language to another. Success can be described in terms of sameness of meaning across languages. In this sense, there should be a unique step in the translation process to find this common ground in meaning that is more or less independent of specific language systems, allowing the comprehension of the source text and production of the target text. For example, Newmark (1988) argues that, when translating, a translator keeps in parallel four levels: the textual, referential, cohesive, and natural (p. 29).

> [The] first and last level is the text; then you have to continually bear in mind the level of reality (which may be simulated, i.e. imagined, as well as real), but you let it filter into the text only when this is necessary to complete or secure the readership's understanding of the text.
>
> *(p. 29)*

The referential level

> goes hand in hand with the textual level. . . . You build up the referential picture in your mind when you transform the SL into the TL text; and, being a professional, you are responsible for the truth of this picture.
>
> *(p. 23)*

Finally, the cohesive level is a generalized level, linking the textual and referential level and following both the structure and the mood of the text (p. 23), and "is a regulator, it secures coherence, it adjusts emphasis" (p. 24).

In this regard, scholars in *interpreting studies* seem to be more radical. In her Interpretive Theory of Translation (ITT), Seleskovitch (1975) proposes a concept of deverbalization in the process of comprehension and reformulation and argues that most of the sounds or graphic signs disappear as soon as comprehension sets in. She points out that people experience deverbalization in everyday communication: we keep in mind facts, notions, events conveyed by words, but we do not retain these words in our memory. Anticipation of sense, which often occurs in oral communication and interpreting, is a proof that, in context and situation, full verbal support is not always necessary for comprehension to take place.

Although there is no consensus as to shared meaning in different language systems, in an artificial neural network, meaning can be more or less simulated, and thus support the belief in common meaning shared across languages. The process of human translation from source text (input data) to target text (output data) can be reflected and demonstrated in a typical artificial neural network, which is discussed in detail in Chapter 3.

Notes

1 Translation scholars have identified and described different forms of equivalence driven by analytical approach and translation purpose, in addition to the evolving if not problematic nature of the term itself. See Bassnett (2014, pp. 33–39) and Munday et al. (2022, pp. 49–72).
2 In mathematics, the dimension of a vector space V is the cardinality (i.e. the number of vectors) of a basis of V over its base field (Dimension (Vector Space), 2022). We introduce some examples to further elaborate this concept in natural language processing in Chapter 3.
3 Numbers in this example are randomly selected to illustrate Lyon's point. Real value numbers are intended to represent meaning as vector space in neural network language models.

2

LEVELS OF ANALYSIS

KEY CONCEPTS

- *Linguistic structure and levels of analysis play a significant role when humans and machines approach translation.*
- *Machine segmentation of large chunks of information relies on both mathematical calculations and human perception of language.*
- *In order for ML tools to work for and interact with humans directly, granularity levels in a machine learning process must be consistent with the nature of human cognitive activity.*

2.1 Introduction

One of the most essential and controversial preliminary steps in language comprehension and production, particularly in translation, is defining the unit with which to operate. As discussed in Chapter 1, every linguistic unit consists of signs and thus has a double structure, that for linguistic form (the signifier) and that for meaning (the signified). Multiple ideas may be positioned within the same unit; for example, the word *mouse* can refer to the rodent or a computer accessory. Sharing the same linguistic form (*mouse* as signifier), these two ideas cannot be separated, but rather are super-positioned. In the flow of language in real-life situations, only one signified is usually retained,[1] preferably that which has priority in the context. In language comprehension and production in translation, there are three elements that play determining roles: form, meaning, and context. While form and meaning can be embodied within a unit, context refers to how a given unit is related to others in the larger environment. And an intriguing question to ask is *Where is the starting point: form, meaning, or context?*

DOI: 10.4324/9781003321538-4

In translation, Vinay and Darbelnet (1995) "define the unit of translation as the smallest segment of the utterance whose signs are linked in such a way that they should not be translated individually" (p. 21). They argue that the signifier takes on a more important role than the signified, and translators must be concerned more with semantics than structure. This is a human approach; it is widely understood that the translator starts with semantics (the meaning) and carries out all translation procedures within the semantic field. In this sense, a unit of translation is not defined exclusively by formal linguistic criteria; rather, it is identified as a unit of thought, taking into account that translators do not translate words, but ideas.

In a machine learning task, these three elements and their relationships – form, meaning, and context – can all be explored in a natural language dataset, or corpus, which includes the unit itself as well as its context, i.e., a combination of other relevant units. A corpus holds all relations of the unit and other units in a distributional structure, which is the main resource for a computer program to generate patterns that correspond to meaning-based human reflections and thoughts. A computer program, whether a machine translation system or a text summarization tool, probably does not understand the underlying meaning of the text in the same way as humans, but it can absorb information and produce results that make sense to humans, in that the output is consistent with human conceptualization of meaning. In this sense, meaning exists only in the human mind during the interaction between human and machine, which includes feeding the dataset in the computer system, designing and optimizing the system architecture, and interpreting and using the machine-generated results. This chapter and the next focus on the machine approach to form, meaning, and context in translation. Chapter 2 describes levels of analysis for form and context. Chapter 3 turns to vector semantics for meaning and context, with the machine approach starting with form and structure, where meaning is extracted through the distributional structure of natural language data in a corpus, where meaning and context lie and co-exist.

2.2 Contextual levels in language comprehension and production

2.2.1 Levels of analysis in translation

Analysis is a key step in the translation process. As Newmark (1988) states, a translator begins translating by "reading the original text for two purposes: first, to understand what it is about; second, to analyze it from the translator's point of view" (p. 8). Further, in terms of linguistic analysis of the source text, Newmark (1988) emphasizes the unit of translation and discourse analysis (pp. 54–67). It is also important to analyze other types of translation-related text, such as the target text, the reference text, and aligned source and target texts. In this chapter, our focus is on one aspect of linguistic analysis, which is how a larger piece of textual information can be segmented into smaller units at various levels. The segmentation in itself shows the relationship between a particular unit and its context. When a translator approaches a text, there are multiple levels of language processing known to be at work, and the translator normally utilizes all of these levels intuitively (see Liddy, 2001, p. 1; Newmark, 1988, pp. 18–24).

Mona Baker (1992) explored equivalence at multiple levels in translation: equivalence at the word level and above the word level, grammatical equivalence, textual equivalence, and pragmatic equivalence. This framework considers form (grammar and number of words) and meaning (idioms and fixed expressions, and pragmatics). Newmark (1988) applied the concept of the translation unit in his theory and pointed out that a sentence is the 'natural' unit of translation, just as it is the natural unit of comprehension and recorded thought. Within the sentence, he identified five further sub-units of translation. The smallest unit of meaning, the morpheme,

> need not be taken seriously, except in the case of prefixes and suffixes, such as 'post-', 'inter-', and '-ism', when they have no direct target language equivalent in the word context. . . . Two sub-units, the clause and the group, are grammatical; the other two, the collocation and the word (including the idiom and the compound, which is a congealed collocation), are lexical.
>
> *(Newmark, 1988, pp. 65–66)*

When a translator translates, the translator must "be looking at the grammatical (the general factors of time, mood, space, logic, agreement) and the lexical (the details) at the same time, making sure that the Functional Sentence Perspective (FSP) is preserved where important" (p. 66). According to Newmark (1988), FSP "links the study of discourse, sentence and emphasis" (p. 60) and "examines the arrangement of the elements of a sentence in the light of its linguistic, situational and cultural context, determining its function within the paragraph and the text" (p. 61).

In oral translation, Chernov (2004) proposes a hierarchy of speech levels as the basis for a probability anticipation mechanism in simultaneous interpreting:

> *Syllable – word – syntagm[2] – utterance – discourse*
>
> *(p. 93)*

These theorizations are self-contained frameworks and represent different approaches to describing the hierarchical structure of a corpus. Machines employ yet another conceptualization of how to organize human thought.

2.2.2 The concept of granularity in NLP

In natural language processing (NLP), a more commonly used term for level of analysis is 'granularity'. Generally speaking, granularity is the concept of breaking down an event into smaller parts or individual granules such that each granule plays a part in the higher level event. Newspaper articles offer a classical example of granularity shifts, with a broad, high-level description in the first paragraph, followed by more detailed descriptions in subsequent paragraphs. Humans shift easily through various levels of granularity to achieve textual understanding. However, for automated identification and extraction, it is important to explicitly recognize the identifiers that indicate a shift in granularity. In natural language discourse, an area of NLP, various approaches and theories are proposed for modeling granularity (Mulkar-Mehta et al., 2011).

Krallinger et al. (2010, pp. 341–382) explore how biomedical text processing systems operate at different levels of granularity, using relevant processing features to detect special characteristics of natural language ranging from a basic level of characters and strings to complex relationships derived from multi-document collections. They point out that levels such as the character and strings level and sentence window level are more suitable for computer processing than human linguistic analysis.

2.2.3 Chunking: a cognitive aspect behind levels of analysis

The human ability to segment an utterance into multiple units at different levels is crucial for language comprehension and production. When reading a piece of text, humans consciously and subconsciously combine units of information – phrases, idioms, proper names, sentences, documents – through meaning to create conceptual chunks. To some degree, comprehension is related to competence in abstracting a collection of ideas. Conceptual chunks are mental leaps that unite separate bits of information that are bound together through meaning, and chunking information makes the mental work of the mind more efficient. Once a person chunks a concept, it is not necessary to remember the underlying details, as long as the main idea – the chunk – is captured. The new logical whole makes the chunk easier to remember and also makes it easier to fit the chunk into the larger picture (Oakley, 2014, pp. 54–57).

Raw information is like puzzle pieces that sometimes do not make much sense individually. Merely memorizing a fact without understanding or context does not help a person grasp how the concept fits together with other relevant concepts. Chunking is like inserting the piece in the puzzle. It is the mental leap that helps a person understand the whole picture (see Oakley, 2014, p. 57).

These cognitive activities can be traced in consecutive interpretation processing. Gillies (2013, p. 112) summarizes the basic interpreting skill set widely recognized in interpreting theory (Gile, 2009; Seleskovitch & Lederer, 1989), which includes active listening and analysis as a key component. In interpreting practice, an interpreter listens for underlying meaning, including the speaker's main points and supporting details, structural transitions, and implicit meaning. Gillies points out that active listening and analysis is about focused listening and concentration throughout the entire speech, without missing a single word of what the speaker says or drifting off in the middle. Practicing the analysis of written and spoken texts without the time pressure of interpreting can help automate the analysis task before attempting to do the same thing in the heat of the interpreting action (p. 111).

Active listening is grounded in analysis, including both general analysis of what the speaker is trying to say and analysis of the hierarchical structure of the speech to distinguish the primary information or main points from lower level, supporting, or ancillary information. Notably, Gillies (2013) proposes the concept of "automizing" the analysis task (p. 111), which implies that there may be an internal cognitive mechanism or language models in the human brain that is able to automate this form of processing (see Chapters 3 and 8).

Given the constraints of time and cognitive load, the interpreter must process the information into larger chunks, rather than attempting to retain the smaller bits of information. Interpreters do not simply write down what they have heard, but rather elements that will trigger their memory for what to say. To some degree, interpreters' notes capture the hierarchical structure of a speech and are typically a demonstration of the results of meaning analysis.

2.2.4 Level of analysis requirements in machine learning

As discussed previously, to some degree, granularity levels in a machine learning process must be consistent with the nature of human cognitive activity in order for ML tools to work for and interact with humans directly. Although there are instances where they are not used directly but instead serve as a basis for machine training of another ML tool that can be utilized by humans, our discussion of the levels of analysis begins with the human framework for linguistic structure and related reasons why machines process information at various levels too.

First, as mentioned earlier, an objective of using ML tools is to scale up and magnify human ability and reduce cognitive load. To this end, various tools have been designed to assist with NLP tasks, such as term extraction tools based on tf-idf (term frequency – inverse document frequency) at the word/term level, phrase representation generation mechanisms in phrase-based statistical machine translation (SMT), and systems that automatically align segments of the source and target text. In many cases, segmentation decisions are made not based on mathematical considerations, but rather to meet human translation requirements and to help humans process natural language, including understanding and producing text or speech. For example, even if input data is sentence by sentence as a parallel corpus with many features based on human information processing, such as segmentation indicated by punctuation, the data cleaning process will deconstruct the text to tokens and usually remove the punctuation that humans rely on for comprehension. Nevertheless, the process starts and ends with human perception, as the data must make sense to humans during input and after output. In this sense, the overarching natural language processing framework for levels of analysis is driven by human rather than internal programming requirements.

Second, when using a neural network for language modeling, the 'meaning' is extracted based on the hypothesis that there is a link between similarity in how words are distributed and what they mean. This distributional hypothesis was first formulated in the 1950s by linguists like Harris (1954) and Firth (1957).

Distributional models of meaning "are generally based on a co-occurrence matrix, a way of representing how often words co-occur" (Jurafsky & Martin, 2020, p. 101). Co-occurrence matrices generally start with a count vector based on units at various levels (term, sentence, document), and the count vector can be further converted to more powerful representation such as embeddings. It is important to understand some basic units in a neural language model, such as tokens and word types, as these units will affect how count vectors are generated.

Finally, the concept of levels of analysis is crucial for data annotation. Starting around 1990, many resources were used to create large, annotated treebanks and other linguistic resources. For example, Universal Dependencies (UD) is a framework for morphosyntactic annotation of human language. UD treebanks are now widely used in natural language processing research, including research on syntactic and semantic parsing (Marneffe et al., 2021, pp. 255–256). Syntactic parsing has been a central task in natural language processing because of its importance in mediating between linguistic expression and meaning. For example, much work has shown the usefulness of syntactic representations for subsequent tasks such as relation extraction, semantic role labeling, and paraphrase detection (Socher et al., 2013, p. 455). To build an automated syntactic parsing system, annotated/labeled data are needed for modeling a supervised classifier at a certain level or levels of analysis (see Chapter 7).

2.2.5 Translation memory: a case study for a balance of form and meaning

Translation Memory (TM) is a fundamental component of modern computer-assisted translation (CAT) tools. It is a language technology that enables the translation of segments (phrases, sentences, paragraphs) of documents by searching for similar segments in a database and suggesting matches that it finds (Raya, 2005). In a TM editor, a larger piece of textual information can be segmented into smaller segments. The segmentation is based firstly on an automatic rule that is typically defined in a TMX file. TMX is the Translation Memory eXchange format; it allows the transfer of translation memories from one translation tool to another (Localization-Related Formats, 2002). In TMX, the 'segtype' attribute (on the fourth line in Figure 2.1) defines the segtype attribute, which can have several values, e.g., 'block', 'paragraph', 'sentence', and 'phrase' (TMX Implementation Notes, n.d.). That is to say, an automatic segmentation tool such as a conventional TM system can segment the larger piece of information by phrase, sentence, paragraph, or block. The 'block' value is used "when the segment does not correspond to one of the other values, for example when you want to store a chapter composed of several paragraphs in a single <tu>" (TMX Implementation Notes, n.d.). A <tu> element indicates a translation unit, which includes both the source and target segments. Figure 2.1 provides an example using the sentences *This is an example. We wrote a TMX document to show how it works.* In this case, segtype="sentence" (in bold). Following this segmentation rule, the TM engine will segment the text into sentences. Figure 2.1 thus shows two translation units: *This is an example.* and *We wrote an TMX document to show how it works.*

```
<?xml version="1.0" encoding="UTF-8"?>
<tmx version="1.4">
        <header
                segtype="sentence"
                adminlang="EN-US"
                srclang="EN-US"
                creationdate="20131117T140541Z"
        >
        </header>

        <body>
                <tu tuid="163323456-0-1">
                        <tuv xml:lang='EN-US'><seg>This is an
example.</seg></tuv>
                        <tuv xml:lang='ZH-CN'><seg>这是例句。</seg></tuv>
                </tu>
                <tu tuid="163323456-0-2">
                        <tuv xml:lang='EN-US'><seg>We wrote a TMX document to
                        show how it works.</seg></tuv>
                        <tuv xml:lang='ZH-CN'><seg>我们编写了此TMX文件来说
                        明其原理。</seg></tuv>
                </tu>

        </body>
</tmx>
```

FIGURE 2.1 An example of sentence segmentation in TMX

In the example in Figure 2.1, larger quantities of information are segmented into smaller chunks in order to help human translators focus on the content and translate the content according to their cognitive habits, e.g., sentence by sentence. The TM tool offers various levels of analysis – phrases, sentences, paragraphs, and blocks – to support human translation. In order for humans to make use of these TM segments in their translation, the segmented results have to be presentable to humans. Otherwise, a translator or linguist will not be able to edit the automated segmentation results.

In the example in Figure 2.2, due to the formatting and the lack of punctuation, many automated segmentation systems that use phrases or sentences as segmentation units tend to separate the text into six segments, namely *romance, fantasy, is finding your, in people, who don't,* and *have it.* For this type of text, segmentation at a higher level, e.g., in paragraphs or blocks, is needed so that the source text can be presented to humans as a whole. Otherwise, human translators have to ignore the segmentation result and analyze the text in a way that makes sense to them, for example, by considering the whole text as one segment: *Romance is finding your fantasy in people who don't have it.* Furthermore, the complex formatting of this text encodes additional information that is communicated to the reader, making

Romance

is finding your

fantasy

in people

who don't

have it

FIGURE 2.2   An example with complex formatting considerations

it challenging for an automated segmentation system to capture. In this case, the translator needs to go back to the original, formatted text in order to fully deliver the meaning conveyed by both words and formatting. We will return to this point in the discussion about translator competence in Section 9.3 of Chapter 9.

The design of TM tools is primarily driven by human needs to the extent possible, instead of the innate requirements of the algorithms. In addition, TM tools not only offer human-friendly language processing features, but also accumulate and store the annotations[3] in parallel corpora. The segmentation, alignment, and other features embedded in the corpora (like data annotation) incorporate human requirements for processing language data, which will be further elaborated in Chapter 7.

As the earlier examples show, the methodology and concept behind translation memory segmentation tools are grounded in features of human cognition. The segmentation of the content in the corpus can be conducted at various levels according to a given context. When localizing embedded subtitles, text overlaid on video frames (Valery & Sene, 2020, p. 119), one has to consider more factors such as the size of the subtitle area and the length of each video frame in order to divide the whole text into multiple subtitle lines. These factors determine whether it is segmented into sentences, phrases, or words. Again, the segmentation for such a document has to make sense to humans, by allowing humans to follow their train of thought. Just like in a translation memory task for written documents, the text is segmented into sentences by using punctuation. Otherwise, the segmentation results will not make sense to humans and therefore lose their value in helping humans process information in a way that works for them.

We must also be aware that translating in a TM environment puts translators at a disadvantage compared to translating in a larger context with both linguistic information and non-linguistic features, such as image and formatting like bold font and line and paragraph breaks. Moreover, Translators may have different approaches or preferences for segmenting a document based upon how they are processing the meaning, whereas TM tools usually do not provide such a degree of flexibility for segmenting the original text. With an increasing number of NLP tools available, translators are able to work in a context-rich environment where TM tools can be used for follow-up data collection, linguistic analysis, and quality assurance (see Chapter 8).

2.3 Drawing parallels between linguistic relations and levels of analysis

2.3.1 Syntagmatic vs. paradigmatic relations

As Harris (1954) states, "language can be described in terms of a distributional structure, i.e., in terms of the occurrence of parts . . . relative to other parts" (p. 146), with each element in a particular position with regard to the element of interest, A:

> The distribution of an element will be understood as the sum of all its environments. An environment of an element A is an existing array of its co-occurrents, i.e., the other elements, each in a particular position, with which A occurs to yield an utterance. A's co-occurrents in a particular position are called its selection for that position.
>
> *(Harris, 1954, p. 46)*

Harris's (1954) work motivated a series of studies that approach meaning through distributional structure, arguing that similarity in meaning results in similarity of linguistic distribution (see Sahlgren, 2008). Words that are semantically related are used in similar contexts: if enough text material is available, and it is found that in the text material that two linguistic entities w_1 and w_2 tend to have similar distributional properties – they occur with the same other entity w_3 – then it can be hypothesized that w_1 and w_2 belong to the same linguistic class, or it can be interpreted that, to some degree, w_1 and w_2 have some common feature in meaning (Sahlgren, 2008, p. 35). In the next chapter, we will see how to reverse-engineer the process in a neural language model by inducing semantic representations from contexts of use (the distributional structure).

In this chapter, let's start with what can be observed and what can be directly induced from elements on the surface, i.e., linguistic relations between elements in the text. Sahlgren (2008) emphasizes the structuralist origins of the distributional methodology, which goes back to the cradle of structuralism with Saussure's *Cours de linguistique générale* (1966/1916), and follows Saussure's theory of classifying functional differences into two kinds of structures: syntagmatic relationships, or those between elements in a linear sequence; and paradigmatic relationships, or those between elements in a class or system. These two main types of distributional models provide information about co-occurrence (syntagmatic) and information about shared neighbors (paradigmatic) (Sahlgren, 2008, p. 33). In other words, the syntagmatic relations show positioning and related entities that co-occur in the text, and the paradigmatic relations show substitution options and relate entities that do not co-occur in the text (p. 39).

Figure 2.3 is a visualization of the two relationships using the sentence *She likes green eggs* as an example, with a notation system using w_n ($w_1, w_2, w_3 \ldots$) to indicate each word in the sentence with a total of n words, and $w_n o_n$ to indicate various options for the position of w_n.

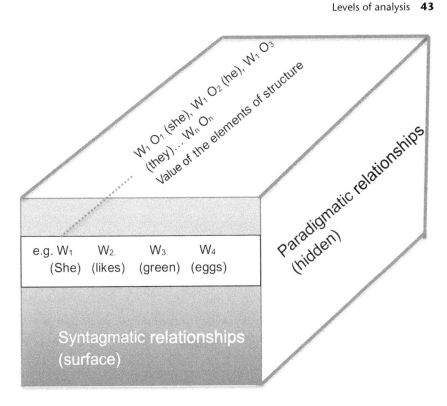

W₁ O₁ (she), W₁ O₂ (he), W₁ O₃
(they)… Wₙ Oₙ
Value of the elements of structure

Paradigmatic relationships
(hidden)

e.g. W₁   W₂.   W₃.   W₄
  (She) (likes) (green) (eggs)

Syntagmatic relationships
(surface)

FIGURE 2.3   The interior relationships within a text

As shown in Figure 2.3, the sentence *She likes green eggs* has two basic relationships: the syntagmatic relationship between each word that recognizes the place and order of each word and "the paradigmatic relationship for terms or units which commute within systems set up to give values to the elements of structure" (Firth, 1957, p. 5). While the distribution of each element (w_n) can be observed (like words that we see), the value for each word w_n is hidden, and we can't observe it directly. Sahlgren (2008, p. 39) uses the concept of substitution to describe the paradigmatic relationship, which denotes that a hidden element is in the same category as an element that can be observed in the actual text sequence. The relationship implies that elements in the same category share some common syntactic and semantic features.

The vocabulary options that can function in a particular position can be seen as instances with certain values that constitute language data. In human cognitive processes, these options might be conscious to a person. For example, when beginning adult learners of English produce *likes* in the second position w_2, they might struggle with other options such as *adores* or *is fond of*. A further abstraction behind these options are the values attached to them, which are semantic features[4] that place them in the same category, such as a verb with the general meaning of *feel affection for*.

In machine learning, a training corpus provides many vocabulary options through co-occurrence of elements. In the structure *she . . . green eggs*, there can be many options for the missing position, such as *likes*, *adores*, *dislikes*, and *abhors*. A neural language network, such as word2vec that will be discussed in the next chapter, can further extract feature vectors that represent different aspects of the word, which is an alignment of "values to the elements of structure" as proposed by Firth (1957, p. 5). These are the hidden values that can define each category in the sequence. For example, the part of speech for w_1 is 'pronoun', and it is not a named entity.[5] Parts of speech (POS) and named entities are useful clues to sentence structure and meaning. They are based on intuitive human summarization but can be leveraged in NLP through sequence labeling tasks, such as POS tagging and named entity recognition (NER) (Jurafsky & Martin, 2020, p. 148).

2.3.2 Linguistic units for machine learning

A sequence w_1, w_2, w_3. . . w_n as a whole is generally dealt with at various levels, and an atomic unit that a language model can train and make predictions on is a 'token', typically a word, character, or subword (see Google Developers, n.d.-c, for a definition and examples).

If a token is a word, the number of tokens in a corpus is the total number N of running words. Tokens are not defined by word type; rather, the term 'type' refers to the unique or distinct words in a corpus. If the set of words in the vocabulary of a corpus is V, the number of word types is the vocabulary size $|V|$. In NLP, references to the number of words in the language are generally references to word types (Jurafsky & Martin, 2020, p. 12). In most cases, the number of word types is not the same as the number of tokens. For example, in a corpus that includes a document about a UN resolution of biodiversity conservation (the English version of a resolution adopted by the General Assembly on 16 April 2021, Symbol A/RES/75/271), there are 583 word types and 2,017 word tokens based on the calculation of Ant-Conc, a corpus analysis toolkit for concordancing and text analysis (Laurence, n.d.), as shown in Figure 2.4. This example illustrates that there is often a large difference between the vocabulary size (number of word types) and the total number of words (tokens) in a corpus. Another linguistic unit in NLP is the lemma, which is the stem of a set of lexical forms that are the same major part-of-speech and have the same word sense. *Cats* and *cat* have the same lemma *cat* but are different word forms. The word form is the full inflected or derived form of the word. In this example, *cats* and *cat* are two inflected word forms. For morphologically complex languages like Arabic, we often need to deal with lemmatization. For many tasks in English, however, word forms are sufficient (Jurafsky & Martin, 2020, p. 12).

There are lemmatization algorithms, which can be complex. This is not surprising, as lemmatization involves a further abstraction around the original word forms and corresponding categorization. In NLP, there is a simpler but cruder method, which mainly consists of chopping off word-final affixes. This naive version of morphological analysis is called stemming. One of the most widely used algorithms is the Porter stemmer (Porter, 2006), which is included in some NLP

Corpus analysis results (processed in AntConc 3.5.8)						
Corpus files	Concordance	Concordance plot	File view	...	**Word list**	Keyword list
UN_resolution.txt	word types: 583; word tokens: 2017					
	rank	frequency	word			
	1	172	the			
	2	145	and			
	...	...	...			
	7	28	biodiversity			
	8	28	for			
	9	27	sustainable			
	...	...	...			

FIGURE 2.4   Number of word types and number of word tokens

packages such as NLTK (Natural Language Toolkit). NLTK includes extensive software, data, and documentation, all freely downloadable from http://nltk.org/ (Bird et al., 2019).

Suppose we have a sentence *They gave the women in these industries some examples of lemmatization*. We can first tokenize it word by word using the nltk.word_tokenize module, and the output of word tokens is: ['They', 'gave', 'the', 'women', 'in', 'these', 'industries', 'some', 'examples', 'of', 'lemmatization', '.']. Then we can use the PorterStemmer module in the NLTK package to stem each word token, and the following is the stemmed output:

They: they
gave: gave
the: the
women: women
in: in
these: these
industries: industri
some: some
examples: exampl
of: of
lemmatization: lemmat

The Porter stemmer can be applied to the following paragraph (cited in Jurafsky & Martin, 2020, p. 21):

> This was not the map we found in Billy Bones's chest, but an accurate copy, complete in all things – names and heights and soundings – with the single exception of the red crosses and the written notes.

The following is the stemmed output:

> Thi wa not the map we found in Billi Bone s chest but an accur copi complet in all thing name and height and sound with the singl except of the red cross and the written note

Returning to the example *They gave the women in these industries some examples of lemmatization*, we can use WordNetLemmatizer in the NLTK package to lemmatize lists of words and join the words in a text. The lemmatized sentence output produced by a command line such as "lemmatized_output = ".join([lemmatizer.lemmatize(w) for w in word_list])" is

> They gave the woman in these industry some example of lemmatization.

Table 2.1 summarizes the outputs after processing the original sentence using NLTK. The words or tokens that are different from the original sentence are *underlined* in the stemmed and lemmatized output.

Note that even though the forms for lemma and stemmed output may be the same, they are generated through different processes. Lemmatization focuses on further categorization that is meaningful for humans and is based on grammar (e.g., from *industries* to *industry* and from *examples* to *example*), whereas stemming focuses on form (e.g., from *industries* to *industi* and from *examples* to *exampl*).

Finally, the concept of *n*-gram is a convenient way for computers to describe various granularity levels. In simple terms, an *n*-gram can be defined as a sequence of *n* words. To some degree, an *n*-gram scheme hard partitions a set of word tokens by defining the length of a sequence, i.e., $n = 1, 2 \ldots n$. The hard partition of a

TABLE 2.1 Tokenization, stemming, and lemmatization

original sentence	They gave the women in these industries some examples of lemmatization.
word tokenized output	'They', 'gave', 'the', 'women', 'in', 'these', 'industries', 'some', 'examples', 'of', 'lemmatization', '.'
stemmed output	*they* gave the women in these *industri* some *exampl* of *lemmat*
lemmatized output	They gave the *woman* in these *industry* some *example* of lemmatization.

longer sequence is a simple and crude way for a computer program to approach the level of analysis. It is widely used in NLP programming. For example, in order to segment phrases, the program can cut a token sequence into a phrase sequence with a fixed phrase length, which varies with the sequence length. This allows the program to roughly divide the granularity levels of a text. As the length of a phrase is usually smaller than that of a sentence, a phrase can be set to be a 5-gram sequence, for example, while a sentence has a higher number of n-gram sequences. An n-gram can also refer to a predictive language model that assigns probabilities to the next word token. In this case, the small letter n refers to the number of grams as in the sequence $w_1, w_2, w_3 \ldots w_n$, while the capital letter N refers to the size of a fixed preceding context to be considered in an n-gram language model. The use of n-grams is discussed in more detail in Chapter 3.

2.3.3 Segmentation based on meaning

Granularity levels in NLP can be confirmed based on the form that corresponds to human units of thought, e.g., punctuation (sentences) and white spaces (words). Recently, neural language models can use a continuous real value vector for each linguistic unit, e.g., word or phrase. Cho et al. (2014) report that both the semantic and syntactic structures of words and phrases can be captured using an RNN Encoder – Decoder. RNN refers to a recurrent neural network, which is one of the architectures for language models (see Chapter 3). Cho et al.'s (2014) research shows that semantically similar words cluster together. For example, France, China, and Russian are clustered, which is consistent with human intuition regarding attributes of countries or regions, and English and French are very close to one another, which is also consistent with human intuition regarding languages or nationality. They also find that most of the phrases about the duration of time that are syntactically similar are clustered together. This is a method for computer programs to capture human understanding of phrases and their meaning. If a computer program does not interact with humans, it is not required to go through such a delivery stage.

Before 2016, when Google, Facebook, and Microsoft launched their Neural Machine Translation (NMT) systems, the most popular MT system was phrase-based Statistical Machine Translation (SMT), as modeling phrases instead of words had significantly improved the SMT approach through the use of larger translation blocks (or 'phrases') and reordering ability. Generally speaking, using phrases instead of words enables conventional SMT to condition on a wider range of context and results in better performance in reordering and modeling long-distance dependencies. Recently, Xu et al. (2020) "propose an attentive phrase representation generation mechanism that is able to generate phrase representations from corresponding token representations" (p. 386). They also incorporate the generated phrase representations into a Transformer translation model to enhance its ability to capture long-distance relationships.

2.4 Application of linguistic levels in machine translation

In a neural network language model, a unit at a certain granularity level is passed to the input layer of the neural network. From the computational perspective, it is not feasible to feed the entire dataset (e.g., 1 billion characters) into the model for training. Therefore, the input data needs to be split into something that is processable. The form of the input data affects that of the output. For example, most machine translation systems use sentences as input, and the MT results are also at the sentence level. A NMT model is based mainly on the encoder-decoder framework: the encoder compresses the input sentences of the source language into an abstraction from which the decoder generates target sentences. One reason to translate at the sentence level is the format of the training data, which is mostly aligned at the sentence level, such as in a translation memory. In addition, there are studies that explore the possibilities of short-single-sentence MT models to be extended to generate larger structures like paragraphs or even entire documents (Li et al., 2015).

An interactive machine translation model, however, usually uses a phrase-based language model. Ortiz-Martínez et al. (2011) describe an example of a session in which a Spanish sentence is translated into English. In this session, the source sentence is *Para ver la lista de recursos*, and the system suggests the translation of the whole phrase *To view the resource list*. The user, usually a translator or editor, can start to interact with the system by accepting or giving new suggestions on a smaller chunk of information. For example, the user might move the mouse to accept the first eight characters *To view*. However, the user may not be satisfied with the suggestion *the* after *To view* and enter *a* instead. This will trigger the system to suggest completing the sentence with *list of resources*, which is a new translation suggestion. If the interaction stops here, the final result will be *To view a list of resources*, instead of *To view the resource list*, which was suggested at the beginning before the user's interaction. The user can keep interacting with the system by changing the options that follow, e.g., change *list* to *listing*, and repeat the interaction until the final suggestion is accepted (Ortiz-Martínez et al., 2011, p. 69).

To some degree, the granularity level of interactive MT is impacted by an internal human analysis framework of levels. The input is fed sequence by sequence. For a computer program, what is more relevant is the length of the sequence. For humans, however, it is the unit of translation that is most accessible when they process the information, which is equal to ordered tokens from a machine's mathematical perspective. Sometimes the length of the sequence is not completely consistent with the concepts of linguistic levels in human minds. For example, a paragraph in a human's eyes might include short sentences so that in terms of length, the paragraph is considered a sentence by an MT system. However, the segmentation levels of the input and output sequences are usually the same, and the levels affect how translators and MT engines interact with each other not only during the interactive MT process but also after the MT results are generated. For example, in an NMT model, an input sequence is mapped to a vector embedding that represents the sequence, which is then converted to an output string of words in the target language at the granularity level. As humans handle both the input and output data, it must be presentable and make sense to humans. In this sense humans, not machines, determine the granularity level in NLP tasks.

2.5 Two approaches to levels of analysis

2.5.1 Sequences vs. meaning units

Note that a sequence is not necessarily a meaningful language unit (e.g., phrase or sentence) in a person's eyes. As discussed previously, meaning only exists in the human mind. The double structure of a sign entails there is no absolute overlapping between the signifier (form) and the signified (meaning). Consequently, a person has to compromise between form and meaning when using language to express ideas. This phenomenon is more obvious in translation. Usually the same meaning or concept in the source language can be expressed in various forms in the target language. An appropriate form can be selected based on the specific context, although that form may not be the preferred choice for everyone or for every situation. Likewise, if the form is prioritized, the emphasis on meaning could be undermined to some degree. A typical example is puns. When a person is asked to translate a restaurant's name "eggcellent," if there is restriction on the form in that the translation has to be one word, the meaning ("egg + excellent") might be compromised if the target language does not have similar linguistic resources to render the meaning. If meaning is prioritized, the translator might need to turn one word into multiple words in the target language, in which case the meaning of the pun may be compromised. If there is an absolute truth about translation solutions, it would be that the preferences underlying such choices are subjective and vary from person to person.

While the term 'sentence' conveys a meaningful unit based on human intuition, a 'sequence' is a concept that applies more to computer programming in that its connotations are more mathematical than linguistic. The term implies that there is a unique timestamp associated with each word; that is, at a certain moment, a person can only utter one word (w_n), and the next word has to follow the previous one. Sequence therefore describes an ordered combination of tokens. It can operate at various levels of granularity, which can be roughly defined by length, whereby the number assigned to n in an n-gram pattern is an important indicator of length. In other words, the concept of 'sequence' is flexible and can include all types of meaning units at various linguistic levels, controlled by the form, or the number of word tokens in the sequence.

2.5.2 Other aspects of comparison

In most NLP processing, punctuation is removed. In translation, however, punctuation is one of the most effective tools for humans to segment a piece of text and analyze discourse. As Newmark (1988) points out,

> Punctuation is an essential aspect of discourse analysis, since it gives a semantic indication of the relationship between sentences and clauses, which may vary according to languages: e.g. French suspension points indicate a pause, where in English they indicate the omission of a passage; exclamation marks in German are used for drawing attention, for emotive effects and emphasis, for titles of notices (but no longer for 'Dear Mary', in letters) and may be doubled; semi-colons indicate cohesion between sentences; French tends to use commas as conjunctions.
>
> *(p. 58)*

Similarly, concepts such as terms, phrases, clauses, sentences, and paragraphs are also designed for the logic of human thinking. To some degree, a human linguistic analysis framework is a social product, which is a learned approach to grouping bits of information to create a new logical whole, as with chunking. It is shared by a group of people with the same or similar cultural features, meaning that there are differences among various groups regarding forms of linguistic levels, like the punctuation systems discussed by Newmark (1988).

2.5.3 Implications for a translator

Translators should be aware of these characteristics so that they can make decisions as to what tasks are suitable for machines to accomplish and what tasks are appropriate for humans. There is no doubt that a computer program works differently from how a human processes textual information. That is the reason both are needed. By understanding the strengths and weaknesses of each approach, human users are able to better interact with and make use of the power of the machine.

These two approaches to levels of analysis do not and should not exclude each other. The architecture of levels of granularity incorporates both computer-specific (character and string levels, sentence window level) and human-oriented concepts (sentences, paragraphs, and passages). In doing so, the architecture can engage users on the levels they can easily process and leverage computing power for the others. For example, the architecture can create sentence segmentation rules using punctuation at the sentence level and apply tokenization at the character and string level to automate follow-up data processing such as POS tagging and parsing. Although there is no NLP processing that is completely unaffected by human intuition, when humans start using NLP tools, they are often impacted by this new approach to language and translation, which differs from familiar human approaches based upon intuition and social perception. By understanding this new approach, humans can also re-examine their existing personal theories of language and translation and possibly gain a deeper understanding in these areas.

Notes

1 An exception is jokes and puns that rely on *double entendre*, or dual meaning of words or phrases, to generate humor.

2   The syntagm is defined as a word combination pronounced as one unit and having sense. It is the smallest unit of sense in Chernov's theory (2004).
3   Annotation refers to the process of adding metadata information to the text in order to augment a computer's capability to perform Natural Language Processing (NLP) (Pustejovsky & Stubbs, 2012, p. ix). See Chapter 7.
4   When humans process information, these features are related to semantics. Semantics are human conceptualizations. In ML, the values are not always semantic in nature, as the values can be anything that computer programs can process.
5   A named entity is, roughly speaking, anything that can be referred to with a proper name: a person, a location, an organization (Jurafsky & Martin, 2020, p. 153).

3

PREDICATIVE LANGUAGE MODELS

KEY CONCEPTS

- *A computer program can generate a sequence through a language model that predicts what word comes next by assigning probability to a sequence of text.*
- *An n-gram language model is a symbol-based, statistical language model that is based on the relationship between adjacent tokens (form).*
- *A neural language model is based on distributional semantics that represents word meaning by taking large amounts of text as input then, through an abstraction mechanism, produces a distributional model, with semantic representations in the form of vectors.*

3.1 Introduction

In translation, prediction happens during both the language comprehension and production process. According to Amos and Pickering (2020), prediction means "pre-activation of any aspect of an utterance that occurs before" the utterance is heard (or read) (p. 706). For example, studies have used neuroscientific and eye-tracking measures to demonstrate prediction of meaning, syntax, and form. Amos and Pickering (2020) argue that

> prediction during comprehension is primarily and routinely a consequence of what we term prediction-by-production – the comprehender uses her production mechanism to predict sequentially, roughly as though she were completing the speaker's utterance herself, but making adjustments for differences between herself and the speaker.
>
> *(p. 709)*

Prediction is particularly obvious in simultaneous interpreting (SI). Simultaneous interpreters need to keep pace with the speaker while planning and producing their

DOI: 10.4324/9781003321538-5

own utterances. Prediction during comprehension allows the interpreter to reduce the lag between input and output and therefore reduce demands on memory. It also frees up capacity to focus attention on production and self-monitoring. Prediction in interpreting is not limited to comprehension; rather, simultaneous interpreters sometimes produce the translated utterance before it has been uttered in the source language, a form of predictive production (Amos & Pickering, 2020, p. 707).

Chernov (2004) proposes a model of the interpreting process that is centered on the psycholinguistic mechanism of "probability anticipation" (p. 91) as investigated in experiments with manipulated input material (Pöchhacker, 2010, p. 160). Specifically, the probability anticipation model hypothesizes that the basic mechanism making SI possible is the probability anticipation of the development of the message (Chernov, 2004, p. 199). Chernov (2004) states that

> the simultaneous interpreter's brain *generates hypotheses in anticipation of certain verbal and semantic developments of the discourse.* These hypotheses are based on subconscious subjective estimates of the range of probabilities within which the given verbal or semantic situation can develop further. In subsequent processes, the interpreter either confirms or rejects hypotheses by checking against critical points of the on-going discourse, concurrently on several levels.
>
> *(p. 93)*

Chernov (2004) further points out that Markov chains or similar linear sequences of elements cannot fully explain speech and postulates that "message development probability anticipation is a multi-level mechanism, operating on a hierarchy of levels" (p. 92).

The concept of prediction probability is useful when visualizing the cognitive activities associated with prediction in translation and interpreting. In natural language processing, predictive language models (LMs) are an approach to examining this cognitive area by means of mathematical formulations, as LMs can produce results that are to some extent consistent with human prediction in language comprehension and generation.

3.2 Language models

3.2.1 Language models for both humans and machines

As mentioned in Chapter 1, language is very unique compared with other human creations. In language use, a specific context triggers humans to produce many combinations of meaningful units, which includes both the units themselves and the order of them. In human language generation processes, it could be thought that there is an internal cognitive mechanism that helps a person search among various options or according to specific linguistic features in order to decide which word to produce next. In many cases, the process of prediction is even obvious for a beginning learner of a language, e.g., when a child is acquiring a language or an adult starts to learn a foreign language. Many beginning learners experience struggling to find the next word in their speech or writing when trying to express their ideas. When a person is proficient enough in using their 'language models' to predict the next word in the sequence or sentence, it happens automatically and subconsciously; most native speakers usually speak or write without giving it too much thought.

A computer program can generate a sequence through a natural language model that predicts what word comes next by assigning probability to a sequence of text, both spoken and written. As discussed in Section 2.3.1 in Chapter 2, an ordered sequence of words $(w_1, w_2, w_3 \ldots w_n)$ represents syntagmatic relationships. In each position of w_n, there are specific linguistic values associated with possible word options. When a language model captures features of these values, e.g., parts of speech and semantics, it can generate and evaluate the results, and produce an optimal outcome that is consistent with the results of human prediction.

Generally speaking, a typical natural language model predicts the next word token, instead of the whole sequence. There is a reason why developers do not work on modeling an entire sequence. As will be discussed in Section 3.4 of this chapter, in a statistical approach to language processing and generation, meaning and associated features related to linguistic forms are investigated by observing the distributional structure of natural language data in a corpus. A language model learns from past experience by analyzing examples and searching for patterns in the language data. Humans are very creative and always produce new sequences. The more word tokens a sequence contains, the lower the probability that the sequence will be included in an existing collection of data. For example, you can easily find the 2-gram sequence *it is* in a corpus, but it is much more difficult to find the 5-gram sequence *It is a giant bird*. A solution is to decompose, or divide up, the problem by segmenting the data into smaller sequences. Generally speaking, a language model subdivides the whole sequence – $w_1, w_2, w_3, \ldots w_n$ – and predicts one word token at a time. In practice, a good language model is expected to assign higher probabilities to sequences that are real and syntactically correct.

Most translation-related NLP tasks are fundamentally sequence-to-sequence problems that can be solved through language modeling, e.g., converting a longer sequence into a shorter one (text summarization), a sequence in language A into a sequence in language B (translation), or a sequence of spoken utterances to written text (speech recognition). In machine learning, the language model learns from input and output data: if the model is fed parallel corpora in a translation memory, for example, the model captures the aligned, equivalent patterns in translation. If the model contains long texts and their short summaries, it aims to accomplish a text summarization task. And if it is a corpus of paired spoken utterances and written text, it learns to convert text between spoken and written forms. What really matters is the training data as examples of input and output data, which is the resource from which the machine learns. The whole process is highly automated, with little or no human intervention required.

3.2.2 n-*gram language models*

As discussed in Section 2.1 in Chapter 2, when using computers to process language information at various levels of analysis, form is a convenient starting point. An *n*-gram is an ordered sequence of *n* words $(w_1, w_2, w_3, \ldots w_n)$. The value of *n* is an indicator of the length of a sequence and the level of granularity of analysis. Typically, the larger the number assigned to *n*, the longer the sequence will be and the greater the probability that the sequence is at a higher level of linguistic analysis. For example, the sentence *it is pitch black at night* can be segmented into the following:

- a one-word sequence of words – *it, is, pitch, black, at,* and *night* – based on a unigram scheme and word level of analysis, or
- a two-word sequence – *it is, is pitch, pitch black, black at,* and *at night* – a 2-gram (also known as bigram) scheme, resulting in a higher probability that the sequence is at the phrase level, as in *pitch black* and *at night,* or
- a seven-word sequence – *it is pitch black at night* – 7-gram scheme at the sentence level.

An *n*-gram model is a symbol-based, statistical language model that can be used to analyze the relationship between adjacent tokens – characters, words, or sequences at other granularity levels – in order to gain insight into how their meanings are related. It is the simplest model that assigns probabilities to word tokens in a sequence. *n*-gram language models are a very successful approach to statistical language modeling and are able to obtain a certain level of generalization by concatenating very short overlapping sequences seen in the training set. As these sequences are ordered in a way that is meaningful to people, this type of investigation can, to some degree, assist computers in capturing and extracting ideas or thoughts that people have created.

3.2.3 *Conditions for prediction in* n-*gram language models*

When a computer program uses an *n*-gram language model to generate a sequence, it keeps adding conditions to the previous probability results. Specifically, in order to estimate the next word, one needs to analyze the training data and compute P(w|h), which is the probability of a word *w* given some history *h*, or the previous $(n-1)$ words. To compute probabilities of entire sequences, the probability needs to be decomposed by using the chain rule of probability (see Equation 3.1; Jurafsky & Martin, 2020, pp. 30–31).

$$P\left(W_{1:n}\right) = P\left(W_1\right)P\left(W_2 \mid W_1\right)P\left(W_3 \mid W_{1:2}\right)K\,P\left(W_n \mid W_{1:n-1}\right) \quad \text{(Equation 3.1)}$$

Table 3.1 shows an example of the computing probabilities of the entire sentence *The cat is extraordinarily frustrating.*

TABLE 3.1 Computing probability of P(w$_{1:n}$)

Time stamp	Probability of the sequence $P(w_{1:n}) = P(w_1)P(w_2 \mid w_1)P(w_3 \mid w_{1:2}) \ldots P(w_n \mid w_{1:n-1})$	Resulting sequence[1]
1	P(The | (start)	(The) . . .
2	P(The | (start)xP(cat | The)	The (cat) . . .
3	P(The | (start)xP(cat | The)xP(is | the cat)	The cat (is) . . .
4	P(The | (start)xP(cat | The)xP(is | the cat) xP(extraordinarily | the cat is)	The cat is (extraordinarily) . . .
5	P(The | (start)xP(cat | The)xP(is | the cat)xP(extraordinarily | the cat is) xP(frustrating | the cat is extraordinarily)	The cat is extraordinarily (frustrating)

As the equation indicates, the joint probability of an entire sequence of words can be calculated by multiplying the conditional probabilities. Intuitively, it seems that new conditions are added to the previous ones. When more word tokens are built into the sequence, the probability of the entire sequence becomes smaller, as the new resulting sequence includes a longer history *h* with more conditions added to the requirements for the next possible word. For example, if the probability of a sequence starting with *the* is 50% (the first timestamp) and, given *the*, the probability of the next word being *cat* is 50% (the second timestamp), then the probability of a sequence being *the cat* is 25%. This is because the new condition (the probability of *cat* given *the*) is multiplied by the first condition (the probability of a sequence starting with *the*).

In practice, the chain rule of probability does not really help in reducing computational complexity. As discussed in Section 3.2.1, humans are very creative in producing new sentences, which may not be captured in a corpus. Take the sequence *the cat is extraordinarily frustrating* as an example. This sequence is probably not included in a training dataset, because it is not very frequent usage in real life. If one wants to compute the exact probability of a word given a long sequence of preceding words, e.g., P(extraordinarily \| the cat is) and P(frustrating \| the cat is extraordinarily), there is no way to estimate by counting the number of times the word *extraordinarily* occurs following *the cat is*, nor the word *frustrating* following *the cat is extraordinarily*, as these instances are not seen in the training dataset. Therefore, a more practical approach is to make future predictions based on the most recent observations, with only a limited history being considered, instead of computing the probability of a word given its entire history. If there are sufficient statistics, it is fine to use longer sequences (e.g., 5-gram). Otherwise, a smaller window is used without looking too far into the past.

The assumption that the probability of a word depends only on the probability of a limited history is called a Markov assumption. Andrey Andreyevich Markov (1856–1922) was a Russian mathematician best known for his work on stochastic processes (Andrey Markov, 2022). The Markov assumption significantly reduces the complexity of a problem (Friedman & Halpern, 2013, p. 264). Based on the assumption, we can generalize the bigram, which looks one word into the past, to the trigram, which looks two words into the past, and so forth to the *n*-gram, which looks *n*−1 words into the past.

$$P\left(W_n \mid W_{1:n-1}\right) \approx P\left(W_n \mid W_{(n-N+1):(n-1)}\right) \qquad \text{(Equation 3.2)}$$

In Equation 3.2, the small letter *n* is the number of word tokens in a sequence $w_1, w_2, w_3, \ldots w_n$, whereas the capital letter N is the size of a fixed preceding context. The equation means that the prediction is based on a fixed preceding context of size N; any input that occurred earlier than that has no bearing on the outcome (Jurafsky & Martin, 2020, p. 175). Take the sequence *the cat is walking in the bedroom* as an example. If we set the context window at 2, the probability of the next word token being *bedroom* given the previous words *the cat is walking in the* is almost equal to the probability of the next word being *bedroom* given the previous word *the*. That is to say, the right side of Equation 3.2 is almost equal to the left side. When $n = 7$ (that is, the seventh word token in the sequence) and $N = 2$, $P(w_7 \mid w_{(7-2+1):(7-1)})$ is equal to $P(w_7 \mid w_{(7-1):(7-1)})$, or, $P(w_7 \mid w_{(7-1)})$. The formula $w_n \mid w_{(n-1)}$ is the generic one for a sequence with *n* word tokens when $N = 2$: $P(w_n \mid w_{(n-2+1):(n-1)}) = P(w_n \mid w_{(n-1):(n-1)}) = P(w_n \mid w_{(n-1)})$. It indicates a bigram model, which predicts the second word token in the bigram given the first token, in this case using the scheme *the cat, cat is, is walking, walking in, in the,* and *the bedroom*.

3.2.4 Neural probabilistic language models

An *n*-gram language model is an approach to statistical language modeling. It estimates words from a fixed window of previous words and obtains a generalization by concatenating very short overlapping sequences seen in the training set. As Bengio et al. (2003) point out, statistical language modeling is "intrinsically difficult because of the curse of dimensionality: a word sequence on which the model will be tested is likely to be different from all the word sequences seen during training" (p. 1137). Mikolov, Yih, and Zweig (2013) also point out weaknesses. They argue that traditional *n*-gram language models treat words as discrete units that have no inherent relationship to one another, and thus cannot achieve a level of generalization that represents text in the corpora where similar words are likely to have similar vectors (p. 746).

Thus Bengio et al. (2003) proposed using neural networks for the probability function. Their study found that this approach allows the model to take advantage of longer contexts and significantly improves on the *n*-gram models. Specifically, they argue that computers should learn a distributed representation for words that allows each training sentence to inform the model about the probability estimation of semantically neighboring sentences. "The model learns simultaneously (1) a distributed representation for each word along with (2) the probability function for word sequences, expressed in terms of these representations" (p. 1137). This means that by "training a neural network language model, one obtains not only the model itself, but also the learned word representations, which may be used for other, potentially unrelated, tasks" (Mikolov, Yih, & Zweig, 2013, p. 746).

In recent years, neural language models (NLMs) have become dominant in solving NLP problems. Many translation-related tasks, such as machine translation, text summarization, and text generation, are handled by NLMs. A neural LM uses neural networks as its architecture to predict upcoming words from prior word context. In the neural network, there are many "small computing units, each of which takes a vector of input values and produces a single output value" (Jurafsky & Martin, 2020, p. 127).

In summary, neural net-based language models have many advantages over the *n*-gram language models:

> they can handle much longer histories and generalize over contexts of similar words. For a training set of a given size, a neural language model has much higher predictive accuracy than an *n*-gram language model. Furthermore, neural language models underlie many of the models for tasks . . . like machine translation, dialog, and language generation.
>
> *(Jurafsky & Martin, 2020, p. 143)*

3.2.5 Embeddings and meaning

In neural language models, the prior context is represented by embeddings of the previous words. Representing the prior context as embeddings, rather than by exact words as used in *n*-gram language models, allows neural language models to generalize unseen data much better than *n*-gram language models. In a certain sense, embeddings are representations of the meaning of words, learned directly from their distributions in texts. These representations are used in every natural language processing application that makes use of meaning. Generally, embeddings are vectors for representing words as a point in a multidimensional semantic space that is derived from the distributions of word neighbors, although the term is sometimes applied more specifically to dense vectors like word2vec (see Jurafsky & Martin, 2020, p. 100). In this book, we use embeddings to refer to dense vectors. Unlike sparse, long vectors with dimensions corresponding to words in the vocabulary, e.g., one-hot encoding, embeddings are a more powerful word representation: "they are short, with the number of dimensions d ranging from 50–1000, rather than the much larger vocabulary size $|V|$" (p. 112), as seen in one-hot encoding. These vectors "are dense: instead of vector entries being sparse, mostly-zero counts or functions of counts, the values will be real value numbers that can be negative" (p. 112).

The implications of the concept and methodology of embeddings are as important in the fields of linguistics and translation as they are in engineering. Since the beginning of reflection on translation centuries ago, meaning has been the center of discussion. There are also many intuitive ways to approach meaning in traditional linguistics and translation, for example through component analysis as discussed in Chapter 1. Yet it was not until theorists developed the methodology of embeddings that they were able to visualize and instantiate the concept of meaning using real value numbers. In this approach, mathematical operations are applied to meaning. For example, the male/female relationship is automatically learned, and with induced vector representations, *king* − *man* + *woman* results in a vector very close to *queen* (Mikolov, Yih, & Zweig, 2013, p. 746). The use of embeddings offers a new dimension of thinking as to what is meant by a word and how the meaning of a word is related to other words semantically. In NLP, this area of study is called vector semantics, and it is the standard approach to representing word meaning, capturing many aspects.

In a feedforward[2] neural network, the computation proceeds iteratively from one layer of units to the next, until the last layer is reached, in a process to obtain predictions by forward propagation. Deep learning includes modern networks that have multiple layers. Neural networks share many of the same mathematical principles as logistic regression. A feedforward neural LM is a standard feedforward network that takes as input at time *t* a representation of some number of previous words and outputs a probability distribution for possible next words. Like the *n*-gram LM, the feedforward neural LM calculates the probability of a word given the entire prior context by estimating based on *N* previous words.

Next we will discuss how meaning is represented in numbers through a neural language model.

3.3 Meaning representation in neural language models

3.3.1 Distributional semantics

In Chapter 1, we discussed two approaches to meaning representation: componential analysis and distributed representation. In both approaches, meaning is represented internally, from the lexeme or the entity in itself. In a human approach, the deconstruction process from a lexeme to its component parts happens through human cognitive activity. In a computer system, the feature extraction and meaning representation are induced externally, from the environment where an entity exists, by observing the distributional structure of natural language data in a corpus.

In a distributional approach to meaning, language data and the structure of the data are the basis for the representation of meaning in the computer program, rather than the human intuition used in translation without computer support. Rapidly increasing computing power allows machine learning to leverage large-scale language data more efficiently. After all, without ML tools, a human would not be able to process such a large amount of information in an entire lifetime.

As discussed in Chapter 2, meaning exists only in the human mind. Then how does NLP programming produce information that renders meaning in computer programs? Generally speaking, there are two strands of thought addressing this question. The first is encoding relevant human linguistic knowledge into the program. An example is WordNet (Fellbaum, 1998), a lexical database that stores words and human judgment-based relationships among them, e.g., synonyms and hyponyms, and linguistic information in the form of parts of speech, e.g., nouns and verbs. The second is capturing similarities from text corpora, for which technical methods can include count-based statistics, modeling using more advanced statistical methods, and increasingly powerful tools from machine learning. In recent years, with the rise of ever-larger text collections on the web, the second strand of thought grounded in corpus-based approaches has come to dominate (Smith, 2019, p. 3).

To capture similarities from text corpora, distributional semantics is applied as a model of word meaning, which is the foundation of meaning in a longer sequence, such as phrases and sentences as discussed in Chapter 2. Distributional semantics is based on the distributional hypothesis arising from the work of Harris (1954), which states that similarity in meaning results in similarity of linguistic distribution. Words that are semantically related are used in similar contexts: if enough text material is available, and in the corpus two linguistic entities w_1 and w_2 tend to have similar distributional properties by occurring with the same other entity w_3, then it can by hypothesized that w_1 and w_2 belong to the same linguistic class, or it can be interpreted that to some degree, w_1 and w_2 have some common meaning features (see Sahlgren, 2008, p. 35). "Distributional semantics reverse-engineers the process and induces semantic representations from contexts of use" (Boleda, 2020, p. 2), in particular from natural language data.

As Boleda (2020) points out, distributional semantics represents word meaning by taking large amounts of text as input, then through an abstraction mechanism, produces a distributional model, with semantic representations in the form of vectors – essentially, lists of numbers that determine points in a multi-dimensional space. "Words are points in a space determined by the values in the dimensions of their vectors, like 0.71028 and 1.76058 for *post-doc*. The words *post-doc* and *student* are closer together in the semantic space than *post-doc* and *wealth*" (p. 3). Thus, they are more closely related semantically and used in more similar contexts.

The collection of vectors in a distributional model constitutes a vector or semantic space, which is characterized by the dimensions of the vectors. In the space, semantic relations can be modeled as geometric relationships. In Boleda's (2020) example, there are two dimensions. The finding shows that the vectors for *post-doc* and *student* are closer in the space than those of *postdoc* and *wealth* because their vector values are closer: the cosine of the angle between the two vectors *post-doc* and *student* is 0.99, which is greater than 0.37, the cosine between *postdoc* and *wealth*. The closer the vectors, the closer the cosines, the more similar the meaning (p. 3).

3.3.2 Vectorization: from text to numbers

3.3.2.1 Words and vectors

Computers cannot process the form and meaning of texts as humans do. A computer processes only binary numbers 0 and 1. When computers are employed in natural language processing, the first step is therefore to convert words to numbers. To do that, numbers can be assigned to words to index them, using label encoding. But these numbers are discrete in nature, and arithmetic operations cannot be performed using the assigned values. These numbers can help identify the corresponding form of a word, but do not contain semantic information. A language sign, as discussed in Chapter 1, has both form (signifier) and meaning (signified). To obtain a representation of meaning, words must be converted to vectors. "A vector is usually a list of numbers, with a known length, which we call its dimensionality" (Smith, 2019, p. 3). Vectors are derived from the distributions of word neighbors and represent an inter-related, continuous, hidden state of words.

Vector or distributional models of meaning are generally based on a co-occurrence matrix, a way of representing how often words co-occur. Converting inputs to numerical representation is the first step to generating a ML algorithm in any domain. In this section, we will use an example: the term-term matrix.

As mentioned in the previous section, in a distributional approach to meaning, language data and the structure of the data set are fundamental for the representation of meaning in the computer program. Table 3.2 shows an excerpt from a document about a UN resolution on biodiversity conservation (the English version of a resolution adopted by the General Assembly on 16 April 2021, Symbol A/RES/75/271) with roughly 2000 words, which is the training corpus for vector learning.

The distributional structure is captured by examining the number of times the target words, such as *conservation*, *restoration*, *development*, and *transboundary*, and the context co-occur, e.g., *approaches and initiatives for* to the left of *transboundary*, and *cooperation, at appropriate levels* to the right. In this example, the context window is relatively small: 4 words to the left and 4 words to the right of the target words.

Table 3.3 is an example of a term-term matrix, also known as a word-word matrix or term-context matrix, in which each cell records the number of times the target word in the row co-occurs with the context word in the column in a

TABLE 3.2 UN corpus excerpt to show target words and their contexts

4 words to the left	Target words	4 words to the right
and implementation for the	conservation	and sustainable use of
cooperation and biodiversity conservation	restoration	and protection, Welcoming regiona
achievements of the Millennium	development	Goals and seeking to
approaches and initiatives for	transboundary	cooperation, at appropriate levels

TABLE 3.3 Co-occurrence vectors for four words in the UN corpus

	. . .	biodiversity	sustainable	global	. . .
conservation	. . .	4	8	0	. . .
restoration	. . .	4	4	0	. . .
development	. . .	1	16	3	. . .
transboundary	. . .	1	0	0	. . .

given context in the training corpus. As shown in the table, there are 0 instances of *sustainable* and *transboundary* co-occur in the context in the training corpus, whereas 16 instances of the word *sustainable* co-occurring with the word *development*. This is not surprising, as intuitively *sustainable* co-occurs with *development* more often than with *transboundary*.

Three of the dimensions, the three words in the row, are hand-picked for pedagogical purposes: *biodiversity*, *sustainable*, and *global*. These three dimensions of the vector for *conservation* – [4, 8, 0] – are the number of instances that *conservation* co-occurs in context with the three hand-picked words.

This example indicates that there is a correlation between distributional similarity and meaning similarity. We can also see from Table 3.3 that the two words *conservation* and *restoration* are more similar to each other than they are to other target words like *development*, because *biodiversity* tends to occur more often in their window (4 times vs. 1 time).

Figure 3.1 is a spatial visualization of word vectors for *development*, *transboundary*, *conservation*, and *restoration* in a three-dimensional space. From the figure, we can see the distance of the word *development* is farther than *transboundary*, *conservation*, and *restoration*, and the distance between *conservation* and *restoration* is much closer, as the meanings of these two words are very close. Though the training corpus includes only one document with roughly 2,000 words, it demonstrates some alignments between the model prediction and human intuitions. The accuracy of the model may improve when we increase vector dimensionality and the amount of the training data (Mikolov et al., 2013, pp. 6–7).

In a real-life corpus, the vocabulary size is much larger than three hand-picked context words. A real vector would have vastly more dimensions and thus be much less dense, as many words may actually appear in the four-word context window to both the left and the right in the training corpus. The length of the vector is generally the size of the vocabulary, often between 10,000 and 50,000 words. Since most of these numbers are zero, the vector representations are sparse. This is a fundamental problem that makes language modeling and other ML challenges difficult to resolve. As Bengio et al. (2003) point out, "if one wants to model the joint distribution of 10 consecutive words in a natural language excerpt with a vocabulary of size 100,000, there are potentially $100000^{10} - 1 = 10^{50} - 1$ free parameters" (p. 1137). One way to solve this issue is to use the shared patterns of the words to describe them, through which the dimensions of the vector are greatly reduced.

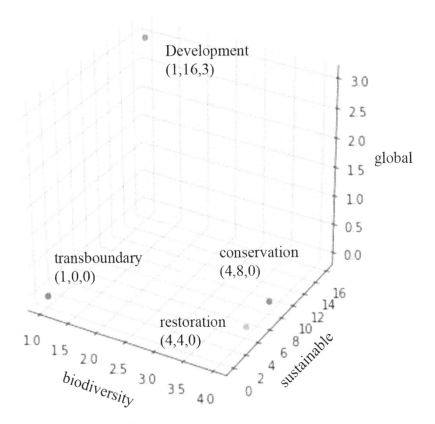

FIGURE 3.1   Spatial visualization of word vectors

The co-occurrence matrix in Table 3.3 shows frequencies of words with other words in each cell. But in most cases, raw frequency is not the best measure of association between words. Raw frequency is very skewed and not very discriminative. For example, words like *the*, *a*, and *I* occur frequently with all sorts of words and do not provide much information about any particular word. Simply by examining co-occurrences with these words, one cannot tell what kinds of contexts are shared by *conservation* and *restoration* in contrast to *development* and *transboundary*. Thus, we need to weight words in the vector. A weighting function can be provided using models such as the PPMI (positive pointwise mutual information) model or the tf-idf (term frequency – inverse document frequency) model, with the former being used for term-term matrices (see Table 3.3) and the latter for term-document matrices. Both algorithms are widely employed to compute word similarity, for tasks like finding word paraphrases, tracking changes in word meaning, and automatically discovering meanings of words in different corpora (Jurafsky & Martin, 2020, pp. 106–112). In translation, the tf-idf model is widely used for automated terminology extraction.

To summarize, in the above approach, a word can be represented as a sparse, long vector with dimensions corresponding to words in the corpus vocabulary or documents in a collection. In the next section, we will introduce a more powerful word representation: short dense vectors. Unlike the vectors produced by the PPMI model or the tf-idf model, these embeddings are short, with the number of dimensions d ranging from 50–1,000, rather than the much larger vocabulary size $|V|$ or number of documents.

3.3.2.2 Feature vectors

Dense vectors entail feature creation, in which the features may or may not have any obvious relation to the original input but do have comparative value in that similar inputs have similar features. In Section 2.3.1 of Chapter 2, we gave an example of paradigmatic relationships in a sequence. As shown in Figure 3.2, specific features can be extracted based on characteristics of each word category.

As discussed in Section 3.2, statistical language models such as n-gram models are based on conditional probability. The generalization is obtained from sequences of words seen in the training corpus to new sequences of words. When a new combination of n words appears that was not seen in the training corpus, n-gram models look at the probability predicted using a smaller context size. In contrast, feature vectors achieve a higher level of generalization that is not possible with classical n-gram language models. For example, if the phrase *the cat is walking in the bedroom* is in the training corpus, the generalization *a dog was running in a room* should be almost as likely, because *dog* and *cat*, as with *the* and *a*, *room* and *bedroom*, etc., have similar semantic and grammatical roles (Bengio et al., 2003, pp. 1137–1140).

Figure 3.2 is a visualization of the generalization obtained when a sequence of words that has not yet occurred has high probability due to the fact that it consists of words that are similar to words in an occurring sequence because they have semantic and grammatical similarity.

If we assign a numeric value to a feature related to 'animal', the values for words *cat* and *dog* must be greater than those for *bedroom* and *room*. Conversely, if the feature is 'space that can be occupied', the values for words *bedroom* and *room* will be greater than those for *cat* and *dog*. These relationships show that the assigned numbers represent meaningful values. They are real value numbers and can be used in mathematical operations. In this sense, feature vectors are in effect distributed representations, as we discussed in Chapter 1. Bengio et al. (2003) state that the feature vectors associated with each word can be "initialized using prior knowledge of semantic features" (pp. 1139–1140). In the case of prior knowledge of semantic features, like parts of speech or name entities, the information can also be passed to the computer program through sequential labeling tasks. The example shown in Figure 3.2 is based on prior human knowledge of semantic features.

Features can also be learned from training data. For example, if *dog* and *cat* are found with similar co-occurrences in a particular corpus, e.g., *dog* and *cat* both appear with *a* and *the* on the left and *is* and *was* on the right side of the word, the

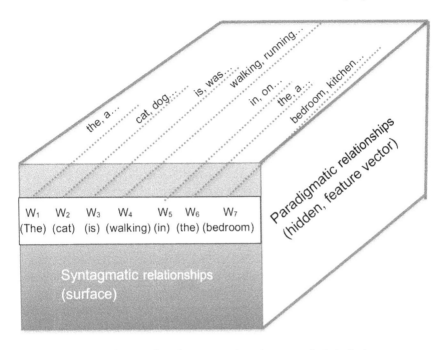

W₁   W₂   W₃   W₄   W₅   W₆   W₇
(The) (cat) (is) (walking) (in) (the) (bedroom)

Paradigmatic relationships
(hidden, feature vector)

Syntagmatic relationships
(surface)

FIGURE 3.2   Generalization based on semantic and grammatical similarity

computer program can learn that they play similar roles syntactically and semantically. Matrices can be applied to extract features from the distributional structure, such as the term-to-term matrices and term-to-document matrices discussed
in Section 3.3.2.1. However, in these models, the length of the vector is generally the size of the vocabulary, often between 10,000 and 50,000 words. This is a
fundamental problem that makes language modeling and other learning problems
difficult.

   This problem can be addressed using neural network language models. In these
models, input and output data are fed to the neural network in order for the neural
language model to work out fixed-sized feature vectors on its own. Dimensions
are learned based on the algorithm and do not have an intuitive interpretation like
'animal' or 'space that can be occupied' as in earlier examples of manually extracted
features.

3.3.2.3 Word2vec

Word2vec is a technique to learn word embeddings using shallow neural networks.
In this approach, the vector-space word representations are implicitly learned
through the input-layer weights, and it has been found that these representations
are surprisingly good at capturing syntactic and semantic regularities in language
(Mikolov, Yih, & Zweig, 2013, pp. 746–751). Instead of counting how often each

word occurs near a target word, which is the term-term matrix solution, word2vec trains a classifier on a binary prediction task to answer the question *Is word w likely to show up near the target word?* In word2vec, what is more important is not the prediction task itself, but rather the resulting learned classifier weights, which are used as the word embeddings.

There are two related models for computing continuous vector representations of words from very large data sets: continuous bag-of-words (CBOW) and continuous Skip-gram model architectures. The CBOW architecture predicts the current word based on the context, and the Skip-gram model predicts surrounding words given the current word. CBOW and Skip-gram models are shallow, two-layer neural networks that are trained to reconstruct linguistic contexts of words. The word2vec tool

> takes a text corpus as input and produces the word vectors as output. It first constructs a vocabulary from the training text data and then learns vector representation of words. The resulting word vector file can be used as features in many natural language processing and machine learning applications.
>
> *(Word2vec, 2013, n.p.)*

Mikolov, Chen, et al. (2013) provide an example of word pair relationships using the Skip-gram model trained on 783 million words with 300 dimensionality.[3] Their research result shows that word vectors can capture a range of syntactic and semantic regularities; for example, Paris − France + Italy = Rome, and Miami − Florida + Baltimore = Maryland (p. 10).

Word2vec methods are fast, efficient to train, and easily available online with code and pre-trained embeddings. Word2vec embeddings (2022) are static embeddings, meaning that the method learns one fixed embedding for each word in the vocabulary. Other methods for learning dynamic contextual embeddings include the popular BERT (Bidirectional Encoder Representations from Transformers) and ELMO (Embeddings from Language Models) representations, in which the vectors for each word vary across contexts. The basic principles of word2vec underlie these more powerful dynamic or contextualized embeddings, which are beyond the scope of this book.

3.4 Predicative LMs and translation

Predicative LMs offer a new dimension of thinking about translation research and practice. First, converting inputs to numerical representation (or features) is the initial step to any ML algorithm in a given domain, and the most effective approach is to use neural language models such as word2vec. Many translation-related tasks, including machine translation, text summarization, and text generation, are handled by neural LMs. They allow us to draw inferences in the translation tasks.

Second, as discussed in Section 3.2.5, the concept and methodology of embeddings offers a new framework to approach the meaning of a sign and how it is related to other signs. As discussed in Chapter 1, in theory, no language system is exactly identical to any other, and thus no absolute equivalence can be found in interlingual translation. Behind the visible element, the signifier, there is an invisible element that represents an interrelated, continuous, hidden state, as shown in a neural network. In the deeper layer of understanding, words are entangled with each other, fluid and susceptible to context, rather than separate, static, and fixed to what the signifier appears to be. Neural language models are effective tools to explore the double structure of signs, which is important for language comprehension and generation in translation.

Third, in the past, many linguistic resources for translators were usually based on the notion that words are discrete entities. For example, regular bilingual dictionaries are in alphabetical order treating each word as a separate entry. Some resources with semantic classification such as thesauri also consider words as separate symbols, even if they classify them further into categories based on similarity of meaning. To some degree, these resources can be misleading in helping translators practice and learn. For example, *faux amis* (false friends) are words that are similar in form and etymology in two languages but which, because of their separate development in two distinct cultures, have taken on different meanings (Vinay & Darbelnet, 1995, p. 68). Neural LMs, such as word2vec, provide a tool to further explore meaning. Even though the dimensions cannot be interpreted directly, they capture syntactic and semantic regularities that are useful. By using neural LMs, one can better explore the logical relationship between words, as shown in the example presented in Table 3.3. Furthermore, the vectorization of words allows us to apply mathematical operations to these feature vectors to explore their semantic relationships. For example, the cosine similarity score, applied to each word paired with other words, indicates mathematically how they are related. This is a type of machine learning largely independent of human intuitive reflection about language.[4] In this sense, neural LMs provide complementary insight into the meaning of words.

Computers are more efficient than humans for processing repetitive language pattern tasks involving immense volumes of language use, due to the repetitive computation involved. In semantics, component analysis done by humans involves only a few features, but when mathematically driven, it involves millions of repetitions. Humans can only focus on the process that makes sense to them, which is the intuitive process of reflection. Humans should focus on the results, rather than the process, given the limitations of human memory and attention mechanisms. Given this dynamic, the division of labor between machines and humans should be reconsidered, which we will address in Chapter 8.

Notes

1   The word token in parentheses is the word predicted by the language model.
2   In a modern neural network that is composed of small computing units, each of these units takes a vector of input values and produces a single output value. When the computation proceeds iteratively from one layer of units to the next, the architecture is called

a feedforward network. When the network has many layers, it is called deep learning (see Jurafsky & Martin, 2020, p. 127).

3 It can be expected that using higher dimensional word vectors will improve the accuracy. Mikolov, Chen, et al. (2013, pp. 6–7) evaluated models with multiple dimensionality options (50, 100, 300, and 600) in order to estimate the best choice of model architecture. In this example, 300 dimensionality is chosen.

4 One of the disadvantages of reduced-dimensionality vectors is that individual dimensions, such as the frequency of other words occurring around a word, are no longer interpretable features that can be mapped back to intuitive building blocks contributing to the word's meaning. The dimensionality and specific features of a vector are not based on human intuitive analysis of language, but rather on mathematical calculation, which is driven by machine learning (see Smith, 2019).

PART II

Machine learning tasks in translation

4
MACHINE TRANSLATION

KEY CONCEPTS

- *In its basic form, a Neural MT (NMT) system is a neural language model with specific conditioning; the relationship between the input and output data is based on the equivalence of meaning in at least two languages.*
- *The transition from rule-based MT (RBMT) to statistical MT (SMT) was a paradigm shift from linguistic rules to statistics. Both SMT and NMT are models that rely on statistical inference and response to linguistic data.*
- *NMT architecture differs from SMT, as NMT models take the form of neural networks composed of a large number of simple components wired together.*
- *Fundamentally, MT aims to solve a human problem. In this sense, MT can learn from the human approach to translation and become an instantiation of human translation processes with its own characteristics.*

4.1 Introduction

This chapter adopts a holistic approach to machine translation (MT) for three main reasons. First, when discussing machine translation with a focus on its impact on the human translation process, it makes sense to broaden attention to the entire localization process, rather than limiting it to activities involving the conversion of meaning from one language to another in the narrow sense. While localization may sound to the layperson like a strictly linguistic process, identical or similar to translation, it is much broader. The Localization Industry Standards Association[1] defines localization as "the process of modifying products or services to account for differences in distinct markets" (LISA, 2003, p. 34), and it has been investigated in both study and practice. While Pym (2014) considers localization as a paradigm of

DOI: 10.4324/9781003321538-7

translation theory (p. 118), this chapter focuses on practice. This chapter situates MT in the broader context of localization, which takes place within a commercial and developmental framework requiring the expertise of translators, language and tools specialists, programmers, engineers, project managers, desktop publishing specialists, and marketing staff (Folaron, 2006; Byrne, 2009, p. 2).

Second, in a holistic approach, MT technologies include not only various types of engines but also other supporting technologies. To integrate MT, technologies used in the localization process need to be updated to maximize MT effectiveness, including the human–machine interaction interface design. For example, interactive MT with computer-assisted translation (CAT) features, MT post-editing interfaces, and CAT tools with MT plug-ins through application programming interfaces (APIs) need to meet the specifications of MT. These language technologies are deployed at different stages of MT implementation, including pre- and post-processing phases.

Third, in a holistic approach, MT is not separate from traditional translation. Rather, MT provides a new dimension for understanding the nature of translation. In essence, language technology, including machine translation, is a form of human reflection about the mental and physical world. Technologies do not emerge from nowhere; rather, they mirror human life, forming a connection making human–machine interaction possible. Humans create each machine system, which is unique in how it processes data. While MT may be a new player in the translation process in a broad sense – to include source text analysis, terminology management, translation proper, editing, and reviewing – as a human creation, MT is defined by human nature.

4.2 The expansion of language technology in localization

4.2.1 MT and CAT: two lines of development

MT was the first computer-based application related to natural language. It is generally agreed that Weaver's memorandum of 1949 brought the idea of MT to general attention and inspired many projects (Liddy, 2001). The first public demonstration of machine translation, the Georgetown-IBM experiment, was performed in 1954. Although a small-scale project of just 250 words and six 'grammar' rules, it raised expectations that automatic systems capable of high quality translation would be developed in the near future (Hutchins, 2006).

The Georgetown-IBM system was a prototype of rule-based MT. For the first time, people realized that computers could not only handle mathematical calculations, but also serve as an 'electronic brain' to process non-numerical language data. It was a great breakthrough in computer science. However, the inadequacies of systems in existence at the time, accompanied by over-enthusiasm, led to the ALPAC (Automatic Language Processing Advisory Committee of the National Academy of Science – National Research Council) report of 1966. The report concluded that MT was not immediately achievable and recommended it not be funded. This had the effect of halting MT and most work in other NLP applications, at least within the United States (Liddy, 2001).

While the ALPAC report ended the golden age of MT funding, it opened a new chapter for commercialized MT. For example, despite the lack of funding available to MT research in the wake of the ALPAC report, SYSTRAN was founded in 1968 and survived by working closely with its clients. Moreover, there were some well-funded MT projects that proved successful in specific domains. METEO was a machine translation system launched in 1977 and fully integrated into the Canadian network for the transmission of meteorological forecasts (Benoit, 1982, pp. 39–40). The Pan American Health Organization Machine Translation System (PAHOMTS) has been in use in the translation unit of PAHO since 1980.

In the late 1980s and early 1990s the first paradigm shift in MT took place, from rule-based to statistical MT, when researchers applied purely statistical, data-driven approaches to the task of translation (Brown et al., 1993). As discussed in Chapter 3, Bengio et al. (2003) developed a language model based on neural networks, which improved the data sparsity problem of traditional SMT models. Their work laid a foundation for applying neural networks to machine translation. One hurdle for NMT system development was that it required significantly more computer power than was available with commercial computer processors. With the advent of GPUs (graphics processing units, which can be up to 100 times more powerful than regular processors), Google NMT, a commercialized system, could be launched in 2016 with impressive MT results (Wu et al., 2016; Tinsley, 2017).

While there have been ups and downs in MT development, MT is not the only solution where computer power is used to solve translation problems. When the ALPAC report of 1966 halted the first big wave of MT funding in the United States, another strand of thought emerged: instead of using computers to translate, they could be used to assist humans to translate. The idea of computers supporting the translation process is directly linked to the development of MT. In 1966, the ALPAC report did support funding for the field of computational linguistics, and in particular what it called "machine-aided human translation," then being implemented by the Federal Armed Forces Translation Agency in Mannheim. As Garcia (2014) points out, a study included in the report "showed that translators using electronic glossaries could reduce errors by 50 percent and increase productivity by over 50 percent" (p. 70). Table 4.1 shows milestones in MT and CAT development. Figure 4.1 compares their timelines.

The idea of databasing translations started to surface in the 1980s. The Translation Support System (TSS) developed by Automated Language Processing Systems (ALPS) in Salt Lake City, Utah, in the mid-1980s is considered the first prototype of a CAT system. In 1990, Trados launched their MultiTerm terminology database, with the first edition of the Translator's Workbench TM tool following in 1992. Also in 1992, IBM Deutschland commercialized its in-house developed Translation Manager 2, while large language service provider STAR AG (also German) launched its own in-house system, Transit, onto the market. Similar products soon entered the arena, such as Déjà Vu, first released in 1993. By the mid-1990s,

TABLE 4.1 MT and CAT development milestones

Year	MT/CAT development	Technology category
1949	Weaver's Memorandum	Rule-based MT
1954	Georgetown-IBM experiment	
1969	ALPAC report	
1968–1980	Early rule-based MT systems	
1980	Database translation	CAT development
mid-1980s	TSS (the first prototype of a CAT system)	
1992	CAT tools (e.g., Trados) and in house tools (e.g., Transit)	
1993	Statistical MT (IBM translation models)	Statistical MT
2003	Neural language model	Neural MT
2016	Google NMT	

translation memory, terminology management, alignment tools, file conversion filters, and other features were all present in the more advanced CAT systems (Garcia, 2014).

Figure 4.1 is a visualization of the CAT and MT development milestones from Table 4.1. In the graph, the x-axis is years and the y-axis is development with a scale showing seven stages. The black solid line reflects the development of MT, progressing from development stage 1 in 1949 with Weaver's memorandum to stage 2 in 1954 with the IBM-Georgetown experiment and stage 3 when the ALPAC report was published. Stage 4 stretches from 1968 to 1980, roughly, as there was still development of MT in some cases like METEO and commercialized MT like Systran. Until the 1990s the development remained flat, but moved to stage 5 in 1993 with the application of statistical MT. The transition to stage 6 occurred around

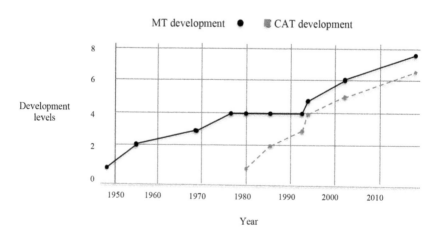

FIGURE 4.1 MT and CAT development timelines

2003 with the beginning of neural MT research, and commercialized neural MT marked the transition to stage 7 in 2016. The dotted line reflects the development of CAT, which began in 1980 when database translation was proposed. The mid-1980s saw the first prototype of a CAT system, leading to commercialized CAT tools in 1992. Since then the development of CAT has been steady and following a trend similar to MT, as CAT is also impacted by the implementation of artificial neural networks.

4.2.2 The role of MT and CAT in a localization process

In an automated localization process, there are two types of localization: automated workflow and automatic translation.

Figure 4.2 shows a localization workflow adapted from Zydron (2009), which was based on OASIS (Organization for the Advancement of Structured Information Standards) Open Architecture for XML Authoring and Localization (OAXAL) architecture. The localization workflow is shown against the gray background. In this process, most traditional CAT tools have automated two thirds of the workflow: the first stage is text extraction and pre-translation, and the third stage is reverse conversion and translation memory/terminology updates. The localization workflow does not include the human translation component. This division of labor has existed since CAT tools were first developed. Then, the improvement of data mining, machine learning, and MT upset this balance. Automation solutions came to focus increasingly on the actual translation stage, which in the past was dominated by humans.

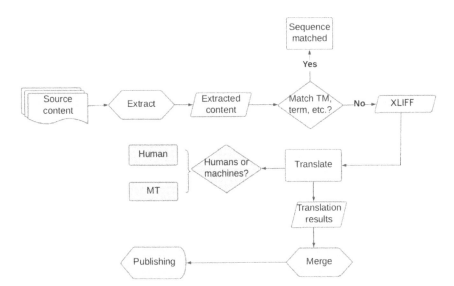

FIGURE 4.2 Automated workflow vs. automatic translation

Source: Adapted from Zydron (2009, n.p.).

When a large chunk of textual information, such as a source text corpus, is fed into a MT system, the system processes the information to perform the pure meaning conversion from one language to another. That is to say, an MT system also includes the components of traditional CAT tools, which include core features such as dividing a text into segments (normally sentences, as defined by punctuation marks), searching a bilingual memory for identical (exact match) or similar (fuzzy match) source and target segments, and searching and recognizing terminology in analogous bilingual glossaries (Garcia, 2014). Looking at segmentation as an example, as discussed in Chapter 2, even if there is no need to segment a larger chunk in machine training, meaningful segmentation is needed in order to improve the effectiveness of human processing during the human–machine interaction. In other words, as long as humans are involved, CAT features – those that support humans instead of machines – have to be included in the MT-driven process, no matter whether these features are shown to human users or not.

4.3 MT paradigms

4.3.1 Interlingua: an ideal level of understanding

In Section 3.2.5 of Chapter 3, we discussed the concept of meaning that can be visualized and instantiated in real value numbers, in particular by using dense vectors. While using embeddings inferred from neural network language models to represent meaning is a more recent development (Bengio et al., 2003), the idea of finding an ideal level of understanding using mathematical methods can be traced back to 1949 when Warren Weaver published his memorandum, in which he compares this level of understanding to "a great open basement" that is common to all languages:

> Think, by analogy, of individuals living in a series of tall closed towers, all erected over a common foundation. When they try to communicate with one another, they shout back and forth, each from his own closed tower. It is difficult to make the sound penetrate even the nearest towers, and communication proceeds very poorly indeed. But, when an individual goes down his tower, he finds himself in a great open basement, common to all the towers. Here he establishes easy and useful communication with the persons who have also descended from their towers.
>
> *(cited in Hutchins, 1999, p. 6)*

This common ground can be understood as the meaning to be rendered across languages. In 1968, Vauquois further elaborated this level of understanding in his paper *A survey of formal grammars and algorithms for recognition and transformation in mechanical translation*. He proposed a concept of a universal 'interlingua' representation of a source language, which represents an ideal level of understanding that is independent of any specific linguistic forms. In this scenario, an MT system

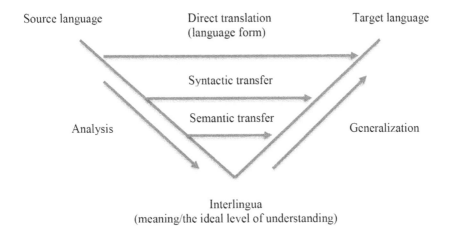

FIGURE 4.3   The Vauquois triangle for MT

Source: Adapted from Vauquois (1968, p. 335).

consists of an analyzer to parse the source language and a generator for each target language to transfer the interlingua representation from one language to another. The Vauquois triangle in Figure 4.3 shows these relationships.

The triangle shows an increasing depth of analysis, moving from the direct translation approach at the top through transfer approaches in the middle to interlingua approaches at the bottom. In addition, a decreasing degree of dependence on the language form (i.e., signifier) happens moving down the triangle. At the direct level at the top, almost all knowledge is at the word level and requires large amounts of transfer between linguistic forms. The dependence decreases to syntactic and then semantic transfer, and finally little specific transfer knowledge based on forms at the interlingua level. We can view the encoder-decoder network of neural machine translation (NMT) as an interlingua approach, with an encoder taking an input sequence and creating a contextualized representation of it, and a decoder generating a task-specific output sequence (see Jurafsky and Martin 2020, p. 208).

Since the first public demonstration of MT in 1954, many paradigms based on the Vauquois triangle have been proposed. They all aim to solve the problem of the conflict between meaning (interlingua) and form (semantic/syntactic structure). This is not an easy task, as many linguistic features come into play, including word order, lexical ambiguity in various contexts, and semantics. The meaning conversion process requires knowledge of morphology, syntax, and semantics for both the target and source languages. Native speakers of a language have this knowledge in implicit form, but coding the knowledge explicitly in computer programs is extremely complex. Bar-Hillel (1959) provides an example in Appendix IV of the *Report on the State of Machine Translation in the United States and Great Britain*: "Little John was looking for his toy box. Finally, he found it. *The box was in the pen.* John was very happy" (p. 2).

In this sentence, *pen* has two meanings in English: (1) a certain writing utensil, (2) an enclosure where small children can play. Most English-Chinese NMT systems in use at this writing still generate a translation with the first, incorrect meaning. Bar-Hillel (1959) argues that

> no existing or imaginable program will enable an electronic computer to determine that the word 'pen' in the given sentence, within the given context has the second of the above meanings, whereas every reader with a sufficient knowledge of English will do this 'automatically'.
>
> *(p. 2)*

Bar-Hillel further points out that the issue is not one that concerns *translation proper*, i.e., the transition from one language to another. Rather the issue concerns a preliminary stage of this process: the determination of the specific contextual meaning of a word that is semantically ambiguous in isolation. In other words, the challenge lies in the analyzer in the Vauquois triangle.

In the next three sections, we consider the three main MT paradigms that aim to address this problem.

4.3.2 Rule-based MT

Rule-based machine translation (RBMT) is the oldest approach, and it is still widely used for a large variety of applications for its high throughput, deterministic translations critical for some use-cases and its powerful customization ability. Generally speaking, the process of rule-based MT strictly follows the Vauquois triangle, with analysis often being very advanced, while generation is sometimes reduced to the minimum. Specifically, RBMT uses a database of rules and lexical items to which the rules apply; further, these rules and lexical items can be understood ("readable") and modified by human interactors, e.g., computer linguists, linguists, and translators (SYSTRAN, 2016).

There are three steps in RBMT: first, the analysis of the sentence in the source language, including part of speech tagging, morphological analysis, semantic analysis, constituent analysis, and dependency analysis. Second, a transfer step creates a series of hard engineered algorithms to represent relevant rules and lexical items based on the analysis, e.g., if the system sees *pen* in English, the system converts it to 笔 (meaning "*pen, pencil, writing brush and other types of writing utensils*" in Chinese). Third, a generation step executes the algorithms to produce the actual target sentence from the internal representation created in the second step.

A word-for-word approach, or direct translation, was the first RBMT technology used in the Georgetown-IBM experiment. In this experiment, the process of transforming the source sentence into the target sentence, i.e., *translation proper*, was divided into three different steps: first, the words in the text were looked up in a bilingual dictionary; second, the equivalent words of the target language were selected; and third, some simple rearrangements of word order were performed and the results were printed out.

Word-for-word RBMT has been further developed in commercial MT systems in terms of the complexity of the analysis. For example, in the early development of SYSTRAN RBMT systems (see Hutchins, 1979), there were four stages in the translation process: input, dictionary lookup, syntactic analysis, and translation. At the input stage, each word was checked against two dictionaries (a high frequency dictionary and a master stem dictionary) for information on grammatical (and some semantic) properties and for possible English equivalents. Syntactic analysis involved four 'passes': (1) to resolve homographs, (2) to establish basic phrase groups, (3) to extend phrase structures and identify specific objects and complements, and (4) to determine the types of clauses, their ranges, and their constituents. The final stage was translation, which incorporated many subroutines using information from the dictionaries and syntactic analysis to select and arrange the English output (pp. 33–34).

From the linguistic standpoint, the main improvement in the early development of SYSTRAN RBMT systems, according to Hutchins (1979), was

> the 'modularity' of its programming, which allows modifications of any part of the translation processes to be undertaken without fear of impairing overall efficiency. Furthermore, the linguistic and computational facets are kept separate, thus avoiding the irresolvable complexities encountered in the Georgetown systems.
>
> *(p. 33)*

This approach used any information, regardless of its source, leading to acceptable English text (p. 34), which is a practice-oriented approach, using applicable rules rather than theoretical linguistic rules, and very pertinent in RBMT development.

The paradigm of RBMT has many restrictions in terms of addressing conflicts between shared meaning and specific linguistic forms, many of which led to the ALPAC report. In this approach, all linguistic rules need to be hard engineered into computer programs, which generates extra effort and makes the system difficult to maintain. Researchers sought different paradigms to achieve a better solution. Due to the rise of CAT and resulting translation memory, bilingual/multilingual data became more sufficient, and attention shifted to the statistical MT paradigm around 1988 when the IBM Watson Research Center started using it (Brown et al., 1993, 1990).

4.3.3 Statistical MT

Technically speaking, statistical machine translation does not follow the process defined by the Vauquois triangle. There is no generation based on analysis, and the transfer component is not deterministic. Instead, for a given source sentence, the engine generates multiple possible translations, each one referred to as a hypothesis, and the system modeling employs probability hypotheses and search algorithms to select the best hypothesis according to the training data. As discussed in Section 4.2.1, researchers started to apply purely statistical, data-driven approaches to the task of translation in the late 1980s and early 1990s (Brown et al., 1990). In particular, IBM translation models draw on the noisy channel model for speech recognition (Brown et al., 1990), which formed the basis of many SMT models now in use today.

What is a noisy channel model, and why is it applied in SMT? Suppose person B tries to listen to or read person A's speech or writing. There is a channel that transmits the signal from person A to B. Yet somehow the original signal is obscured in transmission when disruptions or errors create noise in the channel. Under these circumstances, the noisy channel aims to find the intended signal, and, in this context, anything that obscures the signal can be considered 'noise'. The noisy channel model is applied to machine translation by regarding the target sentence as a distortion of the source sentence through a channel with 'noise', which can be anything that obscures the source sentence. For example, the grammar of the source language (SL) cannot be applied directly to generate an equivalent sentence in the target language (TL). Instead, TL grammar needs to be characterized by observing correspondences between SL and TL grammar, as well as the grammar of the source language.

As Brown et al. (1993, pp. 264–266) describe, a string of English words, e, can be translated into a string of French words, f, in many different ways. In statistical translation, we take the view that every f is a possible translation of e. We assign to every pair of strings (e ~ f) a number Pr (f | e), i.e., the probability of the French translation given the English source e. This relationship can be interpreted as the probability that a translator, when presented with e, will produce f as the translation. However, simply using Pr (f | e) to work out the best possible translation is not adequate, as it distributes probability very widely, with most solutions on ill-formed strings in the target languages. In other words, a target segment hypothesis with the highest probability given a source segment (i.e., a direct model from the source sentence to the target sentence) does not necessarily mean that this hypothesis is fluent in the target language.

Brown et al. (1993, pp. 264–265) use noisy-channel decomposition to address this issue. Intuitively, when a native translator of French produces a string of French words, the translator actually has the string of English words in mind and has translated them mentally. Given a French string f, the job of our translation system is to find the string e that the native speaker had in mind when he produced f. The chance of error can be minimized by choosing the English string e for which Pr(e | f) is greatest. Note that this process involves a form of reverse translation or reverse hypothesis, since English is set as the target language, whereas French is the source language in the problem Pr(e | f). After applying Bayes' theorem,[2] the conditional probability is decomposed into Equation 4.1:

$$\Pr(e \mid f) = \frac{\Pr(e) \text{ g } \Pr(f \mid e)}{\Pr(f)} \qquad \text{(Equation 4.1)}$$

Since the denominator $Pr(f)$ is independent of e, as the segment in French has been given and thus can be considered a constant, finding the estimate of the target sequence in English e, $\hat{e}$, is the same as finding e, so as to make the product $Pr(e)Pr(f \mid e)$ as large as possible. This operation leads to the fundamental equation of machine translation, shown in equation 4.2:

$$\hat{e} = \underset{e}{\textbf{Argmax}} \ \textbf{Pr(e) Pr(f|e)} \qquad \text{(Equation 4.2)}$$

As Brown et al. (1993) state, equation 4.2

> summarizes the three computational challenges presented by the practice of statistical translation: estimating the *language model probability*, $Pr(e)$; estimating the *translation model probability*, $Pr(f \mid e)$; and devising an effective and efficient suboptimal search for the English string that maximizes their product. These challenges are called the language modeling problem, the translation modeling problem, and the search problem.
>
> *(p. 265)*

The application of noisy channels and Bayes' theorem has in effect swapped the dependency relationship between the two events, f and e, i.e., the source language and target language, from $Pr(e \mid f)$ on the left side to $Pr(f \mid e)$ on the right side of Equation 4.1. That is to say, if we want to translate from a French string f to an English string e, which is based on probability $Pr(e \mid f)$, we can convert it to a probability $Pr(f \mid e)$ that operates in the reverse direction as well as a language model $Pr(e)$. As Yee et al. (2019) point out, directly estimating the posterior probability $Pr(e \mid f)$ cannot naturally take advantage of unpaired data (p. 5696). The way a noisy channel model incorporates the language model into its computation allows it to leverage the target language data, which is not paired with that of the source language. This transformation may appear unintuitive; however, it is done for very good reason, as it makes the operation relatively straightforward to implement in computation. In essence, it is more of an engineering achievement than a linguistic achievement, as the hope is that the MT system will work, even if it is not based on how humans actually do the translation. Starting with SMT, the inner workings of machine translation move away from the way humans translate in practice. The noisy channel model is used not only for MT, but also for text generation, text summarization, optical character recognition (OCR), and other NLP tasks.

Around the turn of the century, an extended approach, called phrase-based machine translation (PBMT), was developed. PBMT was based on inducing translations for phrase pairs (Jurafsky & Martin, 2020, p. 229). Before 2016, when commercial NMT systems were launched, PBMT was the simplest and most popular version of statistical machine translation. For PBMT, the system works with larger chunks than words, for example, *in Canada*, *note that*, *interested in*, as well as multi-word idiomatic language use. During decoding, the input sentence is segmented into a sequence of phrases. Note that the word 'phrase' in PBMT refers to any subsequence of words, not necessarily a linguistic phrase. Koehn et al. (2003) suggest that the highest levels of performance can be obtained through "heuristic learning of phrase translations from word-based alignments and lexical weighting of phrase translations" (p. 127).

Typically, a SMT engine consists of multiple modules; for instance, Corbí-Bellot et al. (2005) introduce eight modules in a SMT architecture: de-formatter, morphological analyzer, part-of-speech tagger, structural transfer, lexical transfer, morphological generator, post-generator, and re-formatter, which is similar to an assembly line producing an automatic translation result (p. 81). Kashani et al. (2007) integrated an Arabic-to-English transliteration system into a general-purpose, phrase-based statistical machine translation system and found that the transliteration module can help significantly in the situation where the test data are rich with previously unseen named entities (p. 17).

In SMT, different modules are optimized separately, instead of jointly in one model. In reality, this can be a difficult challenge to resolve, involving considerable work in human feature engineering. Further, adding modules and exceptions confuses the machine. As these modules are added mostly based on human intuitive reflections on the automatic translation process, the focus is on the output rather than machine learning and training processes.

Unlike the traditional phrase-based translation system, which consists of many small sub-components that are tuned separately, neural machine translation attempts to build and train a single, large neural network that reads a sentence and outputs a correct translation. NMT offers end-to-end training, using one model to train everything inside. The architecture of an NMT system is conceptually very simple and has the ability to generalize well to very long sentences.

4.3.4 Neural MT

4.3.4.1 Statistical approaches to MT

In essence, the NMT paradigm is also a statistical approach to machine translation, as it is also based on statistical inference and response to linguistic data. However, NMT architecture is different from that of SMT systems. NMT models take the form of neural networks, which are composed of a large number of simple components wired together. Specifically, a neural translation model consists of two basic parts: an 'encoder' and a 'decoder', which align with the analysis and transfer/generation steps in the Vauquois triangle. In this case, analysis is an encoding process, and the result is a matrix composed of a sequence of vectors, representing the sentence structure and meaning. The transfer and generation steps are combined into a process called decoding, which generates the target words directly. To some degree, compared with the representation provided by RBMT and SMT, the intermediate representation as a result of the analysis or encoding process is the closest state to an interlingua representation. Whereas SMT involves much work in human feature engineering, NMT relies more on machine learning. By feeding the NMT engine with input and labeled output data, the computer program extracts features and works out the meaning representation on its own. NMT involves a higher level of automation.

4.3.4.2 Recurrent neural network

In its basic form, a Neural MT system is a neural language model with extra conditioning. A translation process is one type of sequence generation task. The process can be considered a type of guided target text production with one extra condition: that the meaning of a sequence in the SL be equivalent to that of the sequence in the TL. Similarly, when reading a passage, a human does not absorb the meaning of the words all at once; rather, processing is word by word and comprehension becomes deeper as understanding gradually builds according to what has been processed. In other words, every new comprehension and production step is based on previously accumulated meaning.

An NMT system can be explained intuitively based on a recurrent neural network (RNN). A RNN is any network that contains a cycle within its network connections; that is, any network where the value of a unit is directly, or indirectly, dependent on its previous output. Since it uses its own output subsequently as input, a RNN can be considered a conditional language model (Jurafsky & Martin, 2020, pp. 176–179). "RNN-based language models process a text sequence one word at a time, attempting to predict the next word in the sequence by using the current word and the previous hidden state as input" (p. 179). A hidden state "embodies information about all of the preceding words all the way back to the beginning of the sequence" (p. 179).

As shown in Figure 4.4, the network has an input layer x, a hidden layer s (also called context layer), and output layer y.

> Input to the network in time t is $x(t)$, output is denoted as $y(t)$, and $s(t)$ is state of the network (hidden layer). An input vector $x(t)$ is formed by concatenating vector w representing a current word, and output from neurons in context layer s at time $t - 1$.
>
> *(Mikolov et al., 2010, p. 1046)*

These relationships can be expressed in the formula $x(t) = w(t) + s(t - 1)$ (p. 1046). It is hypothesized that this hidden state represents all the content of the sentence.

4.3.4.3 Attention mechanism in MT

The application of recurrent neural networks in machine translation is critical in solving machine translation and other sequence transduction problems. However,

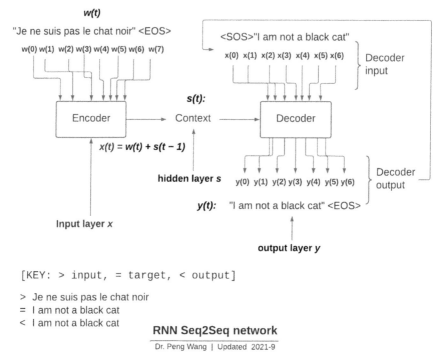

FIGURE 4.4 RNN Seq2Seq network

Source: Adapted from Robertson (n.d.).

passing information forward through an extended series of recurrent connections leads to a loss of relevant information and to difficulties in training. Moreover, the inherently sequential nature of recurrent networks inhibits the use of parallel computational resources, preventing them from being trained with large amounts of data (Jurafsky & Martin, 2020, p. 190; Vaswani et al., 2017).

To address the fundamental constraint of sequential computation, Vaswani et al. (2017) proposed attention mechanisms in machine translation, which brought about the real breakthrough of NMT models.

> Attention mechanisms have become an integral part of sequence modeling and transduction models in various tasks, allowing modeling of dependencies without regard to their distance in the input or output sequences. In all but a few cases, such attention mechanisms are used in conjunction with a recurrent network.
>
> (p. 2)

Based on the attention mechanism, Vaswani et al. (2017) proposed the Transformer, "a model architecture eschewing recurrence and instead relying entirely on

an attention mechanism to draw global dependencies between input and output"
(p. 2). The Transformer allows for significantly more parallelization and can reach
a new state of the art in translation quality after being trained for a relatively short
period of time on GPUs (p. 1). According to Vaswani et al. (2017),

> Self-attention, sometimes called intra-attention, is an attention mechanism re-
> lating different positions of a single sequence in order to compute a represen-
> tation of the sequence. Self-attention had been used successfully in a variety of
> tasks including reading comprehension and abstractive summarization, before
> being applied to machine translation . . . the Transformer is the first transduc-
> tion model relying entirely on self-attention to compute representations of
> its input and output without using sequence aligned RNNs or convolution.
>
> *(p. 2)*

In a self-attention system, the information flows in a single causal, or backward
looking, self-attention layer. A self-attention layer maps sequences of input vectors $(x_1, \ldots, x_n)$ to sequences of output vectors $(y_1, \ldots, y_n)$ of the same length.
When processing each item in the input, the model attends to all the inputs up to
and including the current one. Specifically, the model compares an item of interest,
e.g., x_3, to a collection of other items, i.e., its preceding elements x_1 and x_2, and
to x_3 itself, in a way that reveals their relevance in the current context. The result
of these comparisons is then used to compute an output for the current input. For
example, the computation of y_3 is based on a set of comparisons between the input
x_1, x_2, and x_3. Unlike RNNs, the computations at each time step are independent
of all the other steps and therefore can be performed in parallel (Jurafsky & Martin,
2020, p. 191; Vaswani et al., 2017, p. 2).

Compared with the RNN, the Transformer includes stacked multiple encoders and decoders, which is denoted by *Nx*, implying that encoders and decoders
are stacked *n* times. "Each layer in the encoder has two sub-layers. The first is a
multi-head[3] self-attention mechanism, and the second is a simple, position-wise
fully connected feed-forward network" (p. 3).[4] Intuitively, listeners intend to find
an answer to a specific question in another person's utterance. There is an internal
mechanism in the human brain that directs their mental language model to pay
attention to specific parts of a sentence. For example, if they want to know the
color of a roof, they pay attention to *red* when they hear the statement *There is
a house with a red roof*. Similarly, the multi-head attention mechanism allows the
model to attend to different parts of the sequence according to its context, assigning larger weight to important parts and smaller weight to irrelevant parts. In addition, the position-wise module provides positional encoding that can represent the
position information of a token in a sequence in a dimensional vector, instead of
simply calculating the distances between words/tokens in a sequence.

Vaswani et al. (2017) found that for translation tasks, the Transformer can be
trained significantly faster than architectures based on recurrent or convolutional layers (p. 10). Their research shows these models to be superior in quality while being

more parallelizable. The Transformer generalizes well to other tasks by applying the architecture successfully to English constituency parsing both with large and limited training data. Since 2017, the Transformer model has been widely adopted in the domain of machine learning and has greatly improved the performance of MT.

4.4 MT deployment in the localization process

4.4.1 MT deployment infrastructure

When deploying an MT system, a technical architect typically considers the whole deployment infrastructure. For example, the Tilde MT infrastructure design includes the client, interface, logical, and data layers (Pinnis et al., 2018, p. 1345). However, for linguists, professional translators, and other domain experts, what is most relevant is deployment: how the user interacts with the MT system. In the Tilde MT system, this involves the client and interface layers. The following are popular scenarios for MT deployment:

1   Integrating the MT systems through CAT tool plugins. An MT platform needs to provide integration capabilities for at least the most popular CAT tools so that the tools can access the MT system.
2   Performing translation of text snippets, documents of various popular formats, and websites directly in the MT graphical user interface.
3   Using an MT widget that can be integrated in a website or mobile applications, e.g., Google's Website Translator widget.[5]
4   Integrating the MT external API (application programming interface) in users' translation and multilingual content creation workflow.

Among these deployment scenarios, integrating MT in CAT tools is an efficient way to ensure the quality of output because it leverages both the automatic translation results and human evaluation and editing. In this case, human interaction takes place during the process of translation, and the unit of translation can vary. For example, in Lilt, an interactive MT platform, users (professional translators) interact at the phrase level. In contrast, most CAT tools with MT plugins allow users to edit at the sentence level, although other ML-driven features such as predictive typing are embedded in the platform.

When using other scenarios, MT quality evaluation is crucial, because contaminated indexed content will cause a downward spiral in the quality of the database. When users propagate machine translation with no human improvement and the content is included in the pool of material used to train the MT engine, the system will be polluted with inaccurate translation, causing a decline in the performance of the system, especially a neural MT system. If this problem is to be avoided, human intervention is a necessity. The intervention goes beyond the translation process in the strict sense and takes place before or after machine translation, for example in MT post-editing (MTPE).

One major consideration in MT deployment is how users can best leverage their proprietary linguistic assets to improve the performance of the baseline MT system. Terminology integration and translation memory-MT integration are crucial (see Bulte & Tezcan, 2019). At the user and interface layers, it is important that an MT platform allow users to store linguistic resources for their work, such as parallel and monolingual corpora and multilingual term collections. The connectivity between CAT tools and MT systems is typically through API.

Below the client and interface layers, usually there is a logic layer that offers features such as authentication and authorization when exchanging data. These features can validate a user's identity and grant that user permission to access linguistic resources. Furthermore, in order to provide MT services to clients with security concerns or clients whose data are not allowed to leave the client infrastructure, the MT system can be deployed as an enterprise solution in the client infrastructure.

4.4.2 MT deployment considerations

When deploying MT systems, there are many factors to be taken into consideration, including MT paradigms, communication modes (spoken vs. written translation), the deployment environment (cloud-based or local server), and hardware requirements. Some key considerations in MT deployment are described here:

1 Language pairs

   Some low resource languages such as Arabic and African languages do not have sufficient parallel data, and the language resources are imbalanced. Language pairs with Arabic, for example, have their own features and pose specific challenges for MT. Baniata et al. (2018) point out that SMT performed very well when the translation was between the Palestinian and the Syrian dialects, due to the close linguistic proximity of these two versions of Arabic (p. 3). Another solution for low-resource languages is to use a trained multilingual NMT system that can automatically translate between unseen pairs without any direct supervision. In this solution, a model trained for instance on English/French and Spanish/English is able to directly translate from Spanish to French. Such an emergent property of a multilingual system is called zero-shot translation (Gu et al., 2019, p. 1259).

2 Content types

   An MT solution is closely related to content type. For example, at eBay, MT is used mainly on the following content: search queries, item titles and descriptions, product reviews, product descriptions, and member-to-member communication (Rowda, 2016). These content types vary greatly in their linguistic and stylistic features. For example, as Rowda (2016) notes, queries are hard to translate because, among other things, there is no context. To achieve the best MT performance for different content types, both the MT engines and MT-driven translation workflow need to be customized. On the one hand, if the content type is creative/marketing materials, using CAT with MT plugins or interactive MT is often chosen. On the other hand, if the content is limited to a specific domain, such as weather forecasting, a rule-based MT might work well.

3   Sequence length

The sequence length of the source text impacts the performance of MT engines. Sánchez (2018) compares SMT and NMT output in a case study of MT quality at eBay. In terms of adequacy – whether the translation corresponds to the source text – both SMT and NMT decline with longer segments, whereby short segments include 2–4 words, medium segments 6–12 words, and long segments 12–35 words. However, NMT is better even with shorter segments. In terms of fluency – whether the translation reads well in the target language – SMT and NMT adequacy declines with longer segments, although once again NMT performs better overall.

4   Communication types

There are different technologies for spoken MT, which usually incorporates more ML features. For example, the Microsoft Translator's architecture for spoken MT includes speech recognition and TrueText normalization steps, with the former converting speech audio into text and the latter normalizing the text in order to make it more appropriate for translation. TrueText removes speech disfluencies (filler words such as 'um' and 'ah'), stutters, and repetitions. The text is also made more readable and translatable by adding sentence breaks, proper punctuation, and capitalization. After the converted text is translated using NMT specially developed for real-life spoken conversations, the text is converted to speech again; thus, text-to-speech technology is involved as well (Microsoft Translator, 2018). In this sense, spoken MT is like an accumulative MT, with many pieces of ML technology surrounding the main MT engine.

5   User inputs

Human reactions to different MT paradigms are different. For example, Daems and Macken (2019) find that without knowing whether an MT suggestion came from an SMT or NMT system, translators seem to prefer NMT output (or no MT output) as a starting point for their translations (p. 128). Moreover, characteristics of error types for each MT paradigm also affect a translator's reaction when using MT. Le and Schuster (2016) argued that the quality of NMT is higher than that of SMT. However, as Castilho et al. (2017) point out, the NMT output was rated as more fluent than the SMT output for all language pairs, but the accuracy results were less consistent; depending on the language pair, the NMT output contained more omission, addition, and mistranslation errors (pp. 116–117). In an MT post-editing process, it may take a translator different levels of effort to correct each error type depending on factors such as the translator's preferences and linguistic/cultural proficiency level. Thus, when deploying MT systems, user input is needed to select a solution that effectively uses MT and relevant human resources, as well as post-editing strategies such as the design of an error typology scheme.

4.5 MT as an instantiation of the process of human translation (HT)

Fundamentally, MT aims to solve a human problem, i.e., translating from one language to another. It starts with inputs generated by humans, including the source text, training data, and segmentation rules, and ends with outputs that are presentable to humans. To achieve this purpose, MT can learn from the human approach to translation and become an instantiation of HT processes with its own characteristics. Figure 4.5 offers a framework for the MT translation process and how it parallels the human translation process: (1) extracting the source content; (2) pre-processing the content to include analyzing the document structure, segmentation, domain/topic identification; (3) checking the translation database to make use of legacy linguistic assets; (4) employing machine translation; and (5) finally output desktop publishing. From a theoretical perspective, the framework for the MT process parallels how humans process the source text: separating text from non-translatable content, conducting pre-translation analysis such as text purpose and segmentation, checking memory, deciding whether to use or re-translate what has been translated before, and finally translating and producing the target text.

Newmark (1988) describes the process of translation in four levels: (1) at the SL text level, analyzing the source text from a translator's point of view; (2) at the referential level, progressively visualizing and building up the level of objects and events, real or imaginary, to comprehend the source text and produce the target text; (3) at the cohesive level, tracing the train of thought, the feeling, tone, and various presuppositions of the SL text, in a more general and grammatical manner; and (4) at the level of naturalness, making sure the target language is appropriate to the writer or the speaker in a certain situation (pp. 11–19). Newmark (1988) discusses the importance of resources such as monolingual and bilingual dictionaries and thesauri (pp. 175–176). Of course, translators also check their memory of past translations at the term and sentence levels and utilize glossaries and other personal resources.

What Newmark summarizes is based mainly on translation practice, and it applies to an MT-driven translation process as well. It includes the human analysis/ MT pre-processing stage, analyzing the document structure to conduct tasks, such as extracting translatable strings from formatting, segmentation/chunking, identifying the domain/topic of the source text, and referring to resources/memory check (TM check[6]). The naturalness level is in effect checking the language model to verify the quality, which aligns with the language model in SMT.

The MT framework is an effective way to collect, curate, and manage linguistic assets, including human-annotated language data that is generated from MT post-editing, translation, segmentation, and other human–machine interaction

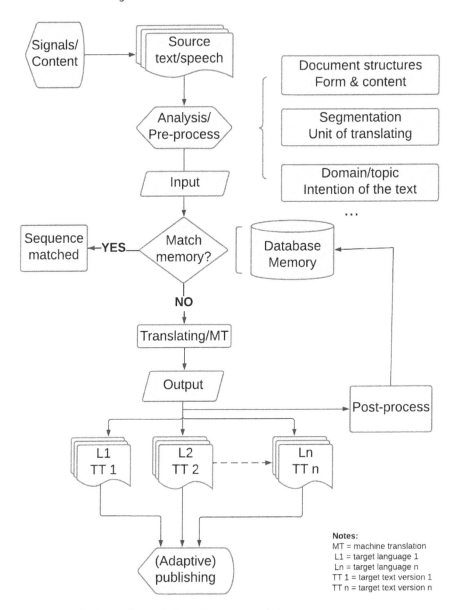

FIGURE 4.5   MT as an instantiation of human translation

activities. These data can empower machine learning to optimize MT systems at a fast pace. In this context, the requirements for human translators are higher, rather than lower, due to the dynamic features of MT systems. While training MT by interacting with an MT system, human translators can also learn from these dynamic systems. We will explore this topic in Chapter 8.

Notes

1 LISA was dissolved in 2011. Yet its definition of localization is still one of the most widely used. Additional background materials are available from other organizations such as the European Telecommunications Standards Institute (ETSI).
2 Bayes' Theorem is widely used in the field of machine learning. It provides a principled way to calculate a conditional probability.
3 Multi-head Attention is a module for attention mechanisms which runs through an attention mechanism several times in parallel (Weng, 2022). The Attention module splits its Query, Key, and Value parameters N-ways and passes each split independently through a separate Head. All of these similar Attention calculations are then combined together to produce a final Attention score (Doshi, 2021).
4 Position-Wise Feed-Forward Layer is a type of feedforward layer consisting of two dense layers that applies to the last dimension, which means the same dense layers are used for each position item in the sequence, so called position-wise (see Vaswani et al., 2022).
5 Google discontinued the Google Translate Widget for commercial use or combined with the Google Cloud Translation API on December 4, 2019.
6 An MT system also has terminology integration, meaning the system can check glossaries as well.

5

MACHINE TRANSLATION QUALITY ASSESSMENT AND QUALITY ESTIMATION

KEY CONCEPTS

- *Using humans alone to assess quality tends to slow down the entire MT process. Therefore, the whole or part of the assessment of MT must be automated to keep up with the speed and efficiency of MT translation.*
- *In terms of MT quality assessment, two important distinctions are (1) whether the assessment is automated and (2) whether the assessment includes editing activities that not only evaluate the MT results but also improve quality through direct human intervention.*
- *There are two types of assessment that depend on whether a reference translation is available: (1) automatic metrics such as BLEU and (H)TER, and (2) quality estimation (QE).*

5.1 Introduction

How to assess quality is one of the most intriguing questions asked in connection with translation. This question cannot be answered simply because any statement about the quality of a translation implies a conceptualization of the goal and purpose of the translation; it presupposes a theory of translation (House, 2014, p. 241). In practice, translations are assessed under differing circumstances: "during translator training, in examinations for official certification, by critics and reviewers, and by the ordinary reader," which consequently allows assessment methods to be developed by actors in different roles, including scholars, teachers, users, and practitioners in the translation industry (Williams & Chesterman, 2002, p. 8).

In translation practice, many standards have been developed with specific focuses and applied in different contexts. For example, the Surface Vehicle Standard (SAE)

DOI: 10.4324/9781003321538-8

J2450 (Vehicle E System Diagnostic Standards Committee, 2016) was issued in 2001, revised in 2005, and stabilized in 2016. It was developed initially as a translation quality metric for use in the automotive industry and then became widely used in other domains. The metric allows an evaluator to tag errors in a translation and compute a weighted, numeric score that represents the quality of the translation. The metric in the 2005 revised version consists of four parts: seven error categories, two sub-categories, two meta-rules to help resolve ambiguities on the assignment of an error to the categories and subcategories, and numeric weights. The error types are applicable to both human and machine translation.

Compared with SAE J2450, Multidimensional Quality Metrics (MQM) aims to provide a comprehensive framework for users to customize and develop their translation quality assessment (TQA) metrics in terms of error typology. By mapping their existing TQA frameworks (e.g., SAE J2450) with MQM, users can apply the same hierarchy of error categories in MQM across projects or in different studies and make meaningful comparisons. MQM is customizable to the user's needs, meaning the user can choose the specific error categories in the framework that are most relevant when evaluating the text (Mariana et al., 2015, p. 137).

In addition to evaluating the quality of the target text, evaluation can also be performed based on translation processes, as well as requirements for language service providers (LSPs) and translation projects. For example, ISO (International Organization for Standardization) 17100:2015 "specifies requirements for all aspects of the translation process directly affecting the quality and delivery of translation services" (ISO, 2015). This standard also provides a guideline for LSPs "concerning the management of core processes, minimum qualification requirements, the availability and management of resources, and other actions necessary for the delivery of a quality translation service" (ISO, 2015). ISO/TS 11669: 2012 (E) provides guidance concerning best practices for all phases of a translation project (ISO, 2012).

Quality assessment for machine translation has some unique features compared with traditional TQA. Human direct assessment (DA) or error annotation does not work for the massive volume of text that MT can produce. In addition, human evaluation of modern high-quality machine translation systems is challenging due to the large volume of MT results and subjectivity of human judgment, and there is increasing evidence that inadequate evaluation procedures can lead to erroneous conclusions. One solution is to automate the assessment process, and a widely used framework for process automation is Bilingual Evaluation Understudy (BLEU) and Translation Edit Rate (TER)[1] (see Section 5.4). Research findings show that automated metrics based on machine learning, e.g., pre-trained embeddings, can outperform human crowdsourcing evaluation results (Freitag et al., 2021, p. 1).

As Castilho et al. (2018) point out, there is a lack of standardization in TQA at the macro and micro level across theoretical, educational, and industry contexts, which yields inconsistency in human TQA procedures, and "there is considerable variation in the correlations between human and machine TQA" (pp. 30–33). For example, automatic metrics have occasionally been shown to be inconsistent with human TQA, and, as discussed previously, each industry standard has its own specific focus. Thus there is no one-size-fits-all solution that applies to all scenarios in TQA for MT.

For this reason, this chapter focuses on fundamental considerations that can support users making decisions about customizing their TQA strategies. For example, the application of MQM can be considered a specific scenario to make the assessment results more comparable across various projects and companies, whereas BLEU is used for MT system development and customization. Furthermore, this chapter focuses on the assessment of translated content. Theoretically speaking, all TQA metrics are potentially applicable to scenarios with both human and machine translation. As long as the approach, whether based on automated or human metrics, is utilized consistently, the assessment result will be useful.

5.2 Fundamental TQA considerations

5.2.1 Retrospective and prospective approaches

House (2014) proposed that there are different ways of assessing (retrospectively) the quality of a translation and different ways of ensuring (prospectively) the production of a translation of specified qualities. This dichotomy is based on time. When the element of time is incorporated into TQA, two fundamental aspects are introduced: quality assessment metrics, including automated and human direct assessment, for the evaluation of completed translations, and methods that help predict the quality of translation. The latter can support the development of effective, situation-driven editing strategies for translation tasks.

5.2.2 Linguistic relationships

Among assessment theories in translation studies (e.g., Chesterman, 1994; House, 2014), a relevant consideration in the context of MT is the concept of linguistic relationships. As Chesterman (1994, p. 153) points out, quality assessment was initially retrospective; it evaluated the relationship between the translated text and its source text, and the source text (plus its author) was taken to be the 'authority'. The goal of translation was a relation of equivalence between source and target text – however equivalence was defined. Chesterman (1994) incorporates the concept of norms (see also Toury, 1995) into his framework and proposes an approach to quality assessment that aims to compare "a given product (or process) to the accepted relevant norms" (p. 153). He points out that this mode of assessment is "objective, text-based, formal, eminently practical, and furthermore manifestly realistic" (p. 153).

As to what norms are considered to be accepted and relevant, specific circumstances must be considered. An extreme case might be the quality assessment of a localized website based upon the customer conversion rate. In this case, business considerations, rather than linguistic features, are prioritized. There are other norms that can be considered, e.g., ISO 17100:2015(en) and ISO/TS 11669:2012(en) focus on services and projects, respectively. This chapter focuses on linguistic relationships, which are the basis of automated and many human assessment metrics.

The concept of linguistic relationships entails a comparison of a text against a reference. Generally speaking, the basis for an automated evaluation metric is a previously completed human translation, as the purpose of machine translation is to generate output that is understandable and readable by humans. By comparing the output of a machine translation engine against a human reference translation, it is feasible to measure factors such as linguistic quality, word order, and other textual features.

Linguistic comparison turns out to be very applicable to the use of automated metrics for MT quality assessment. This approach turns a TQA problem into a linguistic analysis task: evaluating the nature of the relationships between the linguistic features of two sets of texts. As Miller and Beebe-Center (1956) pointed out in their pioneering work:

> The excellence of a translation should be measured by the extent to which it preserves the exact meaning of the original. But so long as we have no accepted definition of meaning, much less of exact meaning, it is difficult to use such a measure. As a practical alternative, therefore, we must search for more modest, yet better defined, procedures.
>
> *(p. 1973)*

They then propose comparing criteria in test translations using a variety of statistical indices. The simplest thing to try first is to ask if they use the same words (p. 76).

The linguistic comparison approach in TQA is language independent. Even though the comparison is linguistic, comparing similarities of words in the reference translation and the MT result, the method of comparison is statistical: how many words or phrases are exactly the same, for instance, between a human translation and an MT result for the same source text? What is important is the statistic; the comparison provides an impression of the quality of the MT results without the need to understand the language(s). The statistical approach can be applied to any language pair.

To some degree, linguistic comparison in MT evaluation emphasizes linguistic more than translational aspects, in the sense that the approach can be applied to natural language processing tasks beyond MT quality assessment. For example, Yeong et al. (2019) employ Bleualign, which uses BLEU scores as a similarity metric to match sentences in the alignment task.

Most automated metrics are based on linguistic comparison and thus evaluative – when a framework is used to compare and find relationships, it usually involves a judgment as to which is better than the other. This might explain why the term MT quality evaluation is widely used in the community of MT system development. In natural language processing research, quality assessment is broadly known as evaluation and includes both human judgment-based and automated methods, and prioritizes how the progress of an intelligent system, such as machine translation, is measured (see Smith, 2019).

5.2.3 Different automation scenarios in TQA

Machine translation quality assessment can be carried out by humans and machines. If it is conducted solely by machines, using fully automated metrics for MT (e.g., BLEU and TER), there is no need to incorporate a human-oriented assessment framework, such as MQM. These error categories are designed primarily for humans, following their thinking patterns, to categorize and annotate errors appearing in translations. These human judgment-based quality frameworks can be considered human metrics, even though further data collection and analysis, e.g., categorizing and counting errors and generating a final quality score, can be automated. This distinction is important, as the methods and procedures of applying an automated metric are different from those involving human judgments of translation quality.

5.2.4 Factors in the TQA workflow

Many factors in the TQA workflow may affect the quality of an MT system, or an MT-driven localization process. One approach to TQA is to assess relevant aspects at various MT implementation stages, including the following:

- before MT: the quality of MT-related strategic decisions for a specific use case in terms of translation purposes, audience, available human resources and linguistic assets, language pairs, and domain identification.
- during the pre-processing stage: the quality of preparations for the use of MT in terms of source text extraction, segmentation, data cleaning, and data synthesis.
- during the MT stage: the quality of implementation of other MT-related tasks, such as translation memory incorporation and terminology integration.
- during the post-translation stage: the quality of post-editing, in-context review, terminology, and translation memory updates.

Each step includes numerous options to consider. For example, in order to convert a source text to a machine-friendly format, it needs to be segmented at a predefined linguistic level, such as sentences. For some content formats, this task can be easily done in some languages by referring to punctuation. However, under some circumstances, it is hard for a machine to decide on the boundaries of a piece of text input, for example, in pdf formatting and other forms of graphic design, there are layers that are hidden intentionally from human eyes. What a machine perceives varies from what humans see. For example, with a brochure containing pictures and text, a design objective is to make the content appealing, rather than ensuring that linguistic content can be easily extracted for translation purposes. Spoken content, such as subtitles, also needs more processing than a regular word document, as such content does not have a naturally occurring splitter like punctuation. These aspects provide approaches to MT quality, which can be specific to a project and examined on a case-by-case basis.

Another approach is the use of effective metrics or frameworks for both machines and humans to measure the performance of an MT engine and quantify the results. This is an efficient and generic way to produce an indicator for TQA. MT and its assessment aim to serve the reader by producing a result that is ready for use. In this sense, MT post-editing (MTPE), editing strategies, and other interventions based on quality assessment or quality estimation results are a natural extension of MT quality considerations.

5.3 Two lines of thought for MT quality assessment

Quality considerations draw attention to an innate dilemma of MT applications. On the one hand, machine translation can improve translation productivity and generate a large volume of translations within a very short period of time. This is a significant strength of machine translation and one of the main reasons that people use MT. On the other hand, in ensuring that a massive amount of MT output is usable and meets expectations, human judgment is perhaps still the most reliable approach, despite its subjectivity and dependence on many external factors. Yet when using humans alone to assess quality, the entire MT process is slowed down, making it impossible to realize the full potential of an MT solution. Therefore, the assessment of MT output must be automated if it is to keep up with the speed and efficiency of the MT solution. Machine intelligence can be utilized to scale and extend human intelligence. The latter resource should be allocated judiciously given the enormous volume of output that an MT engine can produce.

A familiar theme resurfaces: machines and humans do not perceive language and translation in the same way. In terms of MT quality assessment, there are two lines of thought in Figure 5.1 that make helpful distinctions: (1) whether the assessment, or evaluation, is automated; and (2) whether the assessment includes editing activities that aim not only to evaluate the MT results but also improve quality through direct human intervention.

The answer to the first question – whether the MT results will only be evaluated or also edited – leads to two different MT evaluation metrics: automated and human. In machine translation research, the latter is often called human direct assessment (DA). In an automated evaluation system, the reference norm is previously completed human translations, and the process of comparing MT output and reference translations is fully automated. Since it does not require human intervention, it excludes many post-editing and computer-assisted tools that can provide an automated analysis of human annotation and/or edits. When generating the evaluation results through an automated process, machines do not need a linguistic framework. They follow their own algorithm to calculate evaluation scores. In

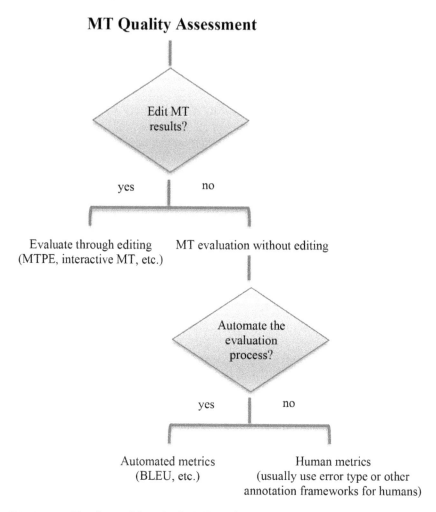

MT Quality Assessment

Edit MT results?

yes

no

Evaluate through editing (MTPE, interactive MT, etc.)

MT evaluation without editing

Automate the evaluation process?

yes

no

Automated metrics (BLEU, etc.)

Human metrics (usually use error type or other annotation frameworks for humans)

FIGURE 5.1   Two lines of thought for MT quality assessment

contrast, when humans evaluate MT results, they usually refer to a framework, such as error categories defined for annotation purposes. If they provide the annotation in a CAT or post-editing tool, the annotated results will be automatically curated. But the evaluation is done by humans, rather than by machines.

The second line of thought involves two different activities in MT assessment: evaluation and editing. These two areas can be a source of confusion among practitioners, as evaluation can be a side product of MT editing, including both post-editing and editing while translating (as shown in interactive MT). When editing is involved, 'quality' can be defined according to how much post-editing effort is needed. There is a difference between reference translations completed with and without the influence of MT. When evaluation is the only task for a human to accomplish, a reference translation is usually unnecessary, as the evaluator will depend on existing linguistic and translation knowledge and expertise to judge the results. In a scenario where the evaluation and editing tasks are combined, which is called evaluation through editing, the evaluation is impacted by the editing process.

In order to reduce the editing effort in a MTPE scenario, editing strategies may set specific requirements for human editors, so that the MTPE result is different from a human translation of the same source text from scratch without leveraging MT. Under these circumstances, the evaluation may be more conservative (see later discussion of TER and HTER). Evaluation through editing is a human metric by nature. However, the edited MT output can serve as a reference translation for an automated metric, where it will also impact the evaluation result. In that case, even though the evaluation is automated, it still has human characteristics as the reference translation is impacted by humans.

As discussed previously, human metrics such as MQM and the stabilized version of SAE J2450 provide useful error typology for error categorization. The application of these metrics relies on specific use cases, including the translation purpose, audience, human resources, and linguistic assets, which are covered in relevant studies and reference documents (Vehicle E System Diagnostic Standards Committee, 2016; Mariana et al., 2015; Lommel et al., 2013). The MT development community tends to use the term 'adequacy' to describe the accuracy of the translation and the term 'fluency' to describe whether the target text is natural and idiomatic in the target language. In quality estimation (QE), 'adequacy' and 'fluency' metrics are incorporated in the algorithms of some applications.

5.4 Automated metrics: using machines to assess machines

5.4.1 An overview of automated metrics

Comparisons conducted by machines are different from those by humans, yet they are a fast and cost-effective way to demonstrate some features of translation quality. In practice, when computer applications are capable of generating a large volume, it is not feasible to rely on human effort to track the quality of the MT output. Under these circumstances, automatic evaluation can be used as a surrogate for human evaluation, evaluating the MT raw results and tracking system development as the machine trains itself.

When developing MT systems, an automated measure of accuracy is preferable for rapid feedback and reliability on the quality of the system at different stages of training. Systems can also be compared with one another; for example, the MT evaluation metric in Microsoft Translator Hub includes scores for the engine after training on a dataset and scores comparing it against a generic purpose engine. This provides indicators of the quality of the MT engine being built, how the engine is improving, and what future direction is needed. Evaluation using automated metrics is more an evaluation of a software application than of translation, although it is also useful for comparing different translation results and text excerpts generated by humans or machines. Automated metrics can also provide a starting point for humans to continue and complete evaluation tasks. Theoretically, automated metrics can be applied at varying levels of linguistic granularity. In practice, linguistic comparison is generally based on the sentence level.

5.4.2 Automated metrics based on n-gram precision

5.4.2.1 The Bilingual Evaluation Understudy score

Of the various metrics for software evaluation, Bilingual Evaluation Understudy (BLEU) was one of the earliest, and it continues to be among the most popular and robust. It was developed in 2002 by a group of researchers at the IBM Watson Research Center (Papineni et al., 2002) as a method for automated evaluation of machine translation. It is also used in other NLP tasks. For example, Bleualign is an MT-based sentence alignment tool, which uses BLEU as a similarity score to find reliable alignments. Specifically, it requires parallel texts (i.e., a text and its translation) as well as an automatic translation of at least one of the texts. The alignment is conducted according to the similarity (modified BLEU score) between the MT results of the source text and the target text sentences in the parallel corpus (Sennrich, 2010; Sennrich & Volk, 2010).

Specifically, the BLEU MT evaluation system requires two ingredients: (1) a numerical 'translation closeness' metric and (2) a corpus of good quality human reference translations. The closeness metric is based on the highly successful word error rate (WER) metric used in the speech recognition community (Papineni et al., 2002, p. 311). BLEU scores on individual sentences will often vary from human judgments. For example, a system that produces the fluent phrase 'East Asian economy' is penalized heavily if all the references happen to read 'economy of East Asia'.

The key to BLEU's success is the similar treatment of all systems and use of multiple human translators with different styles, which are canceled out through comparisons between systems. In practice, a single reference or multiple references might be available to produce a MT result. A single reference translation does not necessarily mean all translations in the corpus are from one translator. Ideally such a corpus will ensure a degree of stylistic variation, which means it is preferable to have translations from different translators.

The cornerstone of the BLEU metric is the precision measure. To calculate precision, we can compare the *n*-grams (in this context, an *n*-gram is an ordered sequence of *n* words) of the candidate with the *n*-grams of the reference translation and count the number of matches, for example, the sum of the candidate translation words (unigrams) occurring in the reference translation is divided by the total number of words in the candidate translation. Unfortunately, MT systems can over-generate what appear to the system as reasonable words, resulting in improbable translations that have a high precision measure. In the first example (see Figure 5.2), out of the total words (unigrams) in the candidate, all of them

Reference translation: *There is a cat on the mat.*
Candidate translation (MT output): *the the the the the the the.*

$$\text{Standard precision measure} = \frac{\text{Reference translation word occurrences in candidate translation}}{\text{Total words in candidate translation}} = \frac{7}{7} = 1$$

FIGURE 5.2 Standard unigram precision measure calculation

(7 in total) find a match in the reference translation. Thus the standard precision measure is $7/7 = 1$.

Since this measure does not accurately evaluate the candidate sentence, a modified unigram precision measure is used. The calculation of this value is shown in the second example (see Figure 5.3). To compute this, one first counts the maximum number of times a word occurs in any single reference translation. For example, in Figure 5.3, there are two reference translations, with 'the' appearing once in reference 1 and twice in reference 2, thus the maximum count of 'the' occurring in the reference translations is 2. The modified count of n-gram matches between the reference translations and the candidate must not exceed the largest count observed in any single reference for that word. Thus, though all the words in the candidate match the unigram 'the' in the references, the count of unigram matches adopted in the modified precision formula in Figure 5.3 is 2, rather than 7, and the resulting score is $2/7 = 0.2857$.

These examples provide only a basic idea about the inner workings of BLEU. In practice, the BLEU algorithm involves many more elements.

The BLEU score is typically measured on a zero to one scale, indicating a probability assigned to the MT output. In practice, that number can be multiplied by a hundred for ease of communication: a BLEU score of 0.2857 will be converted to 28.57. A converted score of 100 means that all of the words of the translation are exactly the same in the human and the machine translated output, including their order. A converted score of 0 means that the human translation is completely different from the machine translation output. In reality, even two high quality human translations of the same source text will not receive a BLEU score of 100, as the words and word order will vary between the two human translations. A BLEU score ranging from 60 to 70 is generally considered high, and very high

Reference translation 1: There is a cat on the mat.
Reference translation 2: The cat is on the mat.
Candidate translation (MT output): the the the the the the the.

$$\text{Modified precision measure} = \frac{\text{Maximum occurrences in reference translation}}{\text{Total occurrences in candidate translation}} = \frac{2}{7} = 0.2857$$

FIGURE 5.3 Modified unigram precision measure calculation for BLEU score

TABLE 5.1 Interpretation of BLEU Score

BLEU Score	Interpretation
< 10	Almost useless
10–19	Hard to get the gist
20–29	The gist is clear, but has significant grammatical errors
30–40	Understandable to good translations
40–50	High quality translations
50–60	Very high quality, adequate, and fluent translations
60–70	Quality often better than human
> 70	Be cautious as it might mean overfitted models rather than extremely high quality

Source: Adapted based on Google Developers (n.d.-b).

BLEU scores above 70 may indicate that the model is not measuring correctly or is overfitting. Table 5.1 is a summary based on Google AutoML Translation, a platform offered by Google which allows users to create and customize translation models.

5.4.2.2 Factors that impact the performance of BLEU

From the algorithm perspective, BLEU has innate disadvantages. First, the unit of comparison is the word. As discussed earlier, this metric attempts to capture allowable variation in word choice by comparing the candidate sentences against (multiple) reference translations. In order to overcome the problem of variation in word order, BLEU uses modified *n*-gram precision, as illustrated previously. This criterion makes this metric biased towards systems based upon statistical approaches, such as statistical and neural MT. For other types of systems, such as rule-based MT, simply using BLEU scores may vastly underestimate its actual quality. There are other examples showing that BLEU's correlation with human judgments might have been overestimated and that BLEU is quite a crude measurement of translation quality (see Callison-Burch et al., 2006, pp. 253–255).

Second, as BLEU is very sensitive to the words that are present in the output of the machine translation engine, a key technology embedded in this metric involves the way that MT output is segmented into words. The performance of this technology varies across languages, which ultimately impacts the BLEU score. For example, with Chinese, Thai, and similar languages, the definition of 'word' is flexible or not completely clear, and there is no space separating word units like in English. The word segmentation employed in the software can have a substantial impact on the BLEU score and how to interpret it.

Thirdly, the number of references used in generating a BLEU score also plays a role. Generally speaking, when multiple references are used, the BLEU score tends to be higher, as Papineni et al. (2002) point out in an example: "on a test corpus of about 500 sentences (40 general news stories), a human translator scored 0.3468 against four references and scored 0.2571 against two references" (p. 315).

Furthermore, a BLEU score by itself is not that meaningful without the context of what is being tested and what the test set is. When comparing BLEU scores between two different systems using two different test sets, the scores are not comparable. The candidates need to be measured against a standard, representative test set or the same test in both scenarios. In many cases, the evaluation system can automatically generate test sets by sampling sentences from the training data. In this process, it is important to ensure that the test data do not overlap with the training set data, which in effect invalidates the evaluation results.

Finally, the main component of BLEU is referred to as "*n-gram precision*, which is the proportion of the matched *n*-grams out of the total number of *n*-grams in *the evaluated translation*. Precision is calculated separately for each *n*-gram order, and the precisions are combined via a geometric averaging" (Banerjee, S., & Lavie, A., 2005, p. 67).

5.4.2.3 *Other* n-*gram based automatic metrics*

Metric for Evaluation of Translation with Explicit ORdering (Meteor) is an automatic metric for MT evaluation that aims to address the weaknesses of BLEU. It evaluates a translation by computing a score based on explicit word-to-word matches between the translation and a given reference translation (Lavie & Agarwal, 2007, p. 228). According to Banerjee, S., & Lavie, A. (2005) and Lavie and Agarwal (2007), Meteor has been demonstrated to correlate strongly with human judgments of translation quality and significantly outperform BLEU. In Meteor,

> [u]nigrams can be matched based on their surface forms, stemmed forms, and meanings. Furthermore, METEOR can be easily extended to include more advanced matching strategies. Once all generalized unigram matches between the two strings have been found, METEOR computes a score for this matching using a combination of unigram-precision, unigram-recall, and a measure of fragmentation that is designed to capture directly how well-ordered matched words are in the machine translation.
>
> *(Banerjee & Lavie, 2005, p. 65)*

Sometimes *F*-measure is used to evaluate MT quality, particularly a model's accuracy. In the context of MT, it is a measure of how closely the hypothesis (MT output) matches the human reference translation. Its calculation employs the variables precision P and recall R. Specifically, precision *P* captures how many words from reference *r* (human reference translation) are present in hypothesis *h*. In other words, it is the proportion of words in the hypothesis *h* (MT output) that is present in reference *r* (human translation). This calculation does not take the position of the word in a sentence into account (see Munkova et al., 2020, p. 1329).

5.4.3 Automated metrics based on edit distance

5.4.3.1 Translation Edit Rate (TER)

Translation Edit Rate (TER) measures the amount of editing that a human would have to perform to change system output so it matches exactly a reference translation (Snover et al., 2006, p. 223). Like BLEU, TER is an automated metric and requires a reference translation. According to research conducted by Snover et al. (2006, p. 223), the single-reference variant of TER correlates as highly with human judgments of MT quality as the four-reference variant of BLEU.

TER is defined as the minimum number of edits needed to change a test translation or MT output (hypothesis) so that it exactly matches one of the references, normalized by the average length of the references (see Figure 5.4).

Possible edits include the insertion, deletion, and substitution of single words as well as shifts of word sequences. Consider the following reference/hypothesis pair, where differences between the reference and hypothesis are indicated by upper case letters:

> REF: SAUDI ARABIA denied THIS WEEK information published in the AMERICAN new york times
>
> HYP: THIS WEEK THE SAUDIS denied information published in the new york times
>
> *(Snover et al., 2006, p. 225)*

Based on the standards set in Snover et al. (2006, pp. 223–225), four edits (one shift, two substitutions, and one insertion) are required to change from the hypothesis to the reference, giving a TER score of $4 \div 13 = 31\%$.

The above explanation of the procedures used to calculate a TER score is simplified by controlling some parameters, including the number of reference translations and definitions of each edit type. Yet it is sufficient to understand the type of calculation underlying TER. In practice, working definitions of such parameters can be decided according to specific use cases and incorporated into algorithms that automate the TER score generation process.

5.4.3.2 Human-targeted TER (HTER)

Human-targeted Translation Edit Rate (HTER) is a human-in-the-loop evaluation. It involves a procedure for creating targeted references. In this approach,

$$\text{TER} = \frac{\text{\# of edits}}{\text{Average \# of reference words}}$$

FIGURE 5.4   TER score

human annotators who are fluent speakers of the target language generate a targeted reference by editing the system hypothesis (MT output). As discussed in Section 5.3, this evaluation task involves editing efforts in addition to evaluation. The editing is done manually by humans, and the MT post-editing (MTPE) process is a typical scenario used to generate targeted references.

The language industry tends to use the term TER to cover both TER and HTER scenarios, as many translation edit rate algorithms are based on post-editing results (targeted references), rather than human reference translations produced without the translator being exposed to the MT results (also known as untargeted references). Yet it is crucial that the differentiation between TER and HTER be clear, as the evaluation results vary given the fact that the reference translations are produced under different conditions.

Snover et al. (2006) compare the number of insertions, deletions, substitutions, and shifts in scenarios with HTER (TER with one human-targeted reference) and with TER (four untargeted references). Here, lower numbers in edit-distance indicate better performance. Snover et al. (2006) found that HTER reduces the edit rate by 33% relative to TER [(49.6–33.5) ÷ 49.6 = 33%]. Substitutions were reduced by the largest factor (from 25.8 to 14.6), most likely because words were often judged synonymous. The majority of the edits were substitutions and deletions in both condition categories, TER and HTER (p. 228).

When revisiting the concept of n-gram-based automated metrics such as BLEU, whether the reference translation is targeted or untargeted also affects the statistical results, which must be considered when controlling the variables in the implementation of MT quality assessment. Both n-gram- and edit distance-based automated metrics share a common feature: they need a reference translation and a hypothesis (MT output) to make the linguistic comparison. In many cases, reference translations are not always available. ML technologies can provide an indicator of MT quality without reference translations, with quality estimation being an example.

5.5 Quality estimation (QE)

Though automated metrics for MT quality evaluation are fast and cost-effective, in many cases a reference translation is not available, much less multiple reference translations, which is preferable. The human reference translation is assumed to be the gold standard, but that is hard to validate. Most source sentences have multiple translations that could be considered high quality translations. Furthermore, automated TQA is retrospective and does not indicate how much time will be required to post-edit the segment or how much the translator should be paid for editing it.

To address these issues, quality estimation (QE) can be used to automatically provide an indication of the quality of machine translation output without access to human reference translations. It is also a method to estimate the level of post-editing effort that will be required. Unlike the retrospective MT evaluation metrics discussed in the previous section, QE metrics are aimed at MT systems in use. In this sense, quality in MT is interpreted in terms of post-editing time and effort.

Specia, Shah, et al. (2013) list a number of applications for QE: (1) deciding which segments require translator revision, or human quality assurance; (2) deciding whether a reader gets a reliable gist of the text; (3) estimating the amount of effort required to post-edit; (4) selecting among alternative translations produced by different MT systems; and (5) deciding whether translations are suitable for self-training of MT systems (p. 79).

QE models are generally trained on publicly available datasets, such as the Europarl parallel corpus (Koehn, 2005). These datasets need to leverage language-specific human annotations for supervision, including direct assessment and post-editing, and these annotations are often costly and time-consuming, particularly for word-level QE, where each token needs a label (Tuan et al., 2021). Specia et al. (2009) describe three types of manually annotated data (MT output): (1) subsets of sentences annotated by humans according to adequacy, with scores from 1 (worst) to 5 (best); (2) sentences annotated by professional translators with quality scores between 1 and 4, with 1 designating a need for complete retranslation and 4 designating fit for purpose; and (3) sentences annotated with post-editing time, determined empirically by recording the amount of time a professional translator required to post-edit the sentence (pp. 30–31).

There are multiple open source MT QE frameworks, including deepQuest, OpenKiwi, QuEst, and QUETCH. To explain the basic inner workings, QuEst can serve as an example (QuEst++, 2022). QuEst was designed to estimate the sentence-level quality of machine translation systems, and it relies heavily on linguistic and textual features. The basic framework includes two main modules: a feature extraction module and a machine learning module. QE is a prediction of quality based on certain features, including language-independent features (such as confidence measures), general linguistic resources (such as part-of-speech taggers), and language-specific features. An example of the latter is incorrect translation of pronouns, which was designed for Arabic-English QE (see Specia, Shah, et al., 2013, p. 81). In the machine learning module, quality is predicted by combining a number of features that describe different aspects of translation fluency and accuracy, source text complexity and 'translatability', as well as MT system confidence (Specia & Soricut, 2013, p. 213). The machine learning module is "independent from the feature extraction code and uses the extracted feature sets to build and test QE models" (Specia et al., 2015, p. 116).

A main component of the machine learning module is Confidence Estimation (CE), which is viewed as a binary classification (Blatz et al., 2003, cited in Specia et al., 2009, p. 28) distinguishing between 'good' and 'bad' translations based upon

> a continuous quality score . . . estimated for each sentence. This problem
> is addressed as a regression task, where algorithms are trained to predict

different types of sentence-level scores. The contribution of a large number of features is exploited by using a feature selection strategy.

(p. 28)

QuEst++ is a new release of QuEst. QuEst++ includes support for word-, sentence-, and document-level QE. It also provides pipelined processing, whereby predictions made at a lower level (e.g., words) can be used as input to build models for predictions at a higher level (e.g., sentences). QuEst++ allows the extraction of a variety of features and provides machine learning algorithms to build and test QE models. Its feature extraction module can extract a variety of attributes from text at three levels of granularity. These are then passed to the machine learning module, which employs them to build a robust QE model (Specia et al., 2015, p. 116).

Tuan et al. (2021) proposes a technique that does not rely on examples from human annotators and instead uses synthetic training data. Their research findings show that the resulting models perform comparably to models trained on human-annotated data, both for sentence and word-level prediction. This is an area showing potential for further exploration. With the rapid improvement of machine learning technologies, QE is becoming more reliable in estimating quality and predicting the required level of post-editing effort.

Note

1 See Snover et al. (2016). In practice, TER is also referred to as "translation error rate"; see for example KatanAI (2015).

6

INTENTIONALITY AND NLP TASKS IN TRANSLATION

KEY CONCEPTS

- *In an MT-driven translation process, a translator is more likely to guide and support translation-related NLP tasks than the core MT technology.*
- *From the perspective of machine learning, there are two basic categories of translation-related NLP tasks: facilitation and intelligent tasks. Facilitation tasks help users improve productivity, whereas intelligent tasks support the development of their customized or personalized ML models.*
- *NLP tasks relevant to a continuous translation process are based on purposes in specific use cases. Machines do not possess intentionality, which is solely in the minds of humans.*

6.1 Introduction

Many natural language processing (NLP) tasks can facilitate ML-driven automation in translation processes. These tasks do not necessarily fall into the category of meaning conversion, i.e., *translation proper*. As stated in Section 4.1 of Chapter 4, it makes sense to discuss these technologies in a larger context such as localization, which takes place within a larger commercial and developmental framework involving the expertise of translators, language and tools specialists, programmers, engineers, project managers, desktop publishing specialists, and marketing staff (Folaron, 2006; cited in Byrne, 2009, p. 2).

As mentioned under 'Natural language processing and translation' in the Introduction to the book, there are three approaches to NLP: symbolic, statistical, and connectionist. Connectionist models usually take the form of neural networks, which are composed of a large number of very simple components wired together. In this book, we will examine the connectionist approach in the context of neural

DOI: 10.4324/9781003321538-9

network models. In 2016, when commercial neural MT was launched, translation research and practice stepped into a new neural NLP era. This chapter is set in this general context.

Two basic translation concepts shape the discussion: (1) language as a sequence, and (2) conversion of meaning and of form associated with meaning, which includes interlingual machine translation as well as intralingual translation, such as from the spoken to written form of a language. First, in the neural NLP approach, language is an inherently temporal phenomenon, consisting of sequences that unfold in time. Second, the translation of meaning and form is basically a conversion problem. Therefore, many translation-related NLP tasks – e.g., optical character recognition (OCR), automatic speech recognition (ASR), as well as machine translation (MT) itself – are based on the sequence transduction model. In addition, some activities beyond the meaning conversion step do not involve conversion challenges, e.g., domain detection, language detection, and automatic terminology extraction. These activities can be captured by other neural network models such as sequence classification. In both cases, data representation is a crucial component supporting effective machine learning. It determines how much useful information can be extracted from raw data for further classification or prediction. Such language data tasks constitute a considerable amount of the translator's work in ML-driven translation.

These sequence models can be further customized into specific NLP tasks with relevant language data to meet various purposes. NLP tasks can be designed for pertinent human needs, and the list of potential neural NLP tasks is dynamic and open-ended. This chapter provides a rough classification of the translation-related NLP tasks based on three considerations.

First, this chapter addresses pertinent NLP tasks that are designed with the user in mind: translators, linguists, localization project managers, and other domain experts. The discussion does not focus on how to develop these technologies but rather how to fully draw upon users' knowledge and expertise to effectively customize and utilize them. In other words, NLP tasks are selected and classified from the perspective of a translator in a translation process, not whether they are suitable for a model customization process or generic data management or annotation project. This user focus is important, because the translation process needs to be driven ultimately by humans, rather than machines.

Second, when a translator customizes and uses NLP tasks in the translation process, there must be a reason behind it. A translator executes tasks, such as source text analysis, term extraction, and text alignment, before, during, and after translation in order to improve productivity, ensure quality, and curate language data. While user purpose and intent must be analyzed on a case-by-case basis, they can be identified in the continuous translation process and categorized based on human need (see Section 6.3).

Third, this chapter distinguishes between *purpose* and *intentionality* as concepts when determining what NLP tasks are needed and how they should be customized in order to leverage the power of machine learning effectively. In this chapter, purposes are task-specific and can be analyzed on a case-by-case basis, whereas intentionality illuminates the relationship between humans and machines from a philosophical perspective. The concept of intentionality proposed by Searle (1980) is borrowed from AI research to illustrate our position on the relationship between humans and machines.

6.2 Classification of NLP tasks from the ML perspective

6.2.1 Two types of NLP tasks

From the perspective of machine learning, there are two basic categories of translation-related NLP tasks: facilitation and intelligent tasks. Facilitation tasks help users improve their productivity. Technologies for these tasks are used to augment human intelligence by automating a designated step without requiring the translator to input, update, or annotate language data. The relationship flows in one direction from machine to user, and the user does not feed language data back into the machine to train it and further develop the ML model.

In addition to improving translator productivity, intelligent tasks, the other type of NLP task, help translators develop their own ML models. Performing these NLP tasks entails not only using the tools to translate but also feeding data into the engines to improve their artificial intelligence. Machine training is a significant aspect of these tasks. When working with intelligent tools, translators need to focus on the translation tasks as well as language data associated with them. Translation is only part of the overall task, and model development is continuous, as language data such as terminology, translation memory, and relevant annotations are accumulated and processed according to specific purposes.

For intelligent NLP tasks, machine training and translation tasks can be conducted in two ways: (1) simultaneously: in an interactive MT environment, a translator edits the MT suggestions to finish the translation task while at the same time the edited data are sent back to the MT engine to train the machine; or (2) separately: language data such as termbase and translation memory are collected from a CAT tool and compiled in a parallel corpus, which then is used to train an NMT engine.

Here the task classification is project-based, from the translator's perspective, rather than technical. When a neural network model for a particular NLP task is optimized directly through the translator's input or additional work on language data (e.g., annotation), it is considered an (artificial) intelligent task. If a NLP task involves machine learning but the model training is not directly relevant to the translation profession, it is still considered a facilitation task that mainly aims to assist translators. For instance, OCR is a seq2seq (sequence to sequence) ML task, but usually the post-recognition verification is conducted by a monolingual person instead of a translator. In this case, the OCR task is mainly a facilitation tool for the translator, though it may be an intelligent tool for other users. In contrast, when a translator plays an important role in creating and ensuring the quality of the training data for a model, e.g., the NMT task involves training and testing data for MT, it is primarily an intelligent tool. In other words, the final criterion to decide whether a task is intelligent or not for a translator must be considered on a case-by-case basis. If the translator uses a tool to conduct a NLP task without updating the system with data, it is a facilitation task. In contrast, if there is a two-way relationship between the translator and the NLP model, i.e., the translator performs the NLP task while also training the system, it is an intelligent task.

6.2.2 Purposes of neural network models in translation

In machine learning, a translator's primary task is not model development, but rather manipulating language data as input and output of the model. Nevertheless, knowledge of some basic neural network models and their functioning in a continuous translation process can help the translator better understand relevant NLP tasks as well as the role that the translator does have in model development. Language data produced by the translator can be used to address two general NLP challenges: sequence classification and sequence prediction. Strictly speaking, in machine learning, classification is essentially a predictive modeling problem. But instead of producing another sequence, as is the case in a seq2seq model, in a classification task, a class label is predicted for a given string of input data.

Both prediction and classification are fundamentally sequential problems. As Jurafsky and Martin (2020) state, "[l]anguage is an inherently temporal phenomenon" and "this temporal nature is reflected in the algorithms we use to process language" (p. 181). In machine learning, an artificial neural network (ANN) such as Transformer and recurrent neural network (RNN) are able to capture the temporal aspects of language as a powerful sequence learning architecture.

6.2.2.1 Sequence prediction

As discussed in Section 4.3.4 of Chapter 4, a Neural MT system is essentially a sequence transduction model with an encoder-decoder structure. In this approach, similar to other sequence transduction models, embeddings are learned from training data so as to convert the input and output tokens to vectors of dimension.

As discussed in Sections 4.3.4.2 and 4.3.4.3 in Chapter 4, RNN-based language models process sequences one word at a time, which may lead to a loss of relevant information and to difficulties in training when passing information forward through an extended series of recurrent connections. Moreover, the inherently sequential nature of recurrent networks inhibits the use of parallel computational resources, preventing them from being trained with large amounts of data

(Jurafsky & Martin, 2020, p. 190; Vaswani et al., 2017). To address this challenge, Vaswani et al. (2017) proposed the Transformer, "a model architecture eschewing recurrence and instead relying entirely on an attention mechanism to draw global dependencies between input and output" (p. 2), which allows the use of parallel computations and a higher training efficiency.

For a sequence prediction task, usually the language data directly created by humans – through human translation, spelling check, and transcription – can be used to train the machine, although additional processing might be needed, such as data cleaning, segmentation, and source-target text alignment. In machine translation, human translation is used to generate parallel corpora to train an NMT engine.

6.2.2.2 Sequence classification

The encoder-decoder artificial neural networks such as RNNs can also be used to classify entire sequences rather than the tokens within them. Examples include domain detection, quality estimation, and sentiment analysis. In these applications, sequences of text are classified as belonging to one of a small number of categories.

Classifying documents into different topic categories can be a useful pre-processing step in translation. For example, to apply RNNs in this setting, the text to be classified is passed through the RNN word-by-word, generating a new hidden layer each time. The hidden layer for the final element of the text is taken to constitute a compressed representation of the entire sequence. In the simplest approach to classification, the hidden layer for the final element of the text serves as the input to a subsequent feedforward network, in which the computation proceeds iteratively from one layer of units to the next as discussed in Chapter 3, that chooses a class via a softmax[1] over the possible classes.

Xing et al. (2010) summarize three large categories of sequence classification methods:

1 Feature-based classification, which transforms a sequence into a feature vector and then applies conventional classification methods.
2 Sequence distance-based classification, which measures the similarity between sequences to determine the quality of the classification.
3 Model based-classification, which uses a hidden Markov model (HMM) and other statistical models to classify sequences.

(p. 3)

Classification tasks need category labels, which usually start with human annotation, i.e., human judgments as to the category. However, some unlabeled data share common features with labeled data and also contain additional features that may provide a more comprehensive description of a class. By incorporating unlabeled data, a more accurate classifier may be built under certain circumstances (Xing et al., 2010, p. 5). In this type of NLP task, a translator usually needs to annotate the language data, which means that there is a secondary layer of data interaction on top of the corpora directly generated in a translation process.

6.3 Purposes of NLP tasks at each step of a continuous translation process

6.3.1 Continuous translation process

In Section 4.5 of Chapter 4, we discussed the translation process in a broad sense, from source content extraction to pre-processing, memory/database check, translation – both human translation (HT) and machine translation (MT) – and publishing. In a continuous translation workflow, there is an extra post-processing step, which accumulates and updates a database (human and/or machine memory) so that it can be leveraged in the next translation task.

In Figure 6.1, we describe some relevant NLP tasks that the translator can conduct at each step of a continuous translation process. For example, NLP technologies such as OCR and document parsing can be used to automatically extract translatable strings from the original content (spoken signals and written text) to produce source text/speech to be further processed. Sequence segmentation from source text/speech to input, and other analytical tasks such as domain detection and quality estimation, can be automated. From input to memory check, functionalities such as terminology extraction and named entity recognition can be used to highlight specific memory. During post-processing, multiple NLP technologies can be used to collect and compile parallel corpora for machine training, including data cleaning using NLP packages, automatic labeling, and automatic alignment. Finally, when the translated content is ready to be published, NLP tasks such as text-to-speech and subtitle synchronization can automate relevant publishing activities.

6.3.2 User purposes at each step of a continuous translation process

As mentioned in Section 6.1, NLP tasks in a continuous translation process are driven by the users' needs, which can be difficult to categorize. The user can always select a particular set of tools, design NLP tasks, and customize these tools according to their purposes, including productivity gains, quality assurance, human value maximization, and continuous machine learning. While human intentions are very individual and difficult to categorize, we can classify them based on shared purposes at each step of a continuous translation process, as shown in the list of examples in Table 6.1.

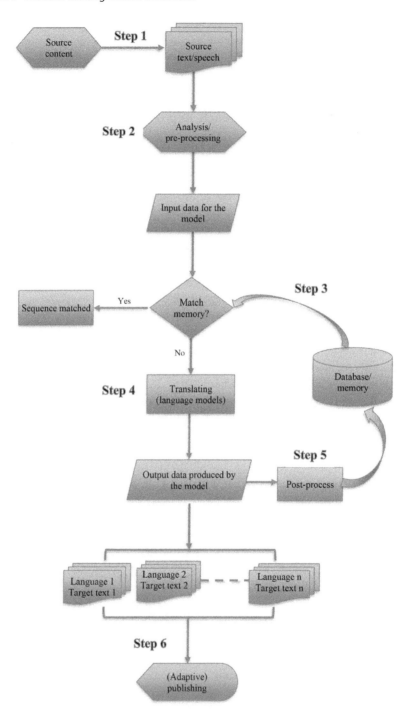

FIGURE 6.1   NLP tasks in a continuous translation process

TABLE 6.1 User purposes and NLP task examples in a continuous translation process

Translation Process Step	User Purpose	NLP Task Examples
1. From content to source text/speech	Extract translatable strings from content in a larger context to prepare source content, quote, etc.	• OCR • Automatic speech recognition • Document parsing • Language detection • Web crawling techniques
2. Analysis/ pre-processing	Prepare the translatable content to follow the cognitive processing features of humans or meet the specifications of CAT or MT environments (tune the inputs)	• Domain detection • Source text analysis/editing • Segmentation • Inline tag alignment
3. Memory match	Leverage past experience/data through human or machine memory systems	• Terminology extraction • Named entity recognition • Translation memory leverage
4. Translating/MT	Convert meaning across languages/cultures by translating (both HT and MT) and editing to ensure the translation quality	• Machine translation • MT quality evaluation • Linguistic quality assurance (LQA) • Automatic post-editing (APE) • MT quality estimation
5. Post-processing	Manage and update human or machine memory systems for future translation tasks	• Corpus compilation and analytics • Data cleaning using NLP packages • Automatic labeling • Automatic alignment
6. Publishing/content delivery	Adapt the target content format to the target locale and culture	• Synthetic media • Subtitle synchronization

The next section will highlight some commonly used intelligent NLP tasks, including the translator's role in each, which involves mostly working with language data.

6.4 Intelligent NLP tasks in a continuous translation process

6.4.1 Extracting translatable strings from content in a larger context

The first step in translation is to review the source content and separate the content from formatting. Humans are usually proficient in singling out linguistic elements from non-linguistic elements, e.g., images and formatting. This process can be automated by using document parsers, such as optical character recognition (OCR) technique and some out-of-the-box solutions, including Pdfplumber, Google Document-AI, and Amazon Textract.

6.4.1.1 Optical character recognition (OCR)

Optical character recognition is

> the task of converting images of typed, handwritten or printed text into machine-encoded text. It is a method of digitizing printed texts so that they can be electronically edited, searched, stored more compactly, displayed on-line, and used in machine processes such as machine translation, text-to-speech and text mining.
>
> *(Sahu & Sukhwani, 2015, p. 1)*

OCR is a typical sequence to sequence learning model. It includes both character recognition and word prediction.

The training data of a typical OCR system is annotated word images. For example, the Modified National Institute of Standards and Technology (MNIST) database of handwritten digits has a training set of 60,000 examples and a test set of 10,000 examples. "The digits have been size-normalized and centered in a fixed-size image" (LeCun et al., n.d.). Though most people who understand the words can annotate the word images, sometimes it is convenient for a translator to verify and annotate OCR results that have multilingual content.

In the past, some functionalities of document parsing and OCR could be utilized in a traditional CAT environment. But with more advanced NLP techniques, it is possible to perform these functions outside a CAT tool environment, using a stand-alone NLP technique for customization based on specific purposes. In translation practice, a translator sometimes needs to verify the OCR results and note patterns in errors to correct them efficiently and consistently. In a separate OCR task, these activities can be automatically documented and then used to train the engine, which helps the translator leverage the linguistic assets created in the process of translation. The same applies to other intelligent tasks covered in this section.

6.4.1.2 Automatic speech recognition (ASR)

As Jurafsky and Martin (2020) note, automatic speech recognition maps any waveform to the appropriate string of words. They point out that "automatic transcription of the speech of any speaker in any environment is still far from solved, but ASR technology has matured to the point where it is now viable for many practical tasks," such as "automatically generating captions for audio or video text" by transcribing movies, videos, or live discussions (p. 548). In translation, ASR tasks are relevant particularly to spoken machine translation and audiovisual translation.

ASR is built on sequence-to-sequence learning modeling. For ASR problems, the training data consist of audio clips of spoken words as input data and a text transcript of what was spoken as output data. The speech data can be further annotated based on linguistic and cultural dimensions. For instance, raw audio data can be categorized and labeled to make the data more usable for machine learning or AI applications, such as annotating the verbal components of speech data (words) as well as non-verbal features like coughing and sneezing, a doorbell ringing, or a barking dog. Again, these tasks do not necessarily need to be performed by a bilingual or multilingual translator. Yet these translation-related activities can be planned in advance in order to make effective use of human and linguistic resources in the translation process.

6.4.1.3 Web crawling techniques

In website localization, web-crawling techniques can be used to extract translatable strings and analyze the linguistic features of the extracted text in order to prepare the source content for the next step. From a business perspective, it can help the translator estimate the word count and linguistic features such as keywords, which is often a basis for cost estimates. For example, tools such as InSite (Complete Website Word Counting with InSite, 2015) and WordCounter (Web Page Word Counter, n.d.) are convenient tools that provide such information. Other tools such as BootCaT (2018) can extract words into a plain text document to generate a corpus for discourse analysis and other follow-up activities that might be necessary in a continuous translation process.

6.4.2 Preparing the translatable content

The second step in a continuous translation process involves optimal preparation of translatable strings and tuning the inputs by analyzing the source text according to human cognitive processing features in an HT scenario. This step can also involve pre-processing content to meet MT specifications. In an ML-driven translation process, some typical pre-processing activities can also be automated.

6.4.2.1 Domain detection

Domain detection is usually conducted for various translation-related tasks. For example, a baseline NMT engine can be further customized and adapted to a particular domain. Each domain-specific MT engine can be further trained on corpora provided by a client, who may not have sufficient previous knowledge of the domain. The domain may also be labeled incorrectly. In this scenario, the ability to detect the domain can help determine which MT engine should be used for the datasets. By labeling the training data, a classifier can be trained how to predict possible domains. It is a classification task where the input is the source sentence and the target is the domain description. The state-of-the-art model for this type of

NLP tasks is normally as follows: (1) the input sentence is tokenized, (2) the tokens are passed into a transformer language model and represented as vectors, (3) the final vector representations are passed into a classifier, and (4) the classifier returns a list of probabilities associated with all possible labels. Humans, who manually tag data, train this type of domain detection modeling.

NLP tasks that are similar to domain detection, such as topic modeling, can be based on ML algorithms that require less manual input than supervised algorithms. However, they require high-quality data in bucket loads. Bucketing (or binning) refers to the transformation of numeric features into categorical features, using a set of thresholds (Google Developers, n.d.-a). In this case, human judgment is also needed for data preparation and feature engineering.

6.4.2.2 Automatic segmentation

In translation, a larger chunk of information is usually segmented into smaller ones, as discussed in Chapter 2. In both HT and MT, sentences are usually the natural segmentation units. Conventionally, sentence segmentation can be produced in a CAT tool environment based on manual sentence boundaries like punctuation. However, this approach does not always work. For instance, in the case of speech translation, the sentence is not a well-defined unit. A speaker may leave a sentence incomplete, make long pauses, or speak for a long period without pausing (Matusov et al., 2005). If speech cannot be segmented into meaningful units like sentences, the speech cannot be properly translated into the target language.

While a human transcriber of speech is usually able to use judgment to segment a raw transcription into meaningful units, this is not always a feasible approach. For example, in spoken machine translation, the pipeline usually includes two independent components: automatic speech recognition and machine translation. Within this pipeline, "ASR provides an error-prone, audio segmented stream of non-punctuated words", whereas "the majority of MT training data consists of nonspeaking style bilingual text data with proper sentence segments and punctuation marks" (Paulik et al., 2008, n.p.). In this case, sentence segmentation of ASR output and punctuation recovery prior to translation play a major role in addressing the mismatch between ASR output and MT training data.

While there are multiple segmentation tools and NLP packages for segmentation, what is relevant to the translator is the training and testing data. In order to train a machine learning-based sentence segmentation system, a set of 'ground truth', human-produced training examples is required. Human insights are also significant when sentence segmentation architecture is based on a decision tree that uses multiple features computed for each boundary (see Paulik et al., 2008). In translation practice, including both HT and MT, automatic segmentation can be an effective measure to improve productivity and ensure quality.

6.4.3 Leveraging past experience/data through human or machine memory systems

The next step in the translation process is to check memory to recycle previous work. A human translator can resort to past experience and recall some memorized information. During this process, some units may require extra mental effort to retrieve, such as specialized terms or proper names. When a computer program processes natural language, these challenges are mirrored in its design and implementation. A program can automatically identify and search an existing database for relevant translation units. Terminology extraction and named entity recognition (NER) are examples of automated recognition tasks that can be leveraged.

6.4.3.1 Terminology extraction

In translation practice, automatic terminology extraction is an effective tool to store, manage, and query relevant specialized concepts in corresponding languages. In particular, term frequency – inverse document frequency (tf-idf) machine learning is a widely used method to automatically extract terms in a document. Specifically, term frequency refers to the frequency of a particular term under investigation in the document. Inverse document frequency examines how common (or uncommon) a word is in various documents in a corpus.

In addition, as Kováříková (2021) points out, terms have specific quantitative features within texts, such as frequency, distribution, and contextual characteristics, which can serve as the basis for statistical methods of automatic terminology extraction (p. 24). For example, terms can be recognized by distribution in various disciplines or entropy[2] of the immediate left or right context.

From a human perspective, terminology is "the study of how specialized knowledge concepts are structured, described, and designated in one or various languages within a specialized domain" (Faber & León-Araúz, 2016, p. 196). In this sense, terminology is a concept and framework primarily for humans to organize their specialized knowledge. When this factor is taken into consideration, automatic terminology extraction can also be customized to cognitive features of individual persons. By using word embeddings and recurrent neural networks, the model can predict individual learners' term recognition based on their annotations, which represent previous schemata of these terms to some degree (Wang, 2021).

6.4.3.2 Named entity recognition (NER)

According to Jurafsky and Martin (2020), a "named entity is, roughly speaking, anything that can be referred to with a proper name: a person, a location, an organization" (p. 148). They cite four entity tags as being the most common – PER (person), LOC (location), ORG (organization), and GPE (geo-political entity) – and point out that tags include other categories, including date, time, and price (p. 153).

In machine learning, automatic NER is a sequence labeling problem. A sequence labeling model assigns "a label chosen from a small, fixed set of labels to each element of a sequence" (Jurafsky & Martin, 2020, p. 182). Following is an example of automatic NER by Stanza, which is an open-source Python natural language processing toolkit supporting 66 human languages. According to Qi et al. (2020), this platform "features a language-agnostic fully neural pipeline for text analysis, including tokenization, lemmatization, part-of-speech and morphological feature tagging, and named entity recognition" (p. 101).

Despite the improvement of automatic NER annotation tools, human judgment cannot be replaced and is required for each annotation. To avoid the risk of introducing bias and reducing annotation quality, the annotation tool must be updated with input from statistical and machine learning methods to support the annotation process (Stenetorp et al., 2012, p. 104). This applies to other annotation tasks as well, which we will discuss in Chapter 7.

6.4.4 Converting meaning across languages and cultures

Humans and machines can both execute meaning conversion tasks. In this step, it is important to reinforce what has been discussed under 'Translation and the language industry' in the Introduction to the book: with the impact of machine translation, the boundaries between 'translating' and 'editing' are frequently blurred, since many human translators are now 'editing' but still feel they are 'translating', even though they are working on the suggestions given by MT and TM. Furthermore, this step also includes quality assurance metrics. Chapter 4 addressed various types of machine translation tasks and machine evaluation metrics. This section will add one more task that has grown in importance in the ML approach to translation: automatic post-editing (APE).

According to Correia and Martins (2019), "APE is inspired by human post-editing, in which a translator corrects mistakes made by an MT system" (p. 3051). Recently, a dual-source transformer architecture has been applied to APE, in which the source sentence and the machine-translated sentence serve as input features and the latter's post-edited version as a target label used to train the model (p. 3051).

In the transformer architecture, the key factor determining APE performance is the human-annotated data. As Chollampatt et al. (2020) point out, adequate supervision in the form of human post-editing with annotation is key. In their study, Chollampatt et al. (2020) compile a large post-edited corpus, SubEdits, which consists of actual human postedits of translations of drama and movie subtitles produced by a strong in-domain proprietary NMT system. Their results show that with a large human post-edited corpus, a strong neural APE model can substantially improve a strong in-domain NMT system.

6.4.5 Continuous learning

The post-processing stage of a continuous translation process is a crucial step in which humans and machines accumulate past experiences and data to further their learning. Translators can learn from the project in addition to fulfilling the translation task, which will improve knowledge and expertise for future projects in the same domain and linguistic style. The translator can also do follow-up research to reinforce knowledge in a particular area. The same applies to a ML-driven translation solution. Relevant computer programs can be utilized to compile corpora, analyze the linguistic features, and process the corpora to make them more ingestible for an ML engine. For example, translation memory can be compiled into a separate parallel corpus, or existing source and target texts can be automatically aligned to optimize use as training data by a machine translation engine. We will further elaborate the concept of continuous learning in Chapters 7 and 8.

6.4.6 Adapting the target content format to the target locale and culture

After the linguistic elements are translated into the target language, the final step is to format the textual information. In effect, many (component) content management systems can manage structured information, starting with the first step in the continuous translation process: when generating the content to be translated or localized. Structured information has a fixed framework, and content can be stored and managed in a separate database according to the structure. For example, in a bicycle owner manual, content can be divided into different parts based upon content, such as bicycle assembly, maintenance and service, general warnings, and important safety information. These sections can be recycled when creating similar content, such as a tricycle owner manual. When each section is translated, the translated part can also be used in a similar manner. Although the translator is usually not involved in the training of the intelligent content management system, it is useful to be familiar with the fundamentals. For example, the Darwin Information Typing Architecture (DITA) was designed specifically for writing, organizing, and linking topic-based content; it benefits those who write and edit technical information (Bellamy et al., 2011). When translators work with technical writers and DITA engineers, relevant knowledge in this area can help them effectively translate and work with other functional departments.

Other intelligent tools are also used in the last step of a continuous translation process, such as speech synthesis or text-to-speech (TTS), which is particularly significant in spoken MT. TTS algorithms aim to convert text into waveforms. It is exactly the reverse of ASR, with similar machine learning principles and possibilities for human involvement.

TTS is part of synthetic media, also known as AI-generated media, generative media, and personalized media, which "refers to any media created or modified by algorithmic means, especially through the use of artificial intelligence algorithms" (W3C, 2020, n.p.). One significant trend in the publishing stage is the rise of implementation of synthetic media, which include not only speech/voice synthesis, but also artificially-generated video, images, or text. AI takes on part (or all) of the creative process, which leads to many ethical concerns. To address these concerns, supporting tools such as automatic fake detection and quality evaluation need to be developed, similar to the many quality evaluation metrics and quality assurance tools that are applied in machine translation.

To sum up, the various steps of a continuous translation process form an ecosystem. The task of managing these ecosystems falls to the translator and, in particular, the localization project manager.

6.5 Integration of NLP tasks

We have discussed examples of intelligent NLP tasks at each step of a continuous translation process, including the translator's interaction with the model while working with the language data. In practice, many more tasks can be created based on a user's intent. The key is creating or selecting the most relevant tools and customizing them in a system, which includes finding the core technology and support tools required to meet a specific translation goal.

These ML-driven NLP technologies are connected and interrelated. In order to optimize performance of the entire system, compatibility and connectivity among these technologies must be considered. In many cases, a feasible solution would be to start with a core technology while adjusting specifications of adjacent tools to maximize overall performance. This solution is driven by identifying one pivotal technology and multiple supporting technologies. For example, in a MT system, as discussed in Chapter 4, multiple components such as segmentation, terminology integration, and automatic text analysis function together with the MT engine as part of the whole system. But they can also be stand-alone tools with their own support technologies. For an MT-driven translation process, each step – preprocessing, memory check, and post-processing – must meet MT engine specifications to maximize the effectiveness of the entire system.

In scenarios where the MT systems integrate CAT tool plugins, typically there are multiple options for the translator to make use of automation: (1) translation memory fuzzy matches that meet a threshold criterion set by the user, (2) the MT result for each sequence (e.g., the whole sentence or individual phrases in the sentence) as suggestions for the translator to choose from, and (3) other features such as predictive typing and fuzzy match repair that automate the translation process.

For instance, Déjà Vu X3 Professional has a feature called DeepMiner, which extracts information from terminology and translation memory databases to create fuzzy match repairs. The machine replaces missing content with the correct term. When the missing content is not in the termbase, the software can perform statistical extraction from translation memory and deduct the translation of the missing content. For example, if the program sees a sentence *It is a cat*, but there is only a French translation (*C'est un chien*) in the translation memory, it can search the termbase to see if there is a translation of *cat*. If there is an entry for the translation of *cat*, the program can automatically replace the word *chien* with *chat* and provide the translation *C'est un chat*. This is an example of a ML technology that, in addition to MT, is integrated into a CAT platform. With the rise of computer power, machine learning has been added to the CAT platform, leading to more intelligent CAT tools.

Similar technologies can be integrated into MT systems as well. For instance, Bulte and Tezcan (2019) propose "a method for augmenting NMT training data with fuzzy TM matches" (p. 1800). Their tests with two language pairs (English into Dutch and English into Hungarian), using the TM of the Directorate-General for Translation of the European Commission, show considerable improvements in MT quality. Highlighting the ease of implementation of this solution, they suggest that their method is promising when a sizable TM is available and there is a repetition across translations.

There is flexibility regarding the main infrastructure. ML technologies can be integrated into MT systems, or CAT systems, or other systems. MT quality has been considered unstable compared with human translation. As a result, in CAT workflows, the MT system is often used as a backup mechanism when the TM fails to retrieve high fuzzy matches above a certain threshold. Yet theoretically, these features can be embedded in any system based on the user's purpose. Lilt, for example, is an interactive MT system. It integrates segmentation and other features into its MT system. As a result, the boundaries between an MT system and a CAT become blurry.

6.6 Intentionality: why machine learning matters in translation

In the Introduction to this book, we discussed Searle's (1980) thought experiment known as the Chinese Room Argument, in which Searle leads those outside the room to believe that he understands Chinese (Cole, 2020). Searle argues that he is simply behaving like a computer performing computational operations on formally specified elements, without any understanding of Chinese. He asserts that he is simply an instantiation of the computer program.

What distinguishes humans from machines is intentionality, which, as Searle (1980) states, is "a product of causal features of the brain" (p. 417). Here, the word 'causal' indicates a relationship between cause and effect. With causal features, the brain is able to produce (i.e., cause) intentional states, which cannot be achieved by a simulation or a computer program. Searle (1980) further points out that instantiating a computer program, as in Searle's thought experiment, is not a sufficient condition of intentionality (p. 417).

> Because the formal symbol manipulations by themselves don't have any intentionality; they are quite meaningless; they aren't even *symbol* manipulations, since the symbols don't symbolize anything. In the linguistic jargon, they have only a syntax but no semantics. Such intentionality as computers appear to have is solely in the minds of those who program them and those who use them, those who send in the input and those who interpret the output.
>
> *(p. 422)*

Intentionality is an innate part of human nature which distinguishes human intelligence from artificial intelligence (AI). Intentionality is a result of a person's mental efforts to focus attention on specific cognitive areas that correlate with previous knowledge and experience. Intentionality is thus individualized from within and varies from person to person,[3] as Locke (1690) set out in *The Essay Concerning Human Understanding*:

> [W]hen ideas float in our mind without any reflection or regard of the understanding, it is that which the French call reverie; our language has scarce a name for it: when the ideas that offer themselves (for, as I have observed in another place, whilst we are awake, there will always be a train of ideas succeeding one another in our minds) are taken notice of, and, as it were, registered in the memory, it is attention: when the mind with great earnestness, and of choice, fixes its view on any idea, considers it on all sides, and will not be called off by the ordinary solicitation of other ideas, it is that we call "intention," or "study."
>
> *(n.p.)*

Since computers and their programs do not have intentionality, they are unfocused. That is not a weakness; it is the reason we use them. Computers and their programs are essentially tools for human beings, no more and no less, no matter how advanced they are. However, anyone who is willing to utilize them for a particular purpose can also bring them to life in their own mind by projecting intentionality on them.

Intention is an area of study in translation theory and practice. A translator begins by analyzing the source text from the translator's point of view, and in doing so determines the intention of the text[4] for the purpose of selecting a suitable translation method and identifying particular and recurrent problems (Newmark, 1988, pp. 11–13). The translator's understanding of the text and search for the intention of the text go together, as intention provides rationale for choices.

Newmark compares translation activity to an iceberg: "the tip is the translation – what is visible, what is written on the page – the iceberg, the activity, is all the work you do, often ten times as much again, much of which you do not even use" (Newmark, 1988, p. 12). In the era of machine learning, we can use machines to explore many areas below the tip of the iceberg, which allows humans to focus on the visible part of the translation activity. A human translator is potentially a speaker, sharing a majority of the cognitive features with the message originator; yet any reconstruction is a new, individual piece of intellectual work, rather than a duplicate. On the other hand, computer programs start with a 'collective' perspective, given the vast amount of data they can process. The translator can customize the computer's approach by projecting intentionality on the computer program to achieve a workflow that conforms with the translator's preferences, including cognitive ones.

A human translator can do better than a machine not due to a particular strength in capturing every aspect of the linguistic features of an utterance, but rather due to the ability to create an experience with relevant intentionality, tapping into potential connections in the hidden part of the iceberg through shared experiences, generating empathy in readers' minds. Communication purposes are satisfied intuitively to some degree in this way. It follows then that there is an issue of the sparsity of individual human experience, since experience is vast, with unknown, hidden potential. As a tool, machine learning can shed light on areas that an individual human cannot cover, offering the translator a feel for what it looks like, while at the same time, machine learning might also generate new hidden and unexpected areas, as ML generates its own rules based on vast amounts of data that no human can process.

Notes

1 Softmax is often used as an activation function of a neural network. As Goodfellow et al. (2016) point out, "[s]oftmax units naturally represent a probability distribution over a discrete variable with k possible values, so they may be used as a kind of switch" (p. 196).
2 Entropy is a very technical term. However, intuitively, one can think about entropy as disorder or uncertainty. That is, we associate entropy with our ignorance of the system, or our lack of information about what microstate it is in. In this sense, entropy is a measure of uncertainty (see Schwartz, 2019, p. 2).
3 According to Searle, there are two types of people who interact with and confer intentionality on computers: those who program them and those who use them. In the discussion in this book, we prioritize users, including translators, project managers, decision makers, and other stakeholders in machine–human interaction.
4 Newmark distinguishes between the intention of text and the translator's intention (Newmark, 1988, pp. 11–13).

PART III

Data in human and machine learning

7

TRANSLATOR–COMPUTER INTERACTION THROUGH LANGUAGE DATA

KEY CONCEPTS

- *There are two fundamental uses of language data: (1) human analysis and learning and (2) machine analytics and learning.*
- *Comparability is a key characteristic of translation-driven language data. In translation, both humans and machines compare pairs of texts to learn, e.g., MT results and human translation to calculate MT quality scores, aligned source and target texts (parallel corpora) to train MT, and texts in different languages on the same topic (comparable corpora) to learn specialized knowledge.*
- *In a typical translation process, translator–computer interaction (TCI) is realized through language data from three perspectives: (1) data design and acquisition, (2) data annotation, and (3) language data use.*

7.1 Introduction

In its foundations, machine learning (ML) is a method of data analysis that automates analytical model building. In other words, data constitute the critical infrastructure necessary to build machine learning systems. In translation, language data largely determine the performance, fairness, robustness, safety, and scalability of translation-related ML systems.

Neural networks are a form of machine learning that uses a layered representation of data. Take a neural MT system pipeline for example. It starts with input data, typically human-friendly linguistic elements in the source language. Then the MT system converts these elements into machine-readable feature vectors that represent syntactic and semantic characteristics. Next, if the network includes deep learning layers, the MT system performs a series of further transformations before converting the feature vectors back into linguistic elements in the target language.

DOI: 10.4324/9781003321538-11

Humans can then edit this final layer to achieve a degree of naturalness that is equivalent or similar to what humans can achieve in their traditional translation or language generation process.

Paradoxically, among AI/ML researchers and developers, aspects of working with language data are often under-discussed, being viewed as 'operational' relative to the lionized work of building novel models and algorithms (Sambasivan et al., 2021, p. 1). For a translator, linguist, or localization project manager, however, working with language data is the most significant part of their practice and research, and their approach to language data is different from that of an AI/ML researcher, developer, or data scientist. Typically, a translator has advanced linguistic and cultural knowledge and can make meaningful analysis of the datasets, both individually for discrete translation tasks and collectively for managing the quality of translation memory through post-editing and annotation by a group of translators. The latter allows for quality control of the language data fed to a neural MT engine to train the model. In contrast, a data scientist or a data engineer uses computer programs and tools to conduct statistical analysis of language data, for example, with software such as Python, R, and Tableau. Similarly, an ML/AI researcher and developer focuses on building novel models and algorithms. While an overlapping of these approaches is unavoidable, the priority for each perspective is clear.

A translator starts with formatted content, including both linguistic and non-linguistic elements, including images, formatting, and audio. In terms of linguistic elements, a linguistic unit consists of signs and thus has a double structure for linguistic form (signifier) and for meaning (signified). In a neural language model, when the input data are prepared and the output data are edited by humans, the data must be presentable and make sense to humans. However, once the data are out of sight of human users, the data do not necessarily have to be meaningful to them. In other words, data can have multiple states. The first state is *parole*, i.e., the concrete instances of language use, which is mainly for humans and demonstrates unique human characteristics. The second state occurs when data are fed to machines, which tokenize, segment, and process the data so that an ML system can digest them and perform mathematical operations. This second state of language data is an engineering and statistical perspective rather than a linguistic or cultural one. The translator interacts with an ML system in the first state and some aspects of the second state − sentence segmentation makes sense to humans, whereas tokenization and stemming do not − by creating and compiling linguistic instances for machine learning, adding human annotations to make reflections understandable by the system, and conducting linguistic analyses to make decisions as to what data are relevant to train the machine.

When discussing human–computer interaction (HCI), many users think first of technological tools − CAT tools for instance − an annotation platform, or an interactive MT system, which provide an HCI interface for the translator. It might be the case that an AI/ML researcher or developer focuses on specific technologies to facilitate HCI. However, the HCI investigation in this approach may make the workflow inconsistent and segmented for the translator, as a translator uses multiple tools, and it can be difficult in theory and practice to connect these separate tech-nologies that are designed for various purposes. What is consistent for the translator is the need to process language data in various states throughout the entire transla-tion process, and the conversion between states is a fundamental characteristic of HCI. Incorporating features that facilitate human insight into language data at or close to the input and output layer of neural networks is part of the translator–com-puter interaction (TCI) process.

7.2 Translation-driven language data

Terms such as *data*, *corpus*, and *information* are often used interchangeably in multi-ple disciplines, e.g., translation studies, NLP, and computer linguistics. In this chap-ter, we point out crucial distinctions between them when examining various states of language data, as ML is pushing the boundaries of the concept of language data. This section aims to clarify these concepts in relation to the continuous translation process discussed in Chapter 6.

7.2.1 Corpus and language data

The concept of 'data' implies an engineering and statistical perspective, rather than a linguistic or translation-related one. *Statistics* is the science of collecting, analyz-ing, presenting, and interpreting data. According to the Encyclopedia Britannica entry for the term *statistics*,

> Data are the **facts and figures** that are collected, analyzed, and summarized for presentation and interpretation. Data may be classified as either quantita-tive or qualitative. Quantitative data measure either how much or how many of something, and qualitative data provide labels, or names, for categories of like items.
>
> *(emphasis added; Williams, n.d.)*

A large amount of data can be analyzed and turned into useful information in many applied fields. The process of "information extraction (IE) turns unstruc-tured information embedded in texts into structured data" (Jurafsky & Martin, 2020, p. 332). For example, the task of relation extraction aims to find and classify semantic relations among the text entities; and temporal expressions such as days of the week (Thursday, Friday, etc.) can also be extracted. In this sense, 'informa-tion' in IE refers to limited types of semantic content that can be extracted from text (p. 332).

In a translator-mediated communication process, large amounts of concrete instances of language use, i.e., *parole*, are created. These linguistic resources are meaningful for humans. For a machine learning system, these linguistic elements – words or lexemes – are categorical data representing discrete, atomic units. They can be converted to continuous, real value numbers (vectors) through feature vectorization, which allow for mathematical operations resulting in machine perception. The language data involved in an ML process can be seen as linguistic elements stripped of meaning, abstracted to a mathematical form.

In addition to naturally occurring text/speech produced in human communication processes, data can be artificial, i.e., generated by a computer simulation. Researchers have studied the ways in which data are often transformed before use, rather than used in their original form (Sambasivan et al., 2021, p. 2). For example, the synthetic data generation approach has been applied to neural machine translation. In a study conducted by Hassan et al. (2017), synthetic data for training NMT systems are generated using seed data to project words from a closely related, resource-rich language to an under-resourced language variant via word embedding representations. Given such uses, it is critical and necessary to differentiate between language data for ML and linguistic elements for humans. This distinction allows activities like data synthesis to be independent of linguistic, cultural, and ethical considerations. Synthetic data are used primarily to address mathematical or engineering problems, but when language data are considered as *parole*, aspects such as fairness and naturalness should be incorporated into the process of analysis. As an example, a translation source text is a fundamental component of a corpus and can be turned into language data for machine learning and analysis, allowing information with limited semantic content to be extracted for a specific purpose.

In summary, the concept of language data in a broad sense includes two fundamental states: one for human analysis and human learning, and another for machine analytics and machine learning. As described previously, the conversion of language data between these two states is a basic form of translator–computer interaction (TCI) in a continuous translation process.

7.2.2 Translation-driven language data

7.2.2.1 Translation-driven corpora

Regarding the state of language data for human analysis and learning, in linguistics and translation research and practice, the most frequently used natural language dataset is the corpus, which is "a large collection of authentic texts that have been gathered in electronic form according to a specific set of criteria" (Bowker & Pearson, 2002, p. 9). A corpus collects *parole* and is primarily designed for human use. In machine learning, most syntactic and semantic relations are examined in a corpus; the relationships within the text itself are generally the focus of investigation. Texts in the corpus are the primary resource allowing observation of the distributional structure of a linguistic unit, i.e., how it is related to other units in the same group of texts in the corpus. These relationships are used to extract feature vectors from linguistic units.

The field of corpus linguistics has made significant contributions to translation theory and practice. Corpus management and analysis skills have become part of translational competence (Zanettin, 2013, p. 20). In particular, Zanettin (2013) proposes the concept of "translation-driven" corpora, i.e., those which are created and/or used for some translation-related purpose (p. 26, 2012, p. 8), in which two dimensions are used to create a typology: (1) monolingual or bilingual/multilingual; and (2) comparable or parallel (2012, pp. 10–11). In this framework, the first type of corpus is the monolingual comparable corpus, which is used to compare translated and untranslated texts in the same language. The second type is the bilingual corpus, which has two sub-types: (a) the parallel corpus, in which source and target texts are paired; and (b) comparable corpora, in which two (sub)corpora – paired on the basis of textual similarity – are compared. A third type of corpus is the multilingual corpus, in which more than two languages are involved. This too can be either parallel or comparable.

It should be noted that the working definition of 'corpus' varies across disciplines and research areas. For example, Schnepp et al. (2010) propose the concept of "synthetic corpora," which are "computer representations of linguistic phenomena. They enable the creation of computer-generated animations depicting sign languages and are the complement of corpora containing videotaped exemplars" (p. 1). In this discussion, we adopt the definition of 'corpus' from corpus linguistics. In this approach, as Biber et al. (1998) point out, corpus-based analysis is comprised of four essential characteristics:

- it is empirical, analyzing the actual patterns of use in natural texts;
- it utilizes a large and principled collection of natural texts, known as a 'corpus', as the basis for analysis;
- it makes extensive use of computers for analysis, using both automatic and interactive techniques;
- it depends on both quantitative and qualitative analytical techniques.

(p. 4)

In this understanding, translation-driven corpora are language data for humans and thus do not include machine-generated, non-authentic texts.

Zanettin (2013) points out that he looks at how corpora and corpus linguistics techniques have been used in translation descriptive research, with the awareness that "[m]illions of people in their everyday life use automatic machine translation systems which rely largely on corpus-based statistical machine translation techniques" (pp. 20–21). In this chapter, our reflections on translation-driven corpora originate mainly through translation practice and practice-oriented translation research. In this approach, translation-driven corpora includes those for both human and machine translation as needed in a given case. In other words, they are collections of authentic texts that have been gathered in electronic form to improve the productivity and effectiveness of both human translators and automatic translation systems.

7.2.2.2 Comparability of translation-driven corpora

Zanettin (2012, 2013) stresses that corpora used in descriptive and applied translation studies usually involve the comparison of at least two main sets of data, which can be called corpus components or subcorpora (p. 26; p. 10). For instance, the British National Corpus (BNC) is often used as a reference for general British English, and parts of it have been used as a comparable component in some corpus-based translation studies (Zanettin, 2012, p. 46). By using a reference corpus in the comparison, linguistic and semantic features of translation-related texts – source and target – can be captured, which can provide insight into a translation process, for example, in terms of text domain and terminology.

In practice, translators are frequently handling and comparing two types of text, e.g., source/target and translated/untranslated text. In effect, a parallel corpus is a special case of comparable corpus, where the comparison is based on content, which indicates the basic translation relationship of equivalence. For instance, one of the earliest parallel corpora was recorded on the Rosetta Stone, a stele inscribed with three versions of a decree issued in Memphis, Egypt, in 196 BC. It included Ancient Egyptian, using hieroglyphic and Demotic scripts, and Ancient Greek (see Rosetta Stone, 2022). It is an early example of how humans associate information by comparing and linking meaning expressed in different languages and scripts. In an ML-driven translation process, bilingual and multilingual parallel corpora are the main data resources for MT training, testing, and evaluation, in addition to being useful for human learning and translation processes.

When comparing two or multiple subcorpora, certain parameters or measurements need to be applied to ensure the effectiveness of comparison. For instance, Zanettin (2012) points out that comparability between two subcorpora in different languages can be ensured through similarity of "sampling techniques" and "balance and representativeness," or by employing the same procedures for generating content, such as using the same web crawling tools (e.g., BootCat) to harvest Internet texts (pp. 150–151). When comparing subcorpora, their scope and size can also be considered. The selection of specific parameters will be driven by the purpose of the comparison and the measurement techniques.

7.2.3 Translation-driven language data

The comparability feature of translation-driven corpora applies to language data in a continuous translation process. For example, in machine translation, the training data are parallel data in a database of aligned source and target segments. For MT domain adaptation and detection, domain specific data are used, which are derived from the comparison of topics or domains. MT results are compared with human translations to generate annotated data for automatic post-editing. In this sense, translation-driven language data are based on comparison.

It is also possible to train an NMT engine on both human translation and synthetic parallel data (see Poncelas et al., 2018). In their research, Poncelas et al. (2018) point out that in many use cases, the amount of good-quality parallel data produced by humans is insufficient to reach the translation standard required. In such cases, it has become the norm to resort to back-translating freely available monolingual data to create an additional synthetic parallel corpus for training an NMT model. In this case, monolingual source text data are translated with an existing MT system, and the MT output can be used with the original monolingual data to generate a training corpus for a new NMT system. The corpus can be used both as a separate standalone dataset, i.e., synthetic, and combined with human-generated parallel data, i.e., hybrid (authentic + synthetic) data. Poncelas et al. (2018) found that using back-translated data as a training corpus affects the performance of an NMT model: when adding back-translated data to a set of human-translated data, they found that translation performance initially improved, but then dropped as more synthetic data were added. However, when using synthetic data alone, astonishingly, the performance is quite good: it was roughly equivalent to the use of authentic data and in some instances even better. This example illustrates that sometimes training results are not always consistent with human intuition, as the concept of 'quality of data' depends on the user: human or machine. In some cases, what is considered good data for humans may not be useful for machines and vice versa.

Thus we expand the concept of translation-driven corpora from translation studies and practice to a broader concept of translation-driven language data, which include all relevant data in a continuous translation process that are used for both humans and machines. In this context, translation-driven language data include: (1) corpora with human generated authentic text, (2) machine generated synthetic data, and (3) language data with a combination of both human generated and synthetic data.

Now that the concept of translation-driven language data has been explained, we turn to the discussion of translator–computer interaction (TCI) through language data from three perspectives: (1) TCI in data design and acquisition, (2) TCI through data annotation, and (3) TCI through language data use.

7.3 TCI in data design and acquisition

7.3.1 Human insights in data design and acquisition

Translator–computer interactions start before the data reach the computer. When translators prepare human-generated language data for ML-driven translation activities, they need to convert the data to a state that maximizes machine power to process it. This conversion and pre-processing of 'raw' language data implies that the translator can consider language data for both human and machine use. As Sambasivan et al. (2021) point out, language data are shaped through the practices of collecting, curating, and sensemaking, which means that language data can be considered inherently socio-political in nature (p. 2). Similarly, Pine and Liboiron (2015) emphasize that techniques of measurement used to produce data are "imbued with judgments and values that dictate what is counted and what is not, what is considered the best unit of measurement, and how different things are grouped together and 'made' into a measurable entity" (p. 1).

The unit of translation is also a means for comparing subcorpora of translation-driven corpora. Many parallel corpora used in translation processes include sentence alignment between the source and target text as a structural feature, and the sentence boundaries indicated by punctuation marks are annotations that writers add when creating text. By applying segmentation rules based on punctuation, computer programs like CAT and automatic segmentation tools use human annotations in parallel corpus design and acquisition.

Terminology is another example. When translators or terminologists identify terms that are associated with specialized knowledge, they organize information about the term using a mental schema to make the term comprehensible to a computer program, although the comprehension is only rudimentary in form. When a CAT tool highlights terms, it provides an option to have the computer program translate the terms and to reduce the translator's cognitive load.

7.3.2 Encoding translator's insights when creating language data

7.3.2.1 Degrees of translator intervention

Generally speaking, if a dataset is created with a high degree of human intervention, it is usually considered high quality, labor-intensive data, which can be a good linguistic resource to train a ML model. By human intervention, we mean how much human intelligence and effort are involved in the database design and compilation. In the following, we focus on the translator, to include translators, interpreters, linguists, terminologists, translation/localization project managers, and other domain experts. With this group in mind, we consider two opposite poles on a continuum of translation-driven language data: (1) general language data with minimum translator intervention and (2) special purpose data created by translators, e.g., translation memory.

(1) Language data with minimum translator intervention

In corpus linguistics, computer science, and natural language processing, large scale datasets are used to analyze specific linguistic behavior, extract meaning representation, and train ML systems to perform NLP tasks. This type of data is usually designed and acquired according to specific criteria, e.g., size limits, topics/domain, clients, authorship, publication date, and languages. The collection of textual items in these datasets relies heavily on computer processing, e.g., using web crawling techniques or computer programs for text formatting and processing. Synthetic data are an extreme case, as the data are created by program simulation with minimum human intervention, rather than in real-life communication processes. Collections of naturally occurring texts, i.e., corpora, can also be compiled with little human intervention. For instance, in web corpus construction, crawling is used to collect human language data. In order to address issues such as redundant or unsuitable content for inclusion in web corpora, crawling algorithms such as focused crawlers can be designed to maximize search variables referred to as document weight or weighted coverage (WC), which can be defined, for example, as high search-engine relevance, documents about specific subjects, or documents in a specific language (Schäfer et al., 2014, p. 9).

In translation, parallel corpora creation relies on multiple ML techniques to collect data, including OCR technologies that digitize translation-related content (source and target texts). Automatic tools are then used to segment and align. These large-scale corpora come from a compilation of different sources, which is not the same as translation memory produced in a translation process. Although the TM includes the translated text, the translator who created the translation usually was not aware of or not directly responsible for the subsequent parallel corpora construction. This type of parallel corpus involves automation rather than translator intervention. Unless the translator further annotates the data, the corpus does not include information about the content of the corpus from the translator's perspective, such as the unit of translation or translation quality.

To some degree, this type of data can be considered general, involving less translator intervention, due to the following reasons:

a   It can be used repetitively for various NLP tasks and for linguistic analysis conducted by humans.
b   The computation of different sources of language data is more relevant to the work of ML developers and data scientists than translators.
c   With the application of computational technologies, the scale of this type of data is usually much larger than the scale of data resulting from translator invention.
d   It is considered data out of context. For example, though each part of the data might come from linguistic resources from a specific project, the project information is usually lost in the massive amount of data after incorporation into the larger dataset, or used repetitively for various projects with their own specific context. Once the data are removed from their specific context (project information, terminology, client requirements, etc.), TCI is no longer possible, unless a user analyzes the data to recover its context.
e   It is usually inactive in a specific translation project. Take translation memory for example. If a TM is not used for a certain period of time, its translations and terminology may be outdated. The TM can be considered inactive or depreciated and should not be presented to translators as suggestions for their translations.

(2) Special purpose data directly created by translators

The translator can also create a corpus while translating. When a translator is working in a CAT tool environment, the translation is automatically stored as aligned source and target segments, which forms a translation memory. The dataset is usually relatively small in size, as the data are created manually. The collection of this type of parallel corpus is dynamic and typically managed under a specific translation project, which includes rich contextual information about clients, project goals, and target audience. In this sense, translation memory associated with a specific translation assignment produces parallel corpora with a high level of TCI.

Translation memory can also be created using automatic or manual methods. In machine translation post-editing (MTPE), a translator can post-edit the MT result to achieve a high-quality translation memory. Compared with the general corpora discussed earlier, the degree of translator intervention is higher.

Furthermore, translator insights can be added to translation memory in the form of annotation based on specific scenarios to select quality data from a large dataset in order to facilitate effective machine learning. For example, a translator can filter translation memory by authors, who have various degrees of translation proficiency levels, and by adding metadata, which is sometimes referred to as 'data about data'. For instance, by adding information about translator proficiency levels, we can instruct the system to choose TM produced by authors with high proficiency levels so that an ML task is trained only on high-quality data. In this context, metadata is "structured information that describes, explains, locates, or otherwise makes it easier to retrieve, use, or manage an information resource" (National Information Standards Organization, 2004, p. 1). Compared with translators directly generating translation memory, annotation with metadata such as author information is a second layer of translator intervention, as contextual information is encoded in the data based on human analysis. Such annotations can improve the effectiveness of machine learning for specialized NLP tasks and can also be used to facilitate human learning. In Chapter 8, we will introduce source-text oriented comparable corpora that can be curated for the purpose of continuous learning.

When translators directly interact with language data, the dataset can be rich in human insights, which can facilitate ML in translation considerably if used strategically. However, there is a fundamental conflict between linguistic resources and language data for ML. Human intervention in language data means reducing, to some degree, the productivity of language data generation; it slows down machine learning, as human interaction yields high quality yet small amounts of data. It is important to balance these two extremes.

7.3.2.2 The dynamic feature of data quality

Human intervention is subjective and context-dependent. When it is incorporated into the data creation process, the concept of data quality becomes dynamic as well. All processes of data generation involve human intervention; as Sambasivan et al. (2021) point out, language data is never "raw" (p. 2). The difference lies in the source of the intervention – whether from translator, AI developer, or data scientist – the degree of intervention, and its impact.

In the previous section, we discussed the degree of translator intervention in the data generation process. In this section, we turn to the quality of the intervention.

Generally speaking, when translators put more effort into a project, the data quality should be higher, making a translation memory corpus with a high degree of TCI valuable for translation-related activities. However, sometimes translation memory can be 'contaminated' by mistakes due to a translator's misunderstanding or the lack of relevant contextual information in the translating or post-editing processes. In this sense, the quality of data is affected by individual factors during data creation.

One must also consider whether the TCI is relevant for translation or NLP tasks. When using linguistic resources, it is important to analyze the data type in terms of TCI. For example, OPUS (https://opus.nlpl.eu) is an online platform where users can access large collections of various parallel corpora (Tiedemann, 2012, p. 2214). If one intends to train a spoken MT, the TED talk corpora can be considered. However, if one intends to train an MT on written translation of political documents, EuroParl can be used. As these examples show, a key indicator to consider is the relevance of the dataset for the NLP task in terms of domain, language pair, and mode of communication (spoken or written).

Now that we have discussed various degrees of TCI from the minimum level of translator intervention to multiple layers of translator insights encoded in data, we will discuss techniques to communicate these human insights to an ML system. Generally speaking, such communication is achieved by means of language data annotation.

7.4 TCI through data annotation

7.4.1 Raw data vs. annotated data

In this section, we focus on human-generated authentic data in corpora to discuss human annotation activities. Language data annotation adds a layer of human intelligence to raw data. Here raw data means unannotated data. In corpus linguistics, the term 'tagged' is often used (see Biber et al., 1998, pp. 257–262). A single corpus annotated with the same specification is called an annotated, or a tagged corpus. A typical example of a grammatically tagged corpus is part-of-speech (POS) tagging. See Figure 7.1 for the POS tagging of the sentence *I do not like green eggs and ham.*

As shown in Figure 7.1, POS tagging assigns each word in the sentence to a category, which is a critical requirement for subsequent analysis.

Both raw and annotated data can be used to train ML algorithms, as functions are learned (or generated) by mapping the relationships between input and the desired output. The main use of raw data is searching for a particular word or sequence of words. In neural language models, the distributional information of linguistic units is the foundation of meaning representation. For example, as discussed in Chapter 3, word2vec uses running text as implicitly supervised training data for a classifier, which avoids the need for any sort of manual annotation of the data. When raw data are annotated, the tags highlight the specific features that are relevant to the learning task.

WORD   PART OF SPEECH

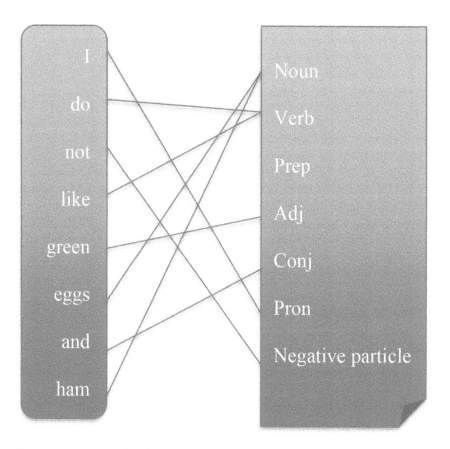

FIGURE 7.1   An example of POS tagging

7.4.2 Framework for human annotations

Before the annotation activities are conducted, it is important to create an annotation framework that includes the categories or metadata of the dataset. The task of creating such a framework and specifically designing a set of metadata usually requires relevant linguistic and translation expertise. For example, to annotate grammatical features, a POS tagset must be standardized and used as a criterion to guide the annotation task.

Translators' domain expertise and relevant linguistic and cultural knowledge are crucial to accomplish this task. One approach is to use a Multidimensional Quality Metrics (MQM) framework that contains a description of translation error types and scoring criteria for the assessment of translation quality (Lommel et al., 2013). A translator can customize MQM error typology into an annotation schema with a specific name and definition of the metadata based on the project requirements. Options include significant error types as the error categories in a MTPE task, allowing post-editors to choose the error categories in their edits, which the linguist can use to analyze MTPE error patterns and train other ML systems, such as automatic post-editing systems.

To improve control of translation memory, the project manager can create an annotation schema that represents translators' competence in producing good translations, including the translator's language proficiency level, translation experience, and familiarity with the translation topic. Such criteria can be saved in a typical translation project management system. Incorporating them into the annotation system makes it possible for the manager to select the most relevant translation memory and check that it was produced by translators who meet certain standards, thus helping to ensure the quality of the translation memory. In this manner, the translator's knowledge and expertise in translation can play a significant role in the design and implementation of a data annotation framework.

For real-world translation-related tasks, the annotation framework can be incorporated into an automated annotation management system. Many CAT tools have an editing feature that allows the user to create different error types, which the system can automatically store. There are also standalone annotation platforms like KEOPS (Keen Evaluation Of Parallel Sentences), which offers a complete tool for manual evaluation of parallel sentences (KEOPS for evaluators, n.d.).

When designing an annotation framework based on existing translation knowledge, as discussed in the case of MQM, it is important to balance the relationship between computational efficiency, the analysis framework, and annotation cost. MQM has 19 core issues, and under each major category, there are subcategories that users can further extend. On the one hand, the higher the number of tags, the more complex the computation and the greater the human cognitive effort required to make judgments regarding the categories, which in turn increases cost. On the other hand, if there are not enough tag categories, the framework does not represent the scenario very well, and the annotations lose significance. Balancing these considerations requires domain expertise, rather than computational knowledge and skill, making a domain expert such as a translator a strong candidate to execute this task effectively.

7.4.3 The role of human annotation in machine learning

The early 1990s saw a shift from rule-based to statistical MT and with it a transition to descriptive approaches in computer program development. Statistical approaches depend on language data, which is in alignment with the history of corpus linguistics, with on-line corpora and analysis tools becoming increasingly accessible and corpus-based studies increasingly common in the 1990s (Biber et al., 1998, p. F33). As an integral part of corpus linguistics, data annotation is significant for these developments. For example, Universal Dependencies (n.d.) is a framework for consistent annotation of grammar (parts of speech, morphological features, and syntactic dependencies) across different human languages. These annotation activities provide a broad range of real-world data with human insights and are valuable resources for linguistic analyses.

From the ML perspective, human annotation seemed very inefficient and slow when first introduced. However, the approach turned out to be very successful, as the annotation offers many benefits that other approaches cannot provide:

1   Generally speaking, human annotation offers high-quality data annotation examples, which can be used to train automatic annotation models such as syntactic parsers and POS (part of speech) taggers. This means reuse of human labor, that is to say, human annotation efforts are embedded in all potential projects that leverage the automatic annotation models based on the initial human inputs.

2   Human annotation offers a method of system evaluation: serving as the 'ground truth' or 'gold standard', human annotation data can be used to evaluate tools, similar to how human translations serve as reference translations in automatic machine translation metrics.

3   Human annotation offers new capabilities that automatic systems cannot yet cover: the more annotated data is used to train the model, the smarter it becomes, and the closer we come to universal usability. Humans are very creative in generating data, which an existing model based on previous human observation cannot fully capture. Humans always take the lead to push the boundaries of data with new feature patterns.

7.4.4 Automatic annotation

Tagging, or annotation, can also be automated. Computer programs that tag an uncoded corpus are called taggers. POS taggers, some of the earliest programs, make use of resources and methodologies such as dictionaries and probabilities with a rule-based component and a morphological analyzer. Parsers are programs that add syntactic analysis to a corpus, identifying subjects, verbs, objects, and more complex syntactic information (Biber et al., 1998, pp. 260–262).

Neural networks have also been integrated into the architecture of automatic labeling programs. For example, Qi et al. (2020) introduce Stanza, an open-source Python natural language processing toolkit that supports 66 human languages. This toolkit features a neural pipeline that takes raw text as input and produces annotations including "tokenization, multi-word token expansion, lemmatization, POS and morphological feature tagging, dependency parsing, and named entity recognition" (p. 101). It is worth noting that the concept of annotation is broadened in their study, as they also consider NLP activities such as tokenization, sentence segmentation, and lemmatization to be annotations in this project. They tokenize the raw text and group tokens into sentences as the first processing step, which "is modeled as a tagging problem over character sequences, where the model predicts whether a given character is the end of a token, end of a sentence, or end of a multi-word token" (p. 102).

7.4.5 Annotation and markup language

From the technical perspective, most annotation projects use some form of XML to encode the tags, and therefore it is helpful to have a basic understanding of markup languages in order to effectively use these standards in actual annotation tasks. A markup language is a human-readable computer language that uses tags to define elements within a document. The two most popular and also most relevant markup languages for translators are HTML (HyperText Markup Language) and XML (eXtensible Markup Language). HTML is used for creating webpages by formatting information on the page, whereas XML was designed to store and transport structured data. While HTML documents use predefined tags, XML files use custom tags to define elements. Localization-related data exchange formats are mostly based on XML. They include (1) TMX format (Translation Memory eXchange), which "allows the transfer of translation memories from one translation tool to another"; (2) TBX (TermBase eXchange) format, which "allows the transfer of glossaries from one translation tool to another"; and (3) XLIFF (XML Localisation Interchange File Format), which "allows the transfer of localizable data extracted from original files from one stage of the localization process to the next, up to merging the localized data back into its original format" (Localization-Related Formats, 2002).

Hanneman and Dinu (2020) show a schematic process in which a TMS (Translation Management System) parses, manipulates, and validates the higher-level document structure in HTML format (p. 1161). In their example, the TMS finds the translatable portions of the input document, performs sentence segmentation on the content, sends it to an underlying MT system for translation, and places the result. Formatting tags within the translatable content (bold, italic, hyperlink, superscript, etc.) are transferred to the MT system to process. These tags are called inline markup/tags, and the proper transfer of these tags from source to target forms a crucial component of the overall quality of the MT system.

Although not always adhering to the strict syntax of a well-defined markup language, most inline tags follow the XML standard and create a hierarchical structure within a segment by introducing either paired tags (opening and closing) or self-closing unary tags. This structure is expected to be preserved in the translation, with paired tags surrounding corresponding text fragments in both the source and target language. This process can include the conversion of HTML predefined tags, like <b> (opening tag) and </b> (closing tag), to XLIFF, like <g id="1" ctype="bold"> (opening tag) and </g> (closing tag), which can be transferred to the MT system. In XLIFF, <g> replaces any inline code of the original document that has a beginning and an end and can be moved within its parent structural element (OASIS, 2008). If the MT system does not transfer these tags in the

	Source text with formatting tags	Target text in Chinese with formatting tags
Website content to be localized	This word is displayed in **bold**	这是个**黑体**字
HTML	\<p\> This word is displayed in \<b\>bold\</b\>\</p\>	\<p\>这是个\<b\>**黑体**\</b\>字\</p\>
XLIFF	\<source\> This word is displayed in \<g id="1" ctype="bold"\><b>\</g\> bold \<g id="1"\></b>\</g\> \</source\>	\<target\> 这是个 \<g id="1" ctype="bold"\><b>\</g\> 黑体 \<g id="1"\></b>\</g\> 字 \</target\>
Tag movement	This word is displayed in \<1\> bold \</1\>	这是个 \<1\> **黑体** \</1\>字

FIGURE 7.2   Projecting source tags into the translated text

correct position, human post-editors must manually correct them in the post-editing process.

Figure 7.2 shows an example of data exchange in HTML, XLIFF, and tag format in an MT system. As shown in the figure, the word *bold* is bolded, which is marked by \<b\> and \</b\> in HTML and \<g id="1"\> in XLIFF. The bold tag is on the last word in the source text, yet in Chinese, the correct tag position should be one character (字, meaning 'character') before the last word. This is due to differences in linguistic structures between English and Chinese. Ideally an MT system can capture this difference. Otherwise, a translator or post-editor needs to manually correct it.

Editing such inline tags in MT is a specialized annotation task, and the translator requires some basic knowledge of the XML markup language to edit accurately. Project managers can provide training to editors to help them understand the meaning of the inline tags. As XML is an extensible markup language, program developers can customize the markup language schema, which makes the meaning of these tags dynamic in different systems. For example, \<1\> may mean bold font in one project but italicized font in another. The translator requires this type of information to perform the tag editing tasks.

7.5 TCI by using language data

In addition to the human element being embedded in the design and compilation of language data and the data annotation process, significant subjective human intervention comes into play when a user analyzes or uses the language data. Generally speaking, there are two basic data use purposes: one is to augment human insights, the other is to facilitate computer analytics and machine learning.

7.5.1 Corpus-based analysis from the translator's perspective

7.5.1.1 Finding patterns in corpora

From the human translator's perspective, the most relevant language data are naturally occurring text or speech in corpora. Given the huge volume of textual information, the translator usually needs to resort to discourse analysis tools to search for information and patterns hidden in the corpus. Concordancing software is designed for word and phrase search and can examine frequencies of words or collocations and find examples of certain words or structures. Discourse analysis tools can perform multiple tasks, such as generating wordlists, lists of lemmas, keywords, collocations and clusters, and word profiles (Zanettin, 2012, pp. 141–146). These tools augment human capabilities by processing large amounts of data that could not be processed without a computer program.

In addition to out-of-box discourse analysis tools, in NLP, a fundamental tool for describing text patterns is regular expression, or regex for short. A regular expression is an algebraic notation used to characterize a set of strings. They are particularly useful for searching for patterns in texts and corpora. A regular expression search function will return all texts that match the pattern (Jurafsky & Martin, 2020, p. 3). For example, a regex in the form of "/[A-Z]/" performs a query to retrieve all upper case letters in the corpus; if a corpus contains only one sentence, e.g., *He lives in the USA*, the searching result will be *H, USA*. Concordancing tools are based on simple regular expressions. Some discourse analysis features are already embedded in traditional linguistic quality assurance tools, like Xbench, and CAT tools. For instance, users can perform concordance searches in the translation memory of most CAT tools, the result of which will gather all translation results that contain a specific sequence, either words or phrases. Some concordancers are standalone tools offering more advanced features of corpus analysis.

7.5.1.2 Corpus-based linguistic analysis

Corpus analysis tools are widely used in translation to observe linguistic patterns in translation-related corpora with the source and target texts. The translator can use regular expression to highlight specific linguistic elements with particular features in the target text, including checking the accuracy of the translation of numbers by using regex /[0–9]/, or verifying the translation of a polysemous word. Rowda (2017) offers an example of using regex to do a translation quality check: In order to find incorrect translations of the word *case* in eBay's product descriptions, i.e., *case* meaning *phone case* rather than other options such as *business case* or *suitcase*, one needs to create a regular expression that finds the Spanish translation of *caso* in the context of mobile phones. First, automatic discourse analysis tools such as Ant-Conc or WordSmith Tools are used to identify context keywords that accompany the translation *caso*. The collocations of the word *case* include context keywords such as Samsung, iPhone, Motorola, and phone. These context words are added to a regular expression: "(?i)(caso.+(iphone | samsung | phone | motorola) | (iphone | samsung | phone | motorola).+caso)." The regular expression returns most of the translations of *case* in the context of mobile phones in this corpus and serves as a starting point for manual verification.

Corpus-based linguistic analysis tools are used in other translation-related tasks. For example, source text analysis based on ML has been applied in the language industry. In this approach, statistics of specific features are analyzed using ML-driven tools, including the number of words, nouns, long words, and complex words. These statistics are good indicators informing the translator's decisions as to whether the source text is suitable for translation and if so, the best method to translate it, whether human translation, MT, or MT with post-editing (MTPE). A translator can also pre-edit the source text based on the analysis result in order to improve the accuracy of the MT engine. In Bar-Hillel's (1959) example of a sentence series – *Little John was looking for his toy box. Finally, he found it. The box was in the pen. John was very happy* – the translator can change *pen* to *playpen* so that the MT system will not mistranslate it (p. 2). In real-life projects, there are usually multiple scenarios for source text creation, including content written by non-native authors, content created by technical specialists for a non-technical audience, and dated content not adhering to brand tone and voice. Corpus analysis can help identify errors in poor source content and predict 'at-risk' content. Sometimes source text needs to be re-written before translation based on the results of the analysis.

More advanced ML driven technologies can be used to conduct translation-driven NLP tasks. Machine translation quality estimation is an example of using ML to estimate the MT quality. Further, by analyzing linguistic features including POS, density of a particular POS (e.g., nouns or adjectives), long words, complex words, short and long sentences, stylistic similarity, and correlations of text features to edit distance and MT quality estimation, one can set up threshold indicators to identify the outliers of an average situation. The outliers can be further examined manually by professional translators to make decisions such as the consistency of the source and target text styles and linguistic features, such as when the target text is more linguistically complex than the source text.

7.5.2 Data analytics for machine learning

7.5.2.1 Using data to train ML models

When using data to train neural ML systems, the characteristics of the dataset are crucial to train, monitor, and upgrade the systems. To find out whether the data are suitable for the task, the data must be cleaned and analyzed to evaluate their quality and relevance to the task. In most ML modeling, there are two basic types of data:

training and testing data. Specifically, the ML model learns from the training data, and it applies its learning and provides output from the testing data. From another perspective, training data influences the model whereas testing data does not. In this sense, data for functions such as tuning or fine-tuning belongs to the category of training data, as tuning is in essence part of the training process.

In neural MT engine training, for example, parallel corpora are usually pre-processed before being used to train the model. Some typical data cleaning activities are removing misaligned sentence pairs, removing repetitions, and tokenization. It is worth noting that many pre-processing tasks can be automated and then post-edited by humans, rather than performed by humans from scratch, unless particular annotation tasks are designed to train a model. For example, computer programs can automatically calculate sentence similarity using word-to-word based, structure-based, and vector-based approaches (Farouk, 2019, p. 1), and in particular, Feng et al. (2022) find that "introducing a pre-trained multilingual language model dramatically reduces the amount of parallel training data required to achieve good performance by 80%" (p. 1). By means of multilingual language models, sentences can be represented across different languages as vectors in a single space, where semantically similar sentences should have similar representations. Based on the sentence embeddings in this space, computer programs can automatically remove sentence pairs not corresponding to translations.

7.5.2.2 Using data to monitor and upgrade ML models

Most models are able to capture only patterns that reflect the training data they have seen. When a ML model is put into use, it starts to interact with the real world through data, which are created or impacted by human behavior. As a matter of fact, models that are dependent on human behavior might be particularly prone to degradation. In this case, continuous model monitoring and learning are necessary.

Again, it is through working with language data that the translator monitors the model and contributes to upgrading processes. An MT system can be trained by feeding it more translations (parallel corpora, translation memories, etc.) produced by translators, editors, or post editors after the translator produces them or simultaneously in an interactive MT scenario. Translators add value to the production and evaluation of the training and testing data in a continuous machine learning process, in particular in areas such as domain adaptation, terminology integration, and translation memory leverage.

8

BALANCING MACHINE AND HUMAN LEARNING IN TRANSLATION

KEY CONCEPTS

- *Learning entails forming a mental model and adjusting the parameters of the model. A significant characteristic of both human and machine learning is the capability to generalize new conclusions based on available observations.*
- *From the perspective of the relationship between samples, population, and inferencing, human learning is in alignment with statistical inference in ML.*
- *The human inference process originates from within. Each person has a unique multilingual language model based upon past experience and their intentions to use the model. Converting generic ML models to personalized tools is an effective way to help humans learn ML technologies and acquire translation-related knowledge and expertise.*

8.1 Introduction

The concept of 'learning' applies to both humans and machines. As Dehaene (2020) states: "To learn is to form an internal model of the external world" (p. 5). Dehaene also emphasizes that "learning is adjusting the parameters of a mental model" (p. 7), highlighting the dynamic features of a learning process, reflecting the diversity and individuality of a learner. All these aspects reflect the fundamental characteristics of not only human learning (HL) but also machine learning (ML).

From the human perspective, when a person learns, for example, a new language, it can be useful to consider two types of learning environments. The first is top-down, starting from known features derived from sampled data, such as grammatical features in a corpus. This approach is based on objective rules, or absolute 'truth', which is independent of an individual learner's cognition or observation. The second is bottom-up, with each learner working with sampled data to extract features or rules on their own, which allows the learner to follow individual

DOI: 10.4324/9781003321538-12

learning preferences. To some degree, the rules extracted in a bottom-up learning process are subjective, in that they depend on the learner's previous knowledge and experience when forming personal understanding. Typically, the top-down approach is driven by an instructor who has mastered the linguistic features and can guide learners. In contrast, the bottom-up approach can begin with learners' personalized inference processes as they extract features on their own. In the top-down teaching environment, instructors give feedback to help learners adjust their language models, whereas in the bottom-up learning approach, learners update their learning models from data or lived experience.

These two basic processes apply to machine learning as well. To automate a process that was originally a human one, a computer program adopts one of two fundamental approaches: machine learning or symbolic reasoning. In machine learning, an algorithm learns rules as it establishes correlations between inputs and outputs. In symbolic reasoning, objective rules are created through human inter-vention and then hard-coded into a static program. Machine learning is bottom-up, similar to human learner-centered approaches. In contrast, symbolic reasoning is top-down, similar to instruction-centered approaches.

There are philosophical considerations behind these two basic approaches. For instance, Lakoff (1987) proposed two basic views of learning, rational thought, and cognition: objectivism and experiential realism (pp. xi–xvii). In the objectivist view of mind, "the world can be described objectively, independent of any par-ticular culture or observer's viewpoint" (Hampton, 1989, p. 131). In an objectivist (human) learning environment, "the teacher is privy in some sense to the answers, that is, to truth, and the learners are there to find out what those answers are" (Kiraly, 2003, p. 5). In a computer setting, these answers, or 'truth' are considered rules in a symbolic reasoning approach. In Table 8.1, the first column summarizes some basic features of objectivism, which is to a very large extent in alignment with symbolic reasoning as we discussed under 'Natural language processing and transla-tion' in the Introduction of the book.

Another view of learning is based on experiential realism, which emphasizes the role of experiences in the nature of learning and rational thought. According to Lakoff (1987), "experience" includes "everything that goes to make up actual or potential experiences of either individual organisms or communities of organisms" (p. xv). As shown in the second column of Table 8.1, thought is dynamic, non-atomistic, and constantly updated with empirical data.

Both views take categorization as the main method for making sense of human experience. As Lakoff (1987) states, "most symbols (i.e., words and mental repre-sentations) do not designate particular things or individuals in the world . . . [they] designate categories" (p. xiii). In an objectivist view, the nature of categories is defined by the properties common to all their members, rather than individuals, as it is believed there is an absolute, objective 'truth' that goes beyond individual observations. In an experientialist view, however, all reasonable thought "grows out of the nature of an organism and all that contributes to its individual and collec-tive experience" (Lakoff, 1987, p. xv). That is to say, empirical data can be either

TABLE 8.1 A comparison of objectivism and experiential realism

Objectivitism/symbolic reasoning/top-down learning	Experiential realism/machine learning/bottom-up learning
1 Thought is the mechanical manipulation of abstract symbols. Symbols that correspond to the external world are internal representations of external reality.	Thought has an ecological structure. The efficiency of cognitive processing in learning and memory depends on the overall structure of the conceptual system and on what the concepts mean. Thought is thus more than just the mechanical manipulation of abstract symbols.
2 Thought is atomistic, in that it can be completely broken down into simple "building blocks" – the symbols used in thought – which are combined into complexes and manipulated by rules.	Thought is not atomistic; concepts have an overall structure that goes beyond merely putting together conceptual "building blocks" using general rules.
3 The mind is an abstract machine, manipulating symbols like a computer, that is, by algorithmic computation.	Conceptual structure can be described using cognitive models, the theory of which incorporates what was right about the traditional view of categorization, meaning, and reason, while accounting for empirical data on categorization and fitting the new view overall.

Source: Extracted from Lakoff (1987, pp. xiv–xv).

specific to each individual or represent the 'experience' of a group of people. An underlying consideration in the experientialist approach is that bottom-up HL and ML can be more flexible in covering both individual and collective learning patterns, depending on the data or observation.

Generally speaking, there has been a transition from the top-down to the bottom-up approach in education, as Kiraly (2014) points out: "In recent years, it has become a commonplace in educational psychology that knowledge is constructed by learners, rather than being simply transmitted to them by their teachers" (p. 1). In translation, the focus in both human and machine training is on the bottom-up, as learners complete project-based work to drive their own learning. This chapter aims to draw parallels between ML and bottom-up HL, as well as exploring how generic ML models can be further personalized in a human learning process when users perform translation-related tasks. In doing so, we will distinguish ML model customization and personalization, in which individual and collective 'experience' (language data) and user intentionality play a significant role.

8.2 Making inferences in learning

The concept of learning can be approached from multiple perspectives. For example, Ambrose et al. (2010) define learning as "a process that leads to change, which occurs as a result of experience and increases the potential for improved performance and future learning" (p. 3). This definition is largely based on learners' developmental processes. In this chapter, however, we approach this concept from the inner workings of machine learning. Mathematical and statistical theories can be used to model the inferences that occur in human learning.

8.2.1 The mathematical analysis of learning processes

In statistical learning theory, the learning problem is considered a problem of finding a desired dependence using a limited number of observations (Vapnik, 2000, p. 17). The first model of a learning machine is called the perceptron, which Rosenblatt (1958) developed. It initiated the mathematical analysis of learning processes (Vapnik, 2000, p. 1). What is unusual about Rosenblatt's model is that it can be generalized. "The perceptron was constructed to solve pattern recognition problems; in the simplest case this is the problem of constructing a rule for separating data of two different categories using given examples" (p. 2). This is different from other types of learning machines that were considered from the very beginning as tools for solving real-life problems (p. 7).

Vapnik (2000) describes a general model of learning from examples through three basic components: (1) a generator (G) of random vectors x, (2) a supervisor (S), and (3) a learning machine (LM), which observes the pairs (x, y) (the training set). The supervisor (S) returns an output value y to every input vector x, according to a conditional distribution function of y given x, or $F(y|x)$. The learning machine (LM) observes the training set, made up of pairs of x and y. After training, on any given value x, the machine returns a value $\hat{y}$, the predicted value of y, also known as the dependent variable. The predicted value $\hat{y}$ is expected to be close to the supervisor's response y. In this model, learning is a problem of choosing from the given set of functions the one $(\hat{y})$ that best approximates the supervisor's response (y) (p. 18).

Vapnik (2000) identifies a paradigm shift in addressing the fundamental question in statistics: "*What must one know a priori about an unknown functional dependency in order to estimate it on the basis of observations?*" (p. ix). According to Fischer's paradigm from the 1920s and 1930s, the answer was restrictive: "one must know almost everything" (p. ix). The paradigm shift from the 1960s to the 1980s showed that "in order to estimate dependency from the data, it is sufficient to know some general properties of the set of functions to which the unknown dependency belongs" (p. ix). This second paradigm offers the fundamental principle of statistical machine learning: in order to statistically analyze the entire group (a population), one can collect a subset of the population data (sampling) and analyze the dataset to draw conclusions about the population (inferencing), with a certain level of significance. This method of inference is based on statistical techniques. In this approach, the size and quality of the sample is a significant factor for the accuracy of the statistical model (pp. ix–xi).

The relationship between sampling and population also explains why a learning machine is data hungry. In order to draw inferences about the population from sampled data, one has to control the sample size and quality, so that the modeling technique can generate a prediction model with good predictive accuracy. Generally speaking, the bigger the sample size and the higher its quality, the more representative of the population the sample will be, facilitating a higher level of accuracy of the statistical inference model.

A neural network language model is fundamentally a statistical learning machine. As discussed in Chapter 3, input and output data are fed to the neural network to develop machine learning patterns, which can be used to generate data that the system has never seen before.

8.2.2 A mental multilingual language model

As Dehaene (2020) states, learning can be described as forming a mental model and adjusting the parameters of the model (p. 5). This definition applies to both HL and ML and assumes there is a mental model in the human brain or a mathematical model in a computer system to estimate dependency and draw inferences about the population based on available observations. A mathematical model used in machine learning is described earlier. In terms of language comprehension and production, for the human mental model, it is reasonable to theorize that translators, speakers, and writers rely on their internal language models to make inferences. This is akin to a 'learning machine' in a person's mind, in which language models are a special mechanism whose architecture can accommodate multiple languages. We can refer to these mechanisms as mental multilingual language models.

There is a vast literature on language acquisition in terms of human language learning mechanisms. In a well-known example, Krashen (1987) proposes five main hypotheses: the acquisition-learning distinction, the natural order hypothesis, the monitor hypothesis, the input hypothesis, and the affective filter hypothesis (pp. 9–31), which can serve as a basis for specific modules of the overall mental language model. In cognitive science, research on learning and cognitive outcomes is also useful for us to explore the mental models of learners. For instance, Kraiger et al. (1993) argue there are three categories of cognitive learning objectives: (1) verbal knowledge, (2) knowledge organization, and (3) cognitive strategies (p. 313). Identifying cognitive learning outcomes entails making the initial assumption that humans make mental effort to acquire and structure knowledge and use cognitive strategies to achieve this purpose. Such an approach implies the belief that humans possess mental mechanisms that can be developed through systematic education and training. While acknowledging the important work that has been done from these perspectives, this chapter aims to use a mathematical approach to examine the mental language model.

According to Shannon and Weaver (1964), in a typical communication process, an information source selects a desired message out of a set of possible messages, which may consist of written or spoken words, or of pictures or music, and the "transmitter encodes this message into a signal which is sent over the communication channel from the transmitter to the receiver" (p. 7). They further clarify that "[w]hen I talk to you, my brain is the information source, yours the destination; my vocal system is the transmitter, and your ear and the associated eighth nerve is the receiver" (p. 7). In this framework, the word *information* "relates not so much to what you do say, as to what you could say. That is, information is a measure of one's freedom of choice when one selects a message" (p. 8).

This is a mathematical theory of communication, in which Shannon and Weaver (1964) emphasize the statistical nature of messages. Specifically, information associated with the communication process, in which messages or signals are generated, "is determined by the statistical character of the process – by the various probabilities for arriving at message situations and for choosing" the next symbols (pp. 17–18). Shannon and Weaver even make an analogy between 'information' and the concept of 'entropy' in thermodynamics, which "is expressed in terms of the various probabilities involved – those of getting to certain stages in the process of forming messages, and the probabilities that, when in those stages, certain symbols be chosen next" (p. 12). Shannon and Weaver's theory is consistent with the predictive language model we discussed in Chapter 3. As to how a message is chosen out of a set of possibilities, Shannon and Weaver (1964) emphasize that "the statistical nature of messages is entirely determined by the character of the source" (p. 18), i.e., the mind of the person who produces the message. In other words, a person possesses a mental language model that guides judgments following rules that involve the analysis of the frequency of past events, which reflects how the person made sense of the real world.

If we observe language development in infants, it is obvious that they are not born with speech or language; language needs to be acquired or learned and does not happen automatically. To cite just two examples from the vast literature on language acquisition, as Brauer (2014) points out, it is interesting to think that a baby has already taken the first steps towards language development before birth. A study conducted by Mampe et al. (2009) shows that newborns' cry melodies are shaped by their native languages. In other words, although humans are not born knowing language, they are born with an innate ability to develop it.

In ML, there is an argument concerning whether one should build a language model for each language or a multilingual language model for many languages. For instance, Aharoni et al. (2019) propose Multilingual Neural Machine Translation, which "enables training a single model that supports translation from multiple source languages into multiple target languages" (p. 3874). In many areas, multilingual NMT offers a more advanced solution than simply combining various bilingual NMT systems. Many NMT technology providers have started to develop bilingual language models, which are still very suitable for specific business needs, while at the same time exploring the potential of and developing Multilingual NMT systems, given their technological capabilities and real-life business applications.

Multilingual NMT is appealing due to its efficiency in terms of the number of required models and model parameters, enabling simpler deployment. Furthermore, multilingual NMT facilitates transfer learning: when low-resource language pairs are trained together with high resource ones, the translation quality may improve. An extreme case of such transfer learning is zero-shot translation (Johnson et al., 2016), where multilingual models are able to translate between language pairs that were not included during training (p. 2). Meanwhile, as Arivazhagan et al. (2019) point out, transfer can also be negative when "high resource languages start to regress due to a reduction in per-task capacity" (p. 2). When we examine a human language learning environment, it is not difficult to find that both transfer and interference exist in cognitive activities. For example, in second language acquisition (SLA), Ellis (1994) points out that transfer errors (interference) are more common in phonology and lexicon than in grammar (p. 62). Take the understanding and translation of the word *drink* for example. Words that accompany the concept of *drink* in English and Chinese have common characteristics: *tea*, *water*, and *alcohol* can all refer to fluids that are ingested, for example. Typically, an English learner will make use of transfer learning by modifying the parameters in the original multilingual language model. However, in English, *drink* is often associated with *alcohol*, whereas in Chinese, it is associated much more frequently with *water* and *tea*. Such discrepancies can lead to transfer errors in translation.

While very promising, in machine learning, it is still unclear how far one can scale the number of languages in multilingual NMT (Aharoni et al., 2019, p. 3874). To some degree, customizing the monolingual language model is a simple start of language model development. As technology advances, the development of multilingual language models will continue through the adjustment of their parameters.

If we proceed with the assumption that humans are born with the ability to develop a language model in their minds, we can hypothesize that this model is more advanced compared to what we have seen in machine learning. It also has the potential to be a multilingual language model – after all, bilingual and multilingual people are all around – even though monolinguals might never activate some model parameters. Again, in the mental multilingual language model, the core capability is the learning mechanism, i.e., the learner's ability to draw inferences to generate new data based on the limited amount of information available. From the perspective of the relationship between samples, population, and inferencing, human learning is in alignment with statistical inference in ML. Whether the calculation is based on numbers, textual information, or other types of input, a deeper discussion of this aspect of human learning is beyond the scope of this book.

8.2.3 Intentions and connectivity of language models in translation

The multilingual language model is like a black box in the human brain, and each person has a unique model based upon past experience performing language tasks, whether translating, speaking, summarizing, or answering questions, among other things. In a typical communication process, the information source, i.e., a participant's mind, creates a new message out of a set of possible messages using the internal language model and generates utterances that the participant delivers. The formulation of an utterance is a natural process resulting from the communicator's mental effort directing the focus of attention to a particular area. The intention to use the language model further customizes the model according to the given context. Thus, in a human language generation process, the inference process originates from within.

When translators participate in a communication process, a translator's internal language model also comes into play. However, in a translator-mediated process, translators are not the originators of the message. Instead of developing their own ideas, they start with utterances produced externally, i.e., language data produced by other speakers and writers. To some degree, their language construction process is not a natural one, as it is guided by the source text or speech, rather than their own original ideas. From this perspective, it could be stated that translators tap into secondary, external intention to generate meaning and messages, which results in a compromise between the translator and speaker or writer. In real-life communication processes, changes usually happen in the transmission of a signal. As Shannon and Weaver (1964) state, "it is unfortunately characteristic that certain things are added to the signal which were not intended by the information source," and these unwanted additions in the transmitted signal are called noise (1964, pp. 7–8).

What really makes a difference between ML and HL is that, as discussed in Chapter 6, intentionality does not exist in a computer program. It starts and ends with data. While humans construct meaning from data, machines can only process it. In contrast to the natural production of speech and text, the translator adopts an external perspective to imbue data with meaning. Translation as a scenario generates complexity that does not occur in conventional communication processes. The addition of the translator adds a third language model to the constellation, and the communication process includes connecting all three, similar to when different computer programs adjust their parameters to migrate and process data, albeit devoid of intentionality.

8.3 Personalized ML tools for human learning

8.3.1 The collective feature of technologies

When abstract thoughts are formulated into language and communicated to others, meaning-making is based upon a shared understanding, which can be a collective understanding if shared among multiple people. Otherwise misunderstanding and miscommunication are likely to occur. This seems to be a prerequisite for successful communication entailing the conversion of ideas to spoken or written form. At the same time, the interpretation of meaning is an individual act, based on an internal language model developed through the knowledge and experience of the recipient of the message. A computer program, however, processes linguistic signs as abstract data, devoid of underlying meaning, but can process data in vast quantities.

Data used to train an ML model come from a group of people, which can result in more diverse and larger datasets than those from an individual. From this perspective datasets for ML models are collective in nature. It seems like AI is creating a virtual agent that represents vast numbers of humans by drawing on big data coming from many individuals' past experiences. With the rapid expansion of computing power, computer programs can process massive amounts of language data, which makes the collective nature of machine learning even more prominent.

In Section 7.3.2 of Chapter 7, we described two types of data based on the degree of human intervention: general data with minimum translator intervention and special data directly created by translators. The greater the degree of human intervention in data construction, the more specific and individualized the data are, with general data involving more automation than human intervention. Balancing the relationship between HL and ML requires addressing the relationship between the collective nature of language data, which varies in degree, and the model trained on it. ML provides a collective approach, facilitating solutions for the translator in rudimentary form, so the translator can focus on other data features that cannot be captured easily.

8.3.2 From generic models to customized and personalized ML technologies

Some technologies are designed to capture collective human behaviors from the start. They aim to address common needs shared by a group of people. When managing human and linguistic resources, a localization project manager focuses on the collective results rather than individual ones. Individual characteristics of the data created in a technological platform, such as a CAT tool, which systematically involves more than one translator, usually decrease as the linguistic assets grow, even though some individual elements can be maintained through data annotation.

In the language industry, technologies are used to improve the productivity and efficiency of the work of either an individual or a group of individuals. For example, a translator uses a translation memory tool to translate as well as manage TM and terminology independently in the translation process, whereas a translation management system is used to manage the whole group's linguistic assets. Distinguishing between individual and group use is important in the context of language data ownership, data security, and data use permissions, as these two approaches may be in conflict in some areas.

Given these considerations, distinguishing between generic, customized, and personalized ML technologies is useful. As discussed in Section 8.2.1, there are three basic components of an ML model: a generator, a supervisor, and a learning machine. These models are generic in nature, with different ML pipelines that consist of multiple steps and techniques to train the model. Considering the purposes of training, there are two basic categories: to meet shared purposes of a group of users, or to meet specific purposes of an individual user. Currently, most language technology suppliers aim to target a certain group of users and serve their needs. In this book, we call these technologies 'customized' tools, though many of them provide a certain degree of personalization within a customized technologi-cal framework, such as allowing each user to enter segmentation rules (e.g., using punctuation to segment sentences) in CAT tools. The collective, virtual agent cre-ated by AI can help users complete tasks, like translation, and it can be customized. For example, an MT engine can be tailored with domain-specific data, which is usually done by an MT engineer or MT project manager, rather than a translator or post-editor. In this example, although the training data are domain specific, the data are collective linguistically and culturally, as the MT trainers are in many cases not directly involved in the data creation process and aim to capture data from all computing resources.

There are potential issues of this type of customization in terms of balancing ML and HL, as these MT trainers do not necessarily learn from the data linguis-tically or culturally. In other words, the data are just for machine learning, and not intended for human learning. Customization also impacts translator–computer interaction (TCI). When an MT system improves its performance after each train-ing, the result is less post-editing work for a human translator and thus fewer TCI opportunities for this type of content. However, knowledge and skills can only be acquired and reinforced through practice and repetition over time. Without suf-ficient engagement with the data in the TCI process, the translator cannot learn effectively. Simply feeding data to machines in a one-way process is insufficient. In this sense, collective customization benefits machine learning more than human learning.

In contrast, if each user, in our case each translator, can train the ML technolo-gies in the translator–computer interaction through activities such as translation, editing, and post-editing, the translator has the opportunity to work with the lan-guage data and thus not only trains the ML system effectively using linguistic and cultural expertise but also learns from the training process. The translator has access to and is able to manage all the language data used in the continuous translation process and can employ other ML learning technologies to learn from the data. Translator-driven customization also solves many data security problems. Strictly speaking, this type of customization is personalization.

A personalized ML technology does not mean that the translator can only use data that the translator creates. On the contrary, the translator can use data from other resources, such as parallel corpora, translation memory from other transla-tors, and web crawlers. However, the data selection is deeply rooted in personal preferences and specific uses of the tools. In addition, the translator has full control of the data before, during, and after the personalization process so that it can be used in multiple NLP tasks. For the translator, only a personalized ML system pro-vides two-way translator–computer interaction. Setting up this direct relationship between translators and the ML systems they are using in the ML training process is crucial if translators are to be motivated to effectively train the model and improve their own learning outcomes.

Personalized ML technologies means decentralization, i.e., the transfer of control and decision-making from a centralized entity to a distributed network.

What needs to be taken into consideration is the interaction of these personalized systems, which helps the translator not only build knowledge and skills through ML-augmented learning processes but also from other translators in the community. Technically speaking, when translators as domain experts – rather than AI/ML developers and data scientists – manage data and personalize ML systems through a decentralized approach, there are fewer learning obstacles. AI/ML developers and data scientists are often managing these processes, however, as there are currently not many translators who have access to human-driven ML systems.

8.3.3 User accessibility to human-driven ML systems in translation

Given the relationship between HL and ML in language model training, ML provides an opportunity for humans to approach their own learning process. This process will be facilitated if the basic principles of ML are intuitive for humans. One significant obstacle for domain experts to learn ML technologies is the lack of access to personalizable ML models.

Here we propose the concept of human-driven ML systems in translation, which allow individual users to personalize and thus learn by manipulating input data and editing or analyzing output data according to the users' purposes and intentions. As mentioned previously, many commercialized language technologies are based on general assumptions about a group of stakeholders' needs, which mostly represent a collective or 'objective' view independent of individual intentions and observations. While these technologies can help users accomplish translation-related tasks, their customized technological architecture is often based on stereotypes built into the generic ML models. The architecture provides limited functionality to make changes using language data to which users have full access. For instance, if translators can only use a neural MT system to translate without being able to train the model based on their needs, they are not fully exposed to dynamics of an ML model, resulting in limited support of their understanding of the inner workings of the model and limited ability to use the model to facilitate their learning.

Ultimately, the goal of users plays a significant role in defining and categorizing these systems. While human intentions are individual and difficult to categorize, we can classify them based on shared purposes at each step of a continuous translation process, as shown in the list of examples in Table 6.1 in Section 6.3.2 of Chapter 6. We start at the end of the scale where ML models have the least amount of personalization, which are the generic models that offer users the greatest flexibility to personalize them based on individual purposes. When categorizing specific use cases, we look to the middle of the scale as a framework where cases can be roughly clustered together. Personalization is the main characteristic when discussing specific use cases of the human-driven ML models (see Figure 8.1).

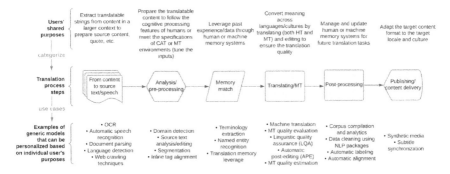

FIGURE 8.1   Shared and individual users' purposes in a continuous translation process

Acquiring ML knowledge and expertise is an immediate goal of using human-driven ML systems. In the long run, these systems must be able to facilitate human learning in a broad sense, e.g., to learn terms and improve translation skills. In the next section, we discuss translation terminology as an example.

8.4 Using human-driven ML systems to facilitate human learning

8.4.1 Individual cognitive aspects of terminology

Translation terminology management is in many aspects a framework for humans to organize, learn, and use specialized knowledge. When a translator tries to identify terms in the source text or reference materials, decisions are usually based on two aspects. The first is specialization, including both specialized knowledge and its corresponding specialized language use. As Faber and León-Araúz (2016) point out, terminology is "the study of how specialized knowledge concepts are structured, described, and designated in one or various languages within a specialized domain" (p. 196). The second is cognitive difficulty level. Regarding this aspect, Muegge (2020) states, "not only the special words that belong to a specific discipline should be managed as part of every translation project, but every 'difficult' word" (p. 23).

These two aspects are related to cognitive features of learners and thus have subjective elements to them. The degree of 'specialization' may be identified by measures such as document comparison, consultation with subject-matter experts, and references to specialized documents and term lists. In comparison, identifying 'difficult' words for translators as learners, who have varying levels of previous knowledge and experience, can be a daunting task, as what is 'difficult' will vary from person to person.

Under these circumstances, a learner can train an ML system to capture basic patterns reflecting a dynamic understanding of what words are 'difficult'. For example, each learner can annotate a term list or a document that includes candidate terms, which provides individualized training sets for an ML terminology extraction system.

Using each training set, the terminology extraction system can return a unique term list for each learner, reflecting their current cognitive states for these words. We will further elaborate this point when discussing intelligent tutors in Section 8.4.4.1.

8.4.2 Vector space and terminological schematic context

Returning to the relationship between form and meaning as a recurring theme in this book, we point out that specialized terms are also linguistic signs with a double structure of signified and signifier. Learning the meaning of a term is about learning not only its form but also the deep structure behind it. In this regard, a continuous vector space in ML can provide useful insights for a person to visualize, build, and expand a semantic field that focuses on the terminology as well as how it facilitates specialized knowledge representation and acquisition for a translator. A semantic field is "based on a meaning representation (a description of meaning taking account of ambiguity, hyponymy and synonym" (Simon-Vandenbergen & Aijmer, 2007, p. 11). In this framework, the meaning of one word depends on the meaning of other words associated with it in a semantic field. We propose a concept of terminological schematic context (TSC), which is a semantic field associated with a specialized term, yet takes an individual's previous knowledge and unique cognitive status into consideration.

In studies of pragmatics and semantics, 'context' is often a cognitive concept. For example, according to Sperber and Wilson (1995), a context is "a psychological construct, a subset of the hearer's assumptions about the world" (p. 15). They point out that it is these assumptions, rather than the actual state of the world, that affect the interpretation of an utterance. In terminological schematic context, specific terms are the anchor. That is to say, each term serves as the learner's starting point to explore other terms that are semantically related to it. When encountering a specialized term, a translator as a learner can activate items in the broader context that are accessible thanks to previous experience.

TSC can provide useful indicators to understand the meaning and evaluate the difficulty level of a term for a learner. For instance, for an English native speaker, *drink* is not a difficult word. It is closely associated with other words in the TSC such as *beer*, *coffee*, and *wine*. The TSC for the Chinese equivalent 喝 (*drink*) is different from that in English, with words such as *soup*, *tea*, and *water* more likely to accompany 喝 (*drink*) than *beer*, *coffee*, or *wine*. That is to say, the distribution of associated words for *drink* in English is different from that of 喝 (*drink*) in Chinese, which generates difficulty for a native English speaker.

The above discussion is based on intuitive reasoning. In machine learning, we can use vector space or semantic space to visualize the TSC of a term based on a specific corpus (see Wang, 2021). In a vector space, semantic relations of words can be modeled as geometric relationships. These relationships are not hard-coded into the program by humans, but learned from the corpus by the computer program. TSC-rich documents can be used as simulated schematic context for terminology. It can be hypothesized that words in a continuous vector space as well as their distance from the term under investigation produced by an ML system are consistent with a person's TSC and can offer useful insight into cognitive activities. Specifically, we can use word embeddings to simulate a vector space. As discussed in Section 3.2.5 of Chapter 3, embeddings are representations of the meaning of words, directly learned from their distributions in texts.

From the technical perspective, embeddings are useful for the computer to use as an input for the next layer of machine learning, but they are not intuitive for humans to understand due to high dimensionality. As introduced in Section 1.3 of Chapter 1, the dimension of a vector space is the cardinality (i.e., the number of vectors) of a basis of a vector space over its base field. In many cases, the embeddings used to train a corpus are high dimensional. For instance, in a research project conducted by Mikolov, Chen, et al. (2013), they evaluate models with multiple dimensionality options (50, 100, 300, and 600) in order to estimate the best choice of model architecture (pp. 6–7).

Thus we require special tools to investigate vector space so that humans can understand its meaning. One way to examine and understand the embeddings is through visualization after dimension reduction. For example, TensorBoard Embedding Projector is a tool to graphically represent high dimensional embeddings (Tensorflow, 2022). It offers three commonly used methods of data dimensionality reduction, which allow easier visualization of complex data: PCA, t-Distributed Stochastic Neighbor Embedding (t-SNE), and custom (Smilkov, 2016, pp. 2–3).

For instance, Figure 8.2 is a visualized vector space trained on a document using t-SNE, in this case the English version of a UN resolution on biodiversity conservation (U.N. General Assembly, 2021). As discussed in Section 2.3.2 in Chapter 2, it has 2,017 word tokens in total. The Gensim Word2Vec model (see Mikolov, Chen, et al., 2013; Mikolov, Yih, & Zweig, 2013; Word2vec Embeddings, 2022) trains the document and also visualizes the vectors, providing insight as to how terms are related to others in the corpus. The learner can refer to the words *assembly* or *nations*, for example, to start understanding, building, and expanding the TSC for these terms. Suppose a learner's previous knowledge related to these two terms is limited to what is included in this document – theoretically, a person will have similar TSC as shown in Figure 8.2, if the model is accurate and competent in generating results in alignment with human cognitive activities.

This simulation of TSC in vector space is an oversimplification, as a person's previous knowledge about *assembly* and *nations* will not be limited to a 2,017-word UN document. Yet we can still see some positive results such as the close relationship between *assembly* and *resolution*, as well as *restoration* and *conservation*. The former relationship is semantic, as a resolution is passed in an *assembly*. The latter relationship is based on semantics as well as the domain, as the two terms are from the domain of biodiversity. The more carefully structured the corpus, the more useful the output in terms of the TSC information for human learning of terminology and specialized knowledge.

The values of vectors are real numbers allowing mathematical calculations, which provides a unique approach to understanding how words are related. For the UN resolution terminology shown in Figure 8.2, we can determine that the most similar words for *conservation* in terms of their real number values are *future*

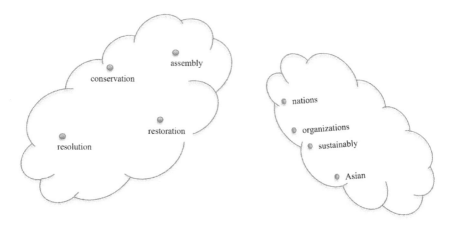

FIGURE 8.2 Using ML to visualize word relationships

and *diversity*, as shown in Figure 8.3. Though the similarity score is not very high, which might be due to the small size of the corpus, it is still reasonable to conclude that these three words are related. However, if we calculate the similarity score between *diversity* and *document*, we find the value is negative, meaning *document* contributes negatively towards the similarity.

We can also use word vectors to do mathematical operations. For example, if we add the vectors of biodiversity and cooperation, the system will return initiatives as the top one result. Such analyses can offer users valuable insights into the meaning of words and the TSCs in this document.

In translation, a translator can also visualize the TSC in both the source and target language and compare them, learning basic differences between two terms,

In [27]	w2v_model.wv.most_similar('conservation', topn=10)
Out [27]	[('future', 0.2758401036262512), ('diversity', 0.27066949009895325), ('multi', 0.26277002692222595), ('environmental', 0.2341262549161911), ('upon', 0.22355292737483978),
	('existing', 0.22006337344646454), ('development', 0.20916648209095), ('restoration', 0.1972241848707199), ('policies', 0.19454489648342133), ('decision', 0.19027021527290344)]
In [28]	w2v_model.wv.similarity('biodiversity','levels')
Out [28]	-0.10396392

FIGURE 8.3 Using word vectors to calculate similarity

such as in the earlier example of *drink*. Such comparisons can be useful when addressing translation-related problems. It is clear that words not burdened with coincidental and misleading resemblances present semantic differences that the wary translator will explore before making translation decisions. The situation is different, however, with *faux amis*, or false friends. When the translator encounters words or phrases that look similar and may be related but differ in the nuance of their meaning, the SL and TL comparison of TSC can be helpful in addressing the translation challenge. As Vinay and Darbelnet (1995) point out: "The parallels between SL and TL are sometimes striking, and we can exploit them productively. At other times, the two languages clearly differ and translators must analyze their differences if they want to understand and bridge them" (p. 28). They propose further that the more two languages are alike in structure and civilization, the greater the risk of confusing the meanings of their respective lexicons, which is the familiar problem caused by *faux amis*. Here as well, TSC can be used as an effective tool to help the translator identify differences between SL and TL terms and choose an appropriate meaning-based translation.

8.4.3 Source-text oriented comparable corpora for ML and HL

As discussed in Section 8.4.2, vector space or semantic space can be used to visualize the TSC of a term based on a specific corpus. While translators do not develop ML models to generalize vector space, they are able to customize these models by means of corpora. As a matter of fact, the relationship between terminology and comparable bilingual corpora is a topic that has been widely discussed in the translation studies literature (e.g., Munday et al., 2022; Bowker & Pearson, 2002). For example, Munday et al. (2022) point out that comparable bilingual corpora "are normally specialized collections of similar STs in the two languages" and "can be 'mined' for terminology and other equivalents" (p. 86). While acknowledging the wide literature in this research field, our discussion on source-text oriented comparable corpora is mainly focused on their application in ML as well as using ML perspectives to complement humans' intuitive reflections on terms and their associated meaning and concepts.

Terminology in the source text can help a translator retrieve relevant documents for specialized knowledge acquisition. In translation, the source text is the starting point not only for the translation process but also for relevant research activities. Some corpus-based approaches to learning have proven to be useful, but they are often post-translation activities. For example, when comparing two varieties of texts in the same language, such as translated and non-translated texts,[1] a translated text must be available, and the criteria, such as the topic, language style, and document length for selecting the non-translated text, must be set before the comparison. In real-life translation scenarios, such a reference translation is often not available. A professional translator frequently resorts to non-translated authentic reference materials in both the source and target language to understand the concept and produce a translation for select terms. For the translator, learning a term involves more than simply knowing its translation. It requires studying relevant specialized knowledge in documents or corpora, which are sources of information about the term in question, associated terms, and their TSC.

Thus, we propose the concept of source-text oriented comparable corpora: naturally occurring, authentic texts in both the source language (SL) and the target language (TL) that are identified based on specialized terminology and content in relation to source texts. This type of corpus includes two subcorpora: one consists of SL documents, which help the translator understand terms in context and associated specialized knowledge. The other consists of TL documents that provide possible translations of these terms. These documents enable the translator to learn terms and specialized knowledge and serve as high-quality data to train the ML model in the SL and TL.

Non-translated texts that are comparable with the source text in terms of terminological content are very useful not only for TSC visualization, but also for other NLP tasks in an ML-driven translation process. In an automated language generation system, for example, naturally occurring comparable subcorpora, guided by the source text, can be used to train a language model to achieve better fluency when producing sentences on the same topic. This is because the terms under investigation will be more frequently relevant when the text content overlaps with that of the source text.

In a human translation process, translators retrieve relevant documents to conduct research on terms and specialized knowledge to solve translation problems. Naturally, translators benefit from these research activities when they find solutions and acquire new terms and associated knowledge. Furthermore, valuable linguistic assets are generated in the process, and they can be used to train ML models that can help humans learn, as shown in the earlier example of the visualization of TSC in vector space. From a technical perspective, the management of translators' research activities can be automated, just like a translation management system. From a practical perspective, however, aspects such as privacy and confidentiality of data collection need to be considered, as well as the ownership of data. Given this situation, one feasible solution is personalization, in which each translator uses a personal source-text oriented comparable corpus generation platform and management system to leverage datasets for relevant NLP tasks.

8.4.4 Personalized intelligent NLP techniques for human learning

8.4.4.1 Machine learning and intelligent tutors

In Chapter 6, we divided NLP techniques into two categories: facilitation and intelligent tools for translators. As discussed in Section 8.3.2, intelligent tools begin with generic ML models and can be further customized and personalized using purpose-driven language data.

In the field of education, ML techniques are used to develop intelligent tools, which include a variety of software applications – simulations; advisory, reminder, and collaborative systems; and games – that model and reason about learners. One example of this approach is the "intelligent interactive tutor" (Woolf, 2009) or "intelligent tutoring system" (ITS) – a computer system that aims to provide immediate and customized instruction or feedback to learners, usually without requiring intervention from a human teacher (Psotka et al., 1988). ITSs are useful integrated educational tools for customizing formal education using intelligent instruction and feedback. The ITS student models, for example, can promote personalized learning, provide real-time learning analysis, use self-adaptive content, and designate targeted practice (see Hu et al., 2020).

ML technology is one of the key tools used to develop intelligent tutors. For example, Woolf (2009) argues that ML techniques can independently observe and evaluate the tutor's actions and identify student learning strategies, such as which activities students select most frequently and in which order. The tutors analyze student behavior and generate feedback using this diagnostic information, leading to improved learning outcomes (pp. 223–297).

In translation, there are areas where ML-driven, interactive intelligent tutors can provide immediate feedback to learners of various linguistic and cultural backgrounds on translation-related tasks and customize their learning content. In most cases, a translation instructor does not have sufficient time to offer a similar amount of such diverse feedback to various learners. To illustrate this approach, we describe an intelligent tutor for translation students in the following section.

8.4.4.2 An intelligent tutor for translation

An ML-facilitated learning process is usually a bottom-up approach that focuses on individual learners. Wang (2021) built a prototype for an intelligent interactive tutor that can collect each learner's feedback on terminology, analyze inputs provided by the learner, and predict the terms that are likely to be the most useful for the learner to learn. In this example, a resolution of the U.N. General Assembly (2021), analyzed in Section 8.4.2, is used to train the term recognition models for different levels of learners. The corpus is annotated to distinguish between beginning, intermediate, and advanced learners based on linguistic and cultural competence for translation tasks. In the study, the task for the students is to understand and analyze the English source text for the purpose of translation. They need to identify new terms that are specialized or difficult for them so that they can focus their translation-related research and learning activities. In this example, the translation students are non-native speakers of English, with beginning learners having the lowest and advanced learners the highest level of linguistic and cultural competence in English, with intermediate learners in between.

In most cases, beginner learners usually focus on individual words, and sometimes have difficulty identifying phrases that have specialized meaning in context. For example, they might recognize *biodiversity conservation* as two separate words, but *biodiversity conservation* has a specialized meaning, referring to the practice of protecting and preserving the wealth and variety of species, habitats, ecosystems, and genetic diversity on the planet, which is important for health, wealth, food, fuel, and services. For specialized documents such as the U.N. resolution, advanced learners who have specialized knowledge will identify *biodiversity conservation* as one term or set phrase, rather than two separate words.

The intelligent tutor can be developed further into a personalized terminology extraction tool that incorporates each learner's level of knowledge about the topic. If a learner has not seen a term before, for example, *migratory*, the learner can identify it as a new term. By annotating the corpus, each learner creates a training dataset that is unique to the individual. The computer program can extract these terms and collocations associated with them, building lists tailored to individual learners. The number of the words associated with the term is also an important indicator of the term's difficulty level for the learner. This tailored term list will be more useful for learners with varying levels of knowledge about a specialized topic than a list generated with a general terminology extraction tool.

Note

1   A monolingual comparable corpus according to Zanettin (2012, pp. 10–11).

9

IMPACT OF MACHINE LEARNING ON TRANSLATOR EDUCATION

KEY CONCEPTS

- *With the impact of machine learning, the translator's role is evolving, with tasks moving from translation proper to translation-related linguistic tasks, which provide new requirements for translator competence.*
- *An educator's role can be considered in two approaches to structuring learning: (1) bottom-up, learner-centered and (2) top-down, educator-guided environments. Both ML and bottom-up human learning can increase learner autonomy.*
- *It is time to rethink the conventional approach to the creation and application of rudimentary ML models. Personalization of these models based on user intention is a more relevant task for translator practice and learning.*
- *The call for human–computer interaction (HCI) has grown in urgency and raises new requirements for translator education.*

9.1 Introduction

From an AI/ML developer or programmer's perspective, Ng (2021) proposes a rule of thumb in terms of what tasks AI technologies can handle. "If a typical person can do a mental task with less than one second of thought, we can probably automate it using ANI[1] either now or in the near future" (n.p.). Specifically, when technical experts design a translation-related ML technology, the following three aspects can be taken into consideration:

1 Even if humans can translate, is it feasible? Obviously, the great demand for translation makes it impossible for humans to bridge the gap alone; we can use AI/ML technologies to address this gap.

DOI: 10.4324/9781003321538-13

2   If a human can accomplish the task, we can probably get data from humans and design machine translation systems to automate the process.

3   If a program makes a mistake, we can gather insights from humans to improve it.

This technical perspective explains why ML permeates so many corners of life, and why ML computer programs seem to catch a glimpse of human intelligence: (1) they can simulate human learning models, if tasks are simple[2]; and (2) language data produced by humans can train, verify, and improve models that are able to predict future activities.

ML generalization capabilities necessitate a higher degree of automation and lower degree of human control. This adds uncertainty to human–computer interaction, which in turn creates challenges for translator education. Education is about humans, and the impact of ML must be taken into consideration, given its dynamics. Translator educators can reflect on the teaching methodology that will best facilitate human learning, and they can predict what new skill sets translators will need. Chapter 8 addressed the relationship between human learning and machine learning. In this chapter we examine this relationship from an educator's perspective.

9.2 New ML-driven translation workflows

9.2.1 A machine-in-the-loop approach to translation

With the implementation of ML, many translators do not start translating from scratch. Rather, ML-driven technologies are applied at each step of a continuous translation process. Inspired by the concept of human-centered machine learning (Tan, 2018), we propose a machine-in-the-loop approach to translation, where humans, in our case translators, take full control of the final outcome, and machines play a supporting role. In this scenario, machines provide suggestions in various forms, e.g., MT, segmentation, and terminology, to improve productivity and translation quality, as well as inspire creativity and help translators overcome cognitive inertia, i.e., the reluctance to engage with new technologies in the translation process and the desire to adhere to 'traditional translation' practices. According to Mclaughlan and Bossarte (2012), cognitive inertia is the human tendency to maintain previously valid beliefs even when new evidence no longer supports those beliefs. This approach achieves what neither a human being nor a machine can achieve on their own.

In a machine-in-the-loop approach, humans are the final decision makers who control translation quality through post-machine evaluation and other editing activities such as MT post-editing, OCR post evaluation, and segmentation verification. There are a few reasons why the entire translation process is human centered: (1) ultimately, translation serves humans. In terms of human experience, only humans can sense what translation results appeal to them most. Some translation is generated to train MT engines, but this can be considered an indirect translation purpose (e.g., back translation in low resource language MT training); (2) humans are capable of conducting advanced, complex mental activities that involve coordination and integration of various sub activities, which is not what machines can achieve at this point; and (3) humans are the real source of creativity. Although machine learning can facilitate a certain degree of generalization, the results are unpredictable in terms of quality and need to be verified and improved by humans.

One important consideration when applying this machine-in-the-loop translation approach is how to maintain and increase creativity. For a human translator, translation is a creative act of an individual, where the 'meaning' of a text is also 'created' anew in an individual act of interpretation and production. Meaning is in the eye of the beholder, or as discussed in Chapter 8, what a person's mental language model produces. As each person's mental model is unique, the meaning created is also unique and contains many original ideas. A machine-in-the-loop approach, however, can mean less human activity for the same amount of translation work compared with a conventional human translation process. Here we argue that humans play a significant role in maintaining and improving creativity in a machine-in-the-loop translation process due to several reasons.

First, when machines assume some tasks conventionally done by translators, the machines help reduce translators' cognitive load, which in turn enables translators to focus on more creative and complex translation tasks.

Second, to some degree, ML models also facilitate creativity when they estimate and predict. As discussed in Section 8.2.1 of Chapter 8, according to statistical learning theory, generalization is an approach that incorporates old knowledge (data) and creates new knowledge (predicted results). In this sense, machines can provide novel suggestions that can inspire human creativity, helping translators find an adequate translation, for example, or consider a wide range of translation options.

Third, translator–computer interaction (TCI) provides a feasible way for humans to gather feedback from computer programs trained on corpora representing a group's language use. In this sense, TCI indicates an indirect individual–group interaction among people, which helps foster creativity. In terms of quantity and immediacy of feedback, it would be challenging for humans to achieve this level of interactivity on their own.

9.2.2 Translation as a language problem

When ML gradually infiltrates the translation and localization workflow, a translator's role tends to move towards what used to be peripheral to the translation. As discussed in Chapter 6, many NLP tasks are linguistically-oriented, translation-related activities that are beyond *translation proper*, i.e., the meaning conversion step. ML shifts the focus to linguistic activities associated with the individual steps of a continuous translation process, e.g., translatable string extraction, source text pre-processing, and terminology identification. Moreover, as discussed in Chapter 4, translation is a special NLP problem that can be solved by neural network language models.

Accordingly, some human cognitive activities such as translating and text analysis (e.g., chunking/sentence segmentation, separating translatable content from formatting, and identifying terminology) are impacted by special NLP techniques when human translators interact with these tools and work with what these tools offer. In particular, neural MT has proved to be effective in many scenarios, and a human translator can analyze the MT output and edit it. Consequently, the translator's task has been shifting from pure translating to tailoring specialized computer programs to make them function optimally, e.g., by preparing for language data at the input layer, working with the data at the end of a neural network and annotating it to provide the modeling with relevant human insights.

9.2.3 Moving beyond routine translation tasks

From a communication perspective, in most cases, there is no absolute linguistic equivalence, as discussed in Chapter 1, and definitions of equivalence have evolved as translation studies has progressed (see Bassnett, 2014, pp. 33–39; Munday et al., 2022, pp. 49–72). To provide another example, the concept of a 'Coast Guard' varies across countries and cultures. The superordinate agencies that oversee the Coast Guard also vary in different countries. In China, it was formerly under the State Oceanic Administration but transferred to the Chinese People's Armed Police Force in 2018. It is now formally under the command of the Central Military Commission. In the United States, the Coast Guard operates under the U.S. Department of Homeland Security during peacetime and can be transferred to the U.S. Department of the Navy under the Department of Defense by the U.S. President at any time, or by the U.S. Congress during times of war. Although these structures differ, we do need to find a term to convey meaning, for example, in a bilateral or multilateral event. Interlocutors use the same term and its literal translation to communicate during such meetings, even though in the back of their minds, they know that their understanding of the term is not the same. Rather, the terms establish sufficient equivalence to conduct a discussion. The degree of consistency between the terms in interlocutors' minds is dependent on the context and other human cognitive factors, such as their background knowledge.

From this perspective, human translators are still essential in ensuring the best communicative experience, even though machines continue to learn by digesting a dynamic influx of language data. Uncertainty and degrees of nonequivalence exist in all translation situations, particularly when the communication occurs in immediate and dynamic settings, such as interpreting. Even if MT attains a very high level of accuracy, it will still not be the preferred solution when the interlocutors' communicative experience is at the forefront and the adequacy of the translation needs to be evaluated. When machines are able to learn patterns by analyzing the linguistic forms, routine and high volume tasks can be automated. Human translators can then focus on their strengths, including the translation purpose as well as communicative and cultural aspects of the translation, taking subtle connotations and nuances into account, including mood, feeling, and emotion. The delegation of such high volume, routine tasks to machines allows human translators to focus on their strengths.

9.2.4 The need for human–computer collaboration

Admittedly, computer scientists and linguists have not always agreed with each other, particularly at the early stage of ML development and implementation. As Jelinek famously stated: "Every time I fire a linguist, the performance of the speech recognizer goes up" (Hirschberg, 1998). At the same time, there is resistance from linguists and translators who are concerned that computer programs will replace them permanently.

This division creates social and cultural challenges that impact translator education. In *Algorithms of Oppression: How Search Engines Reinforce Racism*, Noble (2018) describes the consequences of indifferent attitudes between these two camps. She points out that data discrimination exists in search engines, leading to a biased set of search algorithms that privilege whiteness and discriminate against people of color, specifically women of color. The call for human–computer interaction (HCI) or, rather, collaboration among those who work on both the human and machine sides to address similar issues, has grown in urgency and raises new requirements for translator education.

9.2.5 The evolving role of translators driven by ML

Due to the implementation of ML, the translator's role is evolving, and new and different tasks are emerging, with a tendency to shift from translation proper to translation-related linguistic tasks. One way to categorize these tasks is to cluster tasks around each step of a continuous translation process, including creating, analyzing, and editing source content for translation; estimating human efforts in MT; evaluating and ensuring translation quality; curating, managing, and maintaining the language data; and adapting the target content to the new culture. We will further discuss these tasks in Section 9.3.1 when summarizing competences needed at each step of the continuous translation process. These developments lead to a finer division of labor and new aspects for some traditional roles. For instance, the implementation of NMT raises the requirements for human translators. Translators who can refine MT results constructively add value to the editing process, and other translators may be diverted to other types of NLP tasks, including linguistic analysis in the preprocessing phase (e.g., source text analysis and edits), data compilation and management of parallel corpora and source-text oriented comparable corpora, and postprocessing (e.g., MT postedits annotation and analysis). Reacting to these developments, many companies in the language industry have already strengthened training processes and the application of other NLP tasks, in addition to continuing conventional manual translation and MT post-editing tasks.

Some localization teams have created new professional roles for the deployment of MT. For instance, 'linguistic expert' is a term used in some companies to recruit domain experts and native speakers of specific languages who can help with quality evaluation and data selection for machine training. 'MT evaluators' are usually translators with strong reviewing skills and are specialized in ensuring the accuracy of translation content, terminology, and consistency with style guides in MT-driven translation projects. In a phrase-based interactive MT environment, translators might feel they are translating, but they are actually reviewing and editing the machines' suggestions. Their interaction with the MT engine provides not only the edited translation result, but also training data enabling machines to learn. Thus, they are in effect reviewers, editors, and machine trainers, instead of translators.

Figure 9.1 summarizes translators' primary roles driven by ML in each task category of a translation process. As we discussed under 'Translation and the language industry' in the Introduction to the book, we generally use the concept of the translator in a broad sense, including translators, linguists, project managers, and other domain experts. In Figure 9.1, we flag the translator's role in a narrower sense as limited to the step of Translating/MT. This role can and should be expanded to all the other steps, incorporating roles such as evaluator, editor, terminologist, language analyst, annotator, and culture consultant, all of which add human insights from linguistic and cultural perspectives to an ML-driven translation process. We refer to them as 'primary' roles in the sense that they are categorized based on shared purposes of ML system users. They illustrate the focus of each step, yet are not exhaustive and can be further customized or personalized based on specific user purposes, including the new roles created in the industry that we mentioned earlier.

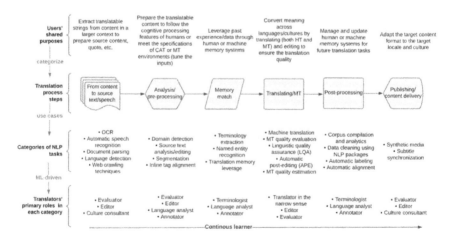

FIGURE 9.1 Translator roles in ML task categories

These roles are closely related. For example, evaluators and editors might well be translators in the narrow sense. Here we intentionally use the term 'editors' instead of 'post-editors'. To some degree, all editing is 'post' the task. However, in most cases, humans do not feel the same when the editing is on different levels of segmentation. As mentioned previously, translators/editors may feel they are translating even if they are editing the MT results in a phrase-based interactive MT. In this sense, they do not feel their cognitive activities lag behind the MT suggestions. In addition, as discussed in Section 5.3 in Chapter 5, there are two lines of thought for MT quality assessment, and editing is a scenario directly following evaluation.

These roles may not necessarily be about the *translation proper*, i.e., the meaning conversion step. For example, evaluators or editors can evaluate or edit the source text (pre-edit) in the analysis/pre-processing step or OCR results in the content extraction step, in addition to translation results in the translating/MT step. The same role names may refer to different job responsibilities and competences depending on the localization steps they are associated with.

These roles may approach the same subject from different perspectives. For instance, the work of both language analysts and annotators focuses on language data. However, the former uses data to answer their questions, whereas the latter adds human insights to the data. Language analysts and annotators mostly work in the steps centering around language data, including analysis/pre-processing, memory match, and post-processing. To some degree, editors can also be annotators when they add extra information, e.g., error categories in the translating/MT step. Here, we consider them two separate roles as they have different focuses, one on editing, the other on annotating.

These roles may indicate different scope of coverage. For instance, terminologists mainly work with specialized terms and their associated concepts in the memory match and post-processing steps, This does not mean terminological considerations are not needed in other steps. However, they are most useful in data match and analysis of both the source and target languages. Similarly, the role of a culture consultant might sound too generic to be applicable in all steps. Indeed, it is mostly relevant to the context extraction and publishing steps when linguistic elements fade into the background and cultural considerations come under the spotlight. Here in this context, any cultural considerations related to a translation or localization process, e.g., legal affairs, custom, and taboo, are relevant to cultural consultants.

In addition, one overarching role is that of continuous learner. The translator needs to be able to learn from the task, data, and ML models to keep up with the dynamics of machine learning. As will be discussed in the next section, ML competence is coupled with continuous learning competence as an overarching construct to allow the translator to effectively function in each step.

With these dynamically evolving roles, it is important to assign tasks and allocate relevant resources to various actors in the translation process, including translators, project managers, and linguistic analysts, in a manner that can allow them to fully leverage their strengths. Accordingly, translator education needs to address the specific features of each role. For example, source-text oriented comparable corpora can help translators understand specialized knowledge and ensure that target texts are idiomatic. For linguistic experts who are focusing on linguistic analysis in one language, bilingual skills may not be a requirement to address in their education and training.

9.3 Translator competences arising from machine learning

9.3.1 Primary competences in a continuous translation process

There is a broad discussion of translator competences in the literature (e.g., Albir, 2010, 2017). As Baartman and Bruijin (2011) state, competence "is generally defined as consisting of integrated components of knowledge, skills, and attitudes . . . and is assumed to be a prerequisite for adequate functioning on the job" (p. 126; see also Lizzio & Wilson, 2004; Eraut, 1994). For translators working in a ML-driven translation process, there are some primary competences useful at each step.

In this section, we consider the most relevant competences that enable a translator to conduct NLP tasks in a continuous translation process. Corresponding to the primary roles in each task category, we list the competences driven by emerging ML applications associated with each step in Figure 9.2. Again we use 'primary' to emphasize that these competences are categorized based on shared purposes of ML system users. They are examples and can be further customized or personalized to

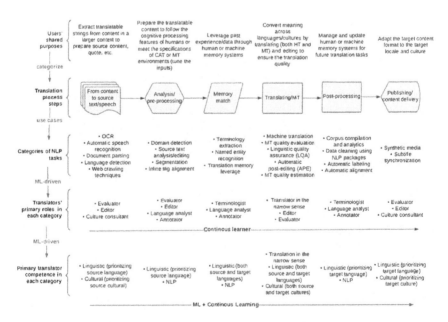

FIGURE 9.2　ML-related competences in a continuous translation process

meet specific user purposes. When a competence is not listed in a particular step, it does not mean that the competence is unnecessary, but that the other competences listed are likely to be more relevant for that step. For instance, one can argue that linguistic and cultural competences are generic and applicable to each step. However, cultural competence stands out in the content extraction and publishing steps when the content involves not only linguistic but also non-linguistic considerations in localizing a product.

Generally speaking, the primary competences needed at each step depend on contextual and project goals. Specifically, there are two considerations when applying the competence and skill set at each step: (1) what roles are needed and how can training be prioritized? (2) what type of tools are most useful? For instance, at Step 5, it is usually more efficient for humans to do in-context review outside the translation memory/CAT environment.

9.3.2 Two overarching ML-driven translator competences

Among the competences listed in Figure 9.2, there are two that are prominent throughout the translation process and thus considered to be overarching constructs, namely, ML-related competence and continuous learning competence. Both of them are about learning, including both machine and human learning.

9.3.2.1 ML-related competence

This competence allows the translator to map translation-related linguistic problems into an NLP task framework. It enables translators to use relevant ML technologies to perform translation tasks more effectively and also to facilitate translation-related learning, as discussed in Sections 8.3 and 8.4 of Chapter 8.

ML-system users need to be able to (1) apply an ML system (i.e., MT) to different tasks, e.g., using MT to translate and generate synthetic data; (2) design their own use case employing multiple ML systems, e.g., using MT and MT quality estimation systems to estimate editing effort; (3) interpret the results generated by an ML system, e.g., understanding BLEU scores produced by an MT automatic evaluation system; and (4) identify and analyze relevant technical details that make the best use of both human and machine power. This entails addressing a series of issues and questions: Should the source text be translated by humans or machines or both, and what might be an appropriate balance? Which MT system is most appropriate for this task? Who would be the best language service suppliers to work with the MT results? We will further discuss these aspects in Section 9.4.2 from the perspective of incorporating ML into the teaching of translation.

A translator may not be able to find the best NLP solution for the translation problem at the beginning of the learning process. A benefit of using tools, though, is that the translator can check the results to judge the quality of the solution. These technologies therefore evolve, and those that function well survive. To acquire this competence, the translator needs to learn the vocabulary of ML and basic functionality of relevant NLP techniques, as well as the capabilities and limits of the ML approach and the associated cost in the event of failure.

9.3.2.2 Continuous learning competence

Continuous learning competence is first and foremost a learning competence, which means learners must not only acquire but also integrate knowledge, skills, and attitudes. The key is accumulating and updating data in ML and offering HL experiences to build ML expertise. In the case of machine learning, a learner should be able to use ML tools to accumulate, annotate, and manage language data to train the machine.

In a human learning scenario, with ML tools available, translators can use advanced technologies to augment their capacity to record, categorize, and analyze language data generated in their ongoing translation and localization projects. Usually a large text corpus contains more data than a human translator can process in a lifetime. With the application of ML and other advanced technologies, the scope of continuous learning can be augmented accordingly.

9.3.3 NLP task-specific competences

9.3.3.1 Translation competence in the narrow sense

This competence covers all types of traditional translation competence, including knowledge, skills, and attitudes required to translate, evaluate, edit, review, and proofread. It involves capabilities that are needed for a translator to function effectively in *translation proper*, i.e., meaning conversion, including translation-related linguistic analysis, as well as semantic and pragmatic considerations involved in the meaning conversion process. These aspects are related to other competences, e.g., linguistic and cultural, but in the translating/MT step, we focus on interlingual translation activities in the narrow sense.

One characteristic of translation competence is the increasingly important role played by editing and evaluating due to the impact of ML. With MT performing the translation task, humans tend to evaluate and edit more, which in many cases requires a higher competence in translation in terms of language proficiency levels, translation strategies, and pragmatics. Simply put, if a human translator cannot provide constructive feedback to the machine translator, that translator is optimally qualified for the evaluation and editing task.

Knowledge and skills about terminology is a part of translation competence when a user considers the translation of terms in the translating/MT step. It can also be included in the memory check and post-processing steps and may focus on identifying specialized terms and concepts or finding an appropriate equivalent of these terms in the target language based on context. In both circumstances, terminology activities are not necessarily about translation in the narrow sense, e.g., identifying terms can be performed only in the source text, and choosing the right term in the target culture might be done only in the target text.

9.3.3.2 Linguistic competence

This competence enables the translator to perform linguistic tasks in a continuous translation process. It includes both knowledge and skills in the source and target languages. A pertinent factor is whether the learner is monolingual or bilingual. In a holistic approach, at each step of a continuous translation process, language requirements differ. In particular, with the impact of ML, linguistic competence in a translation process has some new characteristics.

(1)   Handling small fragments in a translation-related task

As to what tasks are suitable for humans, the length of the text must be taken into consideration. For example, an NLP technique for text classification or domain categorization can handle large amounts of documents in a fast and efficient manner. Yet, it is not very productive for machines to process small fragments of texts that do not have a clear pattern. In contrast, humans can be very flexible in handling fragmented information.

One specific characteristic arising from the application of ML is that a translator, linguist, or other domain expert needs to ensure the consistency of fragmented information in a larger context. Take NMT for example. NMT is driven by its own rules, thus it can work out different translations for the same piece of information. For example, for the concept of 'machine learning in translation', the system may return multiple results such as Machine Learning in Translation, ML in translation, and MLinTrans, just like humans. Under such circumstances, humans must examine the result and ensure coherence in a larger context.

(2)   Evaluating, editing, and adding other human insights

In the era of ML/AI, humans play an irreplaceable role in verifying results of ML techniques and ensuring the quality of the target text due to the fact that humans are the ultimate readers or audience of the ML results. In addition, if human translators take note of error patterns, they can further automate the review and correction process through regular expressions and other automatic discourse analysis tools to scale up their quality assurance efforts.

(3)   Coordinating between linguistic and non-linguistic elements

In many cases, a translation-related ML system, e.g., an NMT engine, is not only based on one system but also integrates other systems such as visuals and sound. This in itself is a great challenge for artificial intelligence. In recent years, there have been studies addressing this challenge. For example, multimodal machine translation involves drawing information from more than one modality based on the assumption that the additional modalities will contain useful alternative views of the input data (Sulubacak et al., 2020). Sulubacak et al. (2020) list some prominent examples of multimodal translation tasks, e.g., image-guided translation (IGT), video-guided translation (VGT), and spoken language translation (SLT), shown in contrast to unimodal translation tasks, such as text-based machine translation (MT) and speech-to-speech translation (S2S), as well as multimodal NLP tasks that do not involve translation, such as automatic speech recognition (ASR), image captioning (IC), and video description (VD). This is a new frontier for ML applications in the language industry, requiring human competence to coordinate among multiple tasks when using and training ML systems. As Stein et al. (2009) point out, humans are capable of Multisensory Integration, which describes a process by which information from different sensory systems is combined to influence perception, decisions, and overt behavior.

9.3.3.3 NLP competence

This competence refers to the knowledge, skills, and attitudes required for the translator (in the broad sense) working in an ML-driven localization process. It includes corpus linguistics, statistical analysis, and other NLP tasks such as using regular expressions (see Section 7.5.1.1 in Chapter 7). It is related to the linguistic competence we discussed in the previous section. However, it is more about language analytic and data annotation tasks, as we discussed in Section 9.2.5 regarding the roles of language analysts and annotators. It is mainly needed in translation analysis-related steps, i.e., analysis/pre-processing, memory match, and post-processing.

With this competence, a translator or linguist is mainly handling language data, including authentic (i.e., corpus) and synthetic data (e.g., data generated by an MT engine). It includes: (1) data preparation, e.g., using NLP tools to crawl the website to create a corpus in the analysis/pre-processing step; (2) data annotation, which is a useful task for multiple steps, aiming to communicate additional human insights to ML systems; (3) data analytics, e.g., source text analysis and improvement in pre-processing, and automatic discourse analysis of the translation memory in post-processing; and (4) other NLP-related tasks, e.g., using regular expressions to search relevant content, which might be useful in all the steps when handling language data.

9.3.3.4 Cultural competence

Computer programs are good at observing linguistic behaviors and providing humans with useful insights. When we delegate some NLP tasks to machines, humans reduce their cognitive loads, which in turn enables them to focus on more creative or complex translation tasks, including cultural ones, as discussed in Section 9.2.3. Thus, it makes sense to place more emphasis on developing cultural competence in translators.

There are many aspects of cultural competence in translator training, which has been discussed widely in the translation literature (e.g., Tomozeiu et al., 2016; Albir & Olalla-Soler, 2016; Albir, 2017; Asiri & Metwally, 2020). First, it includes knowledge, skills, and attitudes about different symbol systems. When symbols are pertinent to translation tasks – be it a sound, a mark on paper, a painting, or a statue – translators need to be familiar with them to solve specific translation problems. Second, cultural competence entails that a translator is able to construct relevant contexts to interpret a message effectively. In real-life translation assignments, translators should be able to apply cognitive strategies to construct the most relevant possible internal representations of phenomena from the outside world, and to process them in a context that maximizes their relevance. Third, cultural competence means a translator is able to acquire and integrate pieces of knowledge, skills, and attitudes and organize them into systematic structures that reflect their relationships. Fourth, cultural competence means a translator is able to transfer. In most cases, there is an imbalance between knowledge structures for different systems or areas as they are learned or acquired in different settings and at different ages of a translator (Wang, 2019, pp. 286–287). It is a prerequisite for a person to transfer his existing knowledge and skills in his original or source culture or professional area to learn the meaning in another culture, as shown in the example of the multilingual language model in Section 8.2.2 of Chapter 8.

9.4 Impact of machine learning on translator education

9.4.1 The educator's role in two approaches to learning environments

We use the term 'educator' in a broad sense in this discussion, referring to a person who provides instruction or education. There are many job titles associated with this term, including teachers, trainers, and instructors.

In Chapter 8, we discussed two types of learning environments which apply to both ML and HL: (1) bottom-up, learner-centered and (2) top-down, educator-guided environments. These two approaches differentiate two basic roles of educators: learning facilitator and knowledge transmission agent. Educators following the top-down approach design teaching materials to transfer knowledge and develop learners' skills, e.g., the general and specific competences at each step of a continuous process. In the learner-centered approach, however, educators step down from a dominant role as the authority in the classroom to a role as a facilitator in the communication and learning process, generally by providing tasks that help learners find patterns on their own and giving feedback.

In both types of learning environments, educators are advanced learners who have mastered the knowledge and skills that they pass to new learners either in educator-guided scenarios or learner-centered scenarios. The former is a traditional teaching environment and the latter is similar to a supervised machine learning environment, with educators organizing training data, i.e., the problems in the tasks as inputs and corrected answers to these problems as outputs.

9.4.2 Incorporating ML into the teaching of translation

In a top-down, educator-guided learning scenario, educators can incorporate the most relevant ML knowledge into their curriculum design in order to improve the overall translator competence as discussed in Section 9.3.

One challenge of incorporating ML knowledge into teaching is its diverse and dynamic features. In Chapter 6, we summarized some typical NLP tasks in a continuous translation process. The list is based on assumptions for a general scenario that might work for many translators. However, in real-life projects, it may not be comprehensive enough, or some of the items may not be relevant to some translators. Thus, there are a few basic considerations when introducing ML knowledge to learners.

Firstly, the purpose of introducing ML knowledge is to augment human knowledge and expertise. That is, the priority is on humans, and how to help translators, project managers, and other domain experts adjust to new ML-driven translation/localization processes. Therefore, fundamental issues for an educator to consider include the true value of humans in an ML-driven translation process and the best way to leverage human capability. For example, if a translator/post-editor reviews 100 sentences of MT results and only 1 sentence needs to be revised, human potential will be underutilized because the task is inefficient, and human intelligence is not fully maximized. In this case, if the instructor teaches students new skills such as MT quality estimation that can identify sentences that need human post-editing, translators will be able to make better use of their time during editing tasks. There are many other NLP techniques that can help us find solutions that maximize human effort and learning, including source-text oriented comparable corpus compilation and analysis, source text analysis and editing from a translator's point of view, and using regular expressions to do linguistic quality assurance of the target text.

Secondly, the teaching of ML knowledge and development of skills must be able to help learners make generalizations, which, as we discussed in Chapter 8, is the essence of both machine learning and human learning. In other words, an instructor should be able to provide students with basic ML technical knowledge that is sufficient for them to make inferences and create new technical solutions based on situations that they have not seen in class. Following are some specific aspects that indicate students' ability to generalize.

1   Students are able to design their own use case using multiple NLP techniques. For example, in Chapter 5, we discussed using human targeted error rate (HTER) to evaluate the accuracy of quality estimation (QE). Another example is source text analysis. There are multiple approaches, including using automatic discourse analysis tools to observe the linguistic behavior, NLP packages to extract relevant features from the text, and named entity recognition (NER) to identify key information (entities) such as proper names and dates/times.
2   Students are able to apply one NLP technique to different tasks. For example, regular expressions (see Section 7.5.1.1 in Chapter 7) can be used in automatic

error recognition during the MT post-editing stage as well as in automatic segmentation in the analysis/preprocessing stage. Another example is using translation memory (TM) for multiple purposes: when students learn how to clean TM to avoid leverage loss (i.e., when some segments are not recognized by another system due to different data formats, system settings, or other factors), they can use the same technique for MT training and data migration across different translation environments.

3   Students are able to interpret the results generated by an automated NLP technique. For example, when students learn about BLEU scores, an automated MT evaluation metric discussed in Section 5.4.1 of Chapter 5, they should be able to tell what factors affect the result and control these variables in order to ensure the credibility and reliability of the BLEU score. Some typical examples are how many reference translations are used in the algorithm, whether the metric is used to measure statistical MT or rule-based MT, and whether the reference translations were previously done by human translators from scratch or MT post-edited results.

4   Students are able to identify and analyze relevant technical details that help them make the best use of both human and machine power. For example, students should be able to figure out where the automation part is for each tool: translation memory includes the automation of segmentation and automatic TM management, including concordance and sometimes regular expressions. MT metrics can be automated: metrics for translation error typology such as MQM are mainly for humans, but the counting and simple analysis of errors can be automated, such as the percentage of each type of error. Having this information, students will be able to draw conclusions as to when and where to use human resources to complement the weaknesses of automation.

Thirdly, even in the top-down teaching approach, much focus has been put on learning in recent years, in recognition of the importance of selecting the most relevant ML knowledge to include in the translation curriculum. Here, the term 'relevance' is a psychological concept that also accounts for the individuality and personality of each learner. As Wilson and Sperber (1994) suggest, "information is relevant to you if it interacts in a certain way with your existing assumptions about the world" (p. 92). Generally speaking, many teaching environments involve the student–instructor relationship in a one-to-many instructional setting, such as classroom lectures. In such settings, instructors need to investigate collective student expectations and learning needs at each step of a continuous translation process, prepare relevant knowledge to share with them, and develop lesson plans for skills development in these areas.

9.4.3 The impact of ML in a learner-centered environment

Learner-centered instruction provides personalized and customized learning, taking into consideration what learners bring to the class, such as their existing knowledge, skills, and attitudes. Time and effort are required for an instructor to analyze learners' backgrounds and individual needs, which results in an increased instructional workload (Pantiru et al., 2012). With a dual focus on both individual learners and learning, the role of an educator in a learner-centered setting has evolved from mere delivery of content and control of the learning environment to actively involving learners in creating their own learning. In particular, the learning environment is a stimulating, dynamic, and interactive one with both teachers and learners working together (see Tawalbeh et al., 2015; Kiraly, 2014, 2015).

A major challenge of a learner-centered approach is insufficient assessment for learning. As Tawalbeh et al. (2015) summarizes, for assessment where teachers assess learners to promote learning, teachers continually provide feedback on learners' progress, and help learners develop self-assessment skills. However, they also point out that the

> tremendous workload produced by multiple assessments that aim for a learner-centered approach to learning in huge classes and the inability to provide results timely, often result in lecturers' maintaining teacher-centered approaches to learning even if they appreciate the benefits of learner-centered approaches.
>
> *(p. 40; see also Bayat & Naicker, 2012)*

To address this challenge, Rich et al. (2014) suggest instructors create learner-centered assessment strategies such as take-home exams, short answer tests, formative summative assessments (FSA), and audience response systems (ARS), and make instruction and assessment responsive to student learning preferences. This means teachers would need to create multiple forms of assessment to match students' learning styles, which may facilitate student performance at their level of competence by removing barriers that uncomfortable test formats can create. Again, the task of learner-centered assessment is time-consuming.

ML technologies can provide a feasible solution to address this issue in translator education. As discussed in Chapter 8, intelligent tools can be customized and personalized through continuous machine learning and human–computer interaction. In that chapter, we also introduced a case study using machine intelligent tutoring systems (ITSs) to provide immediate and customized instruction or feedback to learners. In this approach, machine learning results can offer supplementary insights and references to assist human learning. As ML uses statistical inference, which typically focuses on the material aspect of signs and processes the information from a more general, objective, and 'collective' perspective, the insights it offers can be a useful reference for individual reflection. Therefore, the customization and personalization process can be viewed as a joint machine and human learning process. Once the tool is personalized, it will reflect more personal features than collective ones. At that point, the primary use of the tool is to support translation tasks, rather than offering an opportunity to learn. Nevertheless, humans will end up comparing what is in their minds and what an intelligent tool produces, and that comparison can generate a learning effect. Technology allows us to notice what might have remained concealed previously and thus explore new areas for learning.

9.4.4 Building a learning platform for both educators and learners

Technology is attractive not because of the technology itself, but because communication with it is so engaging. For a computer expert or a passionate gamer, what captivates their attention is the interaction. Unlike humans who in many cases do not give a response, machines always diligently provide you with an answer, even though sometimes it is unsatisfactory, which can motivate you to keep engaging with it. This is human nature: you are interested in something not because the thing itself is interesting, but ultimately you find it interesting because it is relevant to you and satisfies your own needs when you engage with it.

Following this train of thought, we propose establishing a learning platform with personalized systems for both educators and learners, as educators are also advanced learners, which incorporates both top-down and bottom-up knowledge and learning. The personalized feature will allow learners to select the most relevant knowledge and exercises to develop their skills. The platform can be both personal and communicative. Learners can have their own personalized system but be able to learn together with others in their learning community as they customize and accomplish a NLP task together. This community supports beginners and advanced learners, including educators and experienced translators in their (continuous) learning as they translate and localize together.

This learning system can also help learners create, collect, update, manage, and secure their data resources. In Chapter 8, we discussed the collective features of ML technologies. An ML system does not correspond to multiple people similar to NMT customization but rather is tailored to individuals, each of whom has their own internal multilingual language model for processing natural languages in the communication process. The collective, general ML system is the starting point for personalization. Compared with customization that is indirectly working with data generators, a personalized ML system has a much higher probability of being similar to a person's internal language model, and the similarity between these two models will more likely lead to satisfactory results generated by ML systems, in the sense that the results are consistent with what a human language model might produce. In addition, personalized ML systems mean humans have better control and interaction with the language data in the translation process. Learners can use the data for multiple NLP tasks and also find patterns.

9.5 The value of educators in the ML context

As Webb et al. (2021) point out, ML systems are "infiltrating our lives and beginning to become important in our educational systems" (p. 2109). While educators are beginning to use ML methodology and frameworks to innovate our pedagogy, as Webb et al. (2021) demonstrate, the role of educators in the human learning process requires more attention. Now more than ever is the question pertinent: With the growing influence of ML, what is the true value of the educator? In a world of digitized information at our fingertips, we argue that an instructor has an essential role in helping make sense of information, which can be unstructured and disorganized, and in developing technology and information literacy in students, which is an essential part of a communicative, human-centered approach to teaching by leveraging ML capabilities. That is to say, human learners need to interact with other humans and build their shared environment, which is the physical reality on which more abstract knowledge is built. Human instruction is helpful and needed not just because of the quality of information it can provide, but because of the empathy instructors share with their learners. Humans share similar experiences and feelings about language as well as the physical and mental worlds that are conveyed and made sense of through language. Starting from this common ground, learners can verify their hypotheses and inference models with the support of educators as advanced learners, making generalization on a larger scale and transfer to different tasks possible and useful. ML technologies can help instructors focus on the human part of teaching, rather than replacing human instruction.

Notes

1   Artificial intelligence is broadly divided into two stages of development: artificial narrow intelligence (ANI) and the much more complex artificial general intelligence (AGI). All AI systems that are currently available are ANI. This includes systems such as voice assistants or self-driving cars that may seem quite sophisticated. According to Ng (2021), such AI systems are only suitable for areas of activity that have clear boundaries, such as chatbots that draw on databases of typical questions and answers on a particular topic: "Almost all of AI's recent progress is through that type, in which some input data A is used to quickly generate some simple response B. The technical term for building this algorithm is 'supervised learning'" (n.p.).
2   Translation as a whole is not a simple task, but if it can be deconstructed into small components, as discussed in a continuous translation process, AI/ML can handle each component task.

EPILOGUE – HUMAN-CENTERED MACHINE LEARNING IN TRANSLATION

Looking back at the history of human development, one finds that the evolution of humankind is closely linked to the development of tools and technology. When technology frees people from tasks, it allows them to explore new frontiers, physically and mentally. Yet machine learning offers more than progress in the division of labor between humans and machines. Its learning capability enables it to generalize and make predictions independently based on limited observations. In this sense, an ML system is able to create something new, which is not necessarily the same as what human inferences produce.

Confronted with a black box that is subject to less human control than perhaps any other tool in history, people have mixed feelings about its power, with advocates both for and against. This book advocates a holistic approach to ML, which considers the respective roles of both humans and machines so that strengths and weaknesses compensate each other and the translation workflow and learning processes are optimized.

In a neural network language model, machine perception provides us with a tool to examine our cognitive activities when engaging in translation tasks. Although it oversimplifies mental language models in many cases, it provides a preliminary visualization of how our mental language model might work. In other words, machine learning is a form of human reflection of ourselves, both internally of our own cognitive activities and externally of the physical world around us. It is part of us and reflects human nature, which is why we are drawn to it.

Following this train of thought, this book proposes a machine-in-the-loop, human-centered approach to machine learning in translation, where translators take full control of final decisions and are able to personalize generic ML models based on their specific needs. This approach can inspire creativity by providing translators a new perspective of their work. This approach offers what neither humans nor machines can accomplish on their own. However, as machine learning is very new and dynamic, most users lack sufficient relevant competences to implement, customize, and personalize it proactively in their real-life projects.

This book addresses this gap by helping translators understand and adapt to the integration of ML in translation workflows and learning processes. It examines machine learning from the user perspective, in particular translation practitioners with different levels of ML experience and humanities students who are familiar with linguistic and translation theories and aim to use ML technologies in their study and practice. It emphasizes a human-centered approach focusing on translation practitioners in a broad sense, by empowering them with the most relevant knowledge about ML in translation, ML-related communication, and a resource for continuous learning.

Empowering translators with ML knowledge

At the very early stages of AI, when scholars such as Alan Turing and John Searle studied AI and machine learning, it was considered a subdiscipline in the field of intelligence, closely related to philosophy, education, and linguistics. As it developed, AI gradually became an independent discipline within science and technology research. However, with the harvesting of low-hanging fruit in the creation of rudimentary ML models, the language industry is now able to consider how to use these models by implementing, customizing, and personalizing the models for use in real-life scenarios. To achieve this goal, collaboration and communication are needed between computational scientists and translators as domain experts.

This is not an easy undertaking, as these groups of individuals have different levels of exposure to specialized knowledge and skills in machine learning, and, while the development of ML technologies requires an engineering background, their use requires a holistic perspective, considering aspects such as strengths and weaknesses, workflow, as well as ethical issues and consequences. On the one hand, it is important to share relevant technical knowledge with users so that they can make responsible and informed decisions when using ML techniques in translation. For example, if you ask an editor to edit the XML inline tags, you will need to let them know what these tags mean. If you want users to make use of vector space to represent meaning, you will need to give them information about the corpus that generates the vectors so that they can analyze the corpus and the machine-generated insights from the human perspective. By shedding light on relevant technical details, human translators can complete a project more efficiently and effectively. On the other hand, too much technical information is not recommended as it can overwhelm translators rather than helping them focus on what they do best, which is translating and editing.

Empowering translators with ML-related communication

The dichotomy between technology and human beings is in truth a division between human beings themselves, e.g., those with advanced ML knowledge and skills who create technology and those with limited ML competence who are familiar with the business scenarios in which they use technology, either actively or passively. In a translation process, the ML-related communication occurs among and across multiple groups of individuals, including AI/ML developers and programmers, translators who are users of AI/MT programs, and project managers who manage human, data, and technology resources. Specifically, translators interact with computer programs through their work with language data, translating, post-editing, and annotating.

A human-centered approach to machine learning in translation incorporates all types of stakeholders, including educators, ML users, and ML developers/programmers. As ML technology users, translators will benefit from communication with ML developers, who can help address the knowledge gap in the way of translators customizing or personalizing ML technology. ML developers can also benefit from domain experts such as translators, who can help them better understand translation workflows and design user-friendly tools, as well as grasp the ethical and sociocultural aspects of translation.

Due to the large quantity of data an ML system can produce, it makes sense in many cases to use machines to work with or check against other machines. For example, MT speeds up the translation process, which leads to the automation of other steps, e.g., automatic post-editing and automated MT quality evaluation. All these steps require not only technical expertise, but also domain knowledge that differs at various stages of the translation process. The design, development, and upgrading of relevant tools will benefit from effective communication between stakeholders, help ensure quality of the automated results, and take ethical issues into consideration.

Technology should not hinder communication, as can happen when callers reach a customer service center where machine learning tools intended to guide customers to the right human agent cause frustration, because they stand in the way of speaking directly with another human. In a machine translation environment, if the MT deployment is used as an excuse to exclude humans in a translation process, it will lead to a one-sided perspective and generate resistance among translators.

Ironically, the concept of communication implies the existence of barriers and differences. Humans generate messages that reflect their unique cognitive perspectives. Yet, communication processes prioritize commonalities because communication requires a shared understanding to be successful. In this vein, a goal of this book is to maximize a shared understanding of the role of machine learning in translation processes among our various stakeholders.

Empowering translators with continuous learning

In an ML-driven translation process, it is understandable that machine learning is at the center of attention when the objective is to improve the system's performance. However, taking a long view, the question arises whether translators will learn from the ML implementation and customization process. Theoretically, in a human-centered approach, the whole translation process is driven by translators who are in a position to leverage ML results. This role requires a conceptual understanding of ML systems, which has a steep learning curve, at least at the beginning, because these systems are new and dynamic.

Given this situation, we draw attention to the imbalance between ML and HL and the need to develop ML/AI tools to assist translators in ML-driven translation processes. Personalization is an effective way to facilitate interaction between humans and machines, where translators are not only training machines but also learning from ML resources and results. Through customization and personalization, translators can have full control of their linguistic assets and employ ML education tools to facilitate effective human learning. As creators, collectors, and managers of language data, translators and other domain experts have a significant role to play in machine training.

One significant obstacle to domain experts learning ML technologies is the lack of access to personalizable ML models and platforms based on their purposes. In this book, we propose facilitating human learning through human-driven ML systems, which are generic ML models for specific NLP tasks in translation. Such models can be personalized by individual users, whose primary role is to provide relevant language data based on their intentions. A platform with human-driven ML systems incorporating the goals of each step of a continuous localization process is an effective tool to help translators acquire ML knowledge and expertise and learn translation-related skills.

Translator learning is the key to boosting confidence in machine learning. As mentioned earlier, machine learning is like a black box that is subject to less human control than other tools that have preceded it. Technology should not hinder human learning; rather, it should enable and empower translators to keep exploring new frontiers in their physical and mental worlds. Although machine learning has its own capacity to generalize and predict, the ultimate human strength is our unique learning competence. If there is competition between ML and HL, translators will prevail for now because our ability to learn is superior, and the definition of what is better is based on human experience.

REFERENCES

Aharoni, R., Johnson, M., & Firat, O. (2019). Massively multilingual neural machine translation. In *Proceedings of the 2019 conference of the North American chapter of the association for computational linguistics: Human language technologies* (vol. 1, pp. 3874–3884). Association for Computational Linguistics. https://aclanthology.org/N19-1388

Albir, A. H. (2010). Competence. In Y. Gambier & L. V. Doorslaer (Eds.), *Handbook of translation studies: Volume 1* (pp. 55–59). John Benjamins.

Albir, A. H. (Ed.). (2017). *Researching translation competence by PACTE Group*. John Benjamins.

Albir, A. H., & Olalla-Soler, C. (2016). Procedures for assessing the acquisition of cultural competence in translator training. *The Interpreter and Translator Trainer*, *10*(3), 318–342. https://doi.org/10.1080/1750399X.2016.1236561

ALPAC. (1966). *Languages and machines: Computers in translation and linguistics. A report by the Automatic Language Processing Advisory Committee*. National Academy of Sciences, National Research Council. https://nap.nationalacademies.org/resource/alpac_lm/ARC000005.pdf

Ambrose, S. A., Bridges, M. W., DiPietro, M., Lovett, M. C., & Norman, M.K. (2010). *How learning works: Seven research-based principles for smart teaching*. Jossey-Bass.

Amos, R., & Pickering, M. (2020). A theory of prediction in simultaneous interpreting. *Bilingualism: Language and Cognition*, *23*(4), 706–715. https://doi.org/10.1017/S1366728919000671

Andrey Markov. (2022, July 20). *Wikipedia*. https://en.wikipedia.org/w/index.php?title=Andrey_Markov&oldid=1099443977

Arivazhagan, N., Bapna, A., Firat, O., Lepikhin, D., Johnson, M., Krikun, M., Chen, M. X., Cao, Y., Foster, G. F., Cherry, C., Macherey, W., Chen, Z., & Wu, Y. (2019). Massively multilingual neural machine translation in the wild: Findings and challenges. *CoRR*, abs/1907.05019, 27 pages. https://doi.org/10.48550/arXiv.1907.05019

Asiri, S. A. M., & Metwally, A. A. (2020). The impact of linguistic and cultural competence on translation quality: Pedagogical insights into translation problems. *Journal of Language Teaching and Research*, *11*(30), 509–520. www.academypublication.com/issues2/jltr/vol11/03/22.pdf

Baartman, L. K. J., & de Bruijin, E. (2011). Integrating knowledge, skills and attitudes: Conceptualising learning processes towards vocational competence. *Educational Research Review, 6*(2), 125–134. https://doi.org/10.1016/j.edurev.2011.03.001

Baker, M. (1992). *In other words: A coursebook on translation*. Routledge.

Banerjee, S., & Lavie, A. (2005). METEOR: An automatic metric for MT evaluation with improved correlation with human judgments. In *Proceedings of the ACL workshop on intrinsic and extrinsic evaluation measures for machine translation and/or summarization* (pp. 65–72). Association for Computational Linguistics. https://aclanthology.org/W05-0909

Baniata, L., Park, S., & Park, S. (2018). A neural machine translation model for Arabic dialects that utilizes multitask learning (MTL). *Computational Intelligence and Neuroscience, 2018*, 10 pages. Article ID: 7534712. https://doi.org/10.1155/2018/7534712

Bar-Hillel, Y. (1959). *Report on the state of machine translation in the United States and Great Britain. Appendix IV*. United States Office of Naval Research. https://aclanthology.org/www.mt-archive.info/50/Bar-Hillel-1959.pdf

Barrow, H. (1996). Connectionism and neural networks. In M. A. Boden (Ed.), *Artificial intelligence. Handbook of perception and cognition* (pp. 135–155). Academic Press.

Bassnett, S. (2014). *Translation studies* (4th ed.). Routledge.

Bayat, A., & Naicker, V. (2012). Towards a learner-centered approach: Interactive online peer assessment. *South African Journal of Higher Education, 26*(5), 891–907. https://doi.org/10.20853/26-5-200

Bellamy, L., Carey, M., & Schlotfeldt, J. (2011). *DITA best practices: A roadmap for writing, editing, and architecting in DITA*. Pearson Education.

Bengio, Y., Ducharme, R., Vincent, P., & Janvin, C. (2003). A neural probabilistic language model. *Journal of Machine Learning Research, 3*, 1137–1155. www.jmlr.org/papers/volume3/bengio03a/bengio03a.pdf

Benoit, T. (1982). The METEO system. In V. Lawson (Ed.), *Practical experience of machine translation* (pp. 39–44). North-Holland. https://aclanthology.org/www.mt-archive.info/70/Aslib-1981-Thouin.pdf

Berlinski, D. (2011). *One, two, three: Absolutely elementary mathematics*. Pantheon.

Biber, D., Conrad, S., & Reppen, R. (1998). *Corpus linguistics*. Cambridge University Press.

Bird, S., Klein, E., & Loper, E. (2019, September 4). Preface. *Natural Language Processing with Python*. www.nltk.org/book/ch00.html

Boleda, G. (2020). Distributional semantics and linguistic theory. *Annual Review of Linguistics, 6*, 213–223.

BootCaT. (2018, March 15). *BootCaT: Simple utilities to bootstrap corpora and terms from the web*. Retrieved July 18, 2022, from https://bootcat.dipintra.it/

Bowker, L., & Pearson, J. (2002). *Working with specialized language*. Routledge.

Brauer, J. (2014). The brain and language: How our brains communicate. *Frontiers for Young Minds, 2*(14). https://kids.frontiersin.org/articles/10.3389/frym.2014.00014#ref2

Brown, P. F., Cocke, J., Pietra, S. D., Pietra, V. J., Jelinek, F., Lafferty, J. D., Mercer, R. L., & Roossin, P. S. (1990). A statistical approach to machine translation. *Computational Linguistics, 16*(2), 79–85.

Brown, P. F., Pietra, S. D., Pietra, V. J., & Mercer, R. L. (1993). The mathematics of statistical machine translation: Parameter estimation. *Computational Linguistics, 19*(2), 263–311. https://aclanthology.org/J93-2003

Buckner, C., & Garson, J. (2019). Connectionism. In E. N. Zalta (Ed.), *The Stanford encyclopedia of philosophy*. Retrieved from https://plato.stanford.edu/entries/connectionism/

Bulte, B., & Tezcan, A. (2019). Neural fuzzy repair: Integrating fuzzy matches into neural machine translation. In *Proceedings of the 57th annual meeting of the Association for Computational Linguistics* (pp. 1800–1809). Association for Computational Linguistics. https://aclanthology.org/P19-1175.pdf

Byrne, J. (2009). Localisation – when language, culture and technology join forces. *Language at Work – Bridging Theory and Practice, 3*(5). https://doi.org/10.7146/law.v3i5.6190

Callison-Burch, C., Osborne, M., & Koehn, P. (2006). Re-evaluating the role of bleu in machine translation research. In *11th conference of the European chapter of the Association for Computational Linguistics* (pp. 249–256). Association for Computational Linguistics. https://aclanthology.org/E06-1032/

Castilho, S., Doherty, S., Gaspari, F., & Moorkens, J. (2018). Approaches to human and machine translation quality assessment. In J. Moorkens, S. Castilho, F. Gaspari, & S. Doherty (Eds.), *Translation quality assessment* (pp. 9–38). Springer. https://doi.org/10.1007/978-3-319-91241-7_2

Castilho, S., Moorkens, J., Gaspari, F., Calixto, I., Tinsley, J., & Way, A. (2017). Is neural machine translation the new state of the art? *The Prague Bulletin of Mathematical Linguistics, 108*, 109–120.

Chernov, G. V. (2004). *Inference and anticipation in simultaneous interpreting: A probability-prediction model*. John Benjamins.

Chesterman, A. (1994). Quantitative aspects of translation quality. *Lebende Sprachen, 39*(4), 153–156. https://doi.org/10.1515/les.1994.39.4.153

Cho, K., van Merrienboer, B., Gulcehre, C., Bahdanau, D., Bougares, F., Schwenk, H., & Bengio, Y. (2014). Learning phrase representations using RNN encoder-decoder for statistical machine translation. *CoRR, abs/1406.1078*, 15 pages. https://doi.org/10.48550/arXiv.1406.1078

Chollampatt, S., Susanto, R. H., Tan, L., & Szymanska, E. (2020). Can automatic post-editing improve NMT? In *Proceedings of the 2020 conference on Empirical Methods in Natural Language Processing (EMNLP)* (pp. 2736–2746). Association for Computational Linguistics. https://aclanthology.org/2020.emnlp-main.217/

Chollet, F. (2017). *Deep learning with Python*. Manning.

Christie, A. (1987). *The mystery of the blue train*. Turabian.

Cole, D. (2020). The Chinese room argument. In E. N. Zalta (Ed.), *The Stanford encyclopedia of philosophy*. Stanford University Press. https://plato.stanford.edu/entries/chinese-room/

Complete Website Word Counting with InSite. (2015, July 15). *Inspyder*. Retrieved July 18, 2022, from www.inspyder.com/products/InSite/Website-Word-Count

Corbí-Bellot, A., Forcada, M., Ortiz-Rojas, S., Pérez-Ortiz, J., Ramírez-Sánchez, G., Sánchez-Martínez, F., Alegria, I., Mayor, A., & Sarasola, K. (2005). An open-source shallow-transfer machine translation engine for the Romance languages of Spain. In *EAMT 2005 conference proceedings* (pp. 79–86). https://aclanthology.org/2005.eamt-1.12.pdf

Correia, G. M., & Martins, A. F. T. (2019). A simple and effective approach to automatic post-editing with transfer learning. In *Proceedings of the 57th annual meeting of the Association for Computational Linguistics* (pp. 3050–3056). Association for Computational Linguistics. https://aclanthology.org/P19-1292/

Daems, J., & Macken, L. (2019). Interactive adaptive SMT versus interactive adaptive NMT: A user experience evaluation. *Machine Translation, 33*, 117–134. https://dl.acm.org/doi/abs/10.1007/s10590-019-09230-z

Dehaene, S. (2020). *How we learn: Why brains learn better than any machine . . . for now*. Viking.

Dimension (Vector Space). (2022, June 30). *Wikipedia*. https://en.wikipedia.org/w/index.php?title=Dimension_(vector_space)&oldid=1075564704

Doshi, K. (2021, January 16). Transformers explained visually (Part 3): Multi-head attention, deep dive. *Towards Data Science*. https://towardsdatascience.com/transformers-explained-visually-part-3-multi-head-attention-deep-dive-1c1ff1024853

Edgar, T., & Manz, D. (2017). *Research methods for cyber security*. Elsevier.

Ellis, R. (1994). *The study of second language acquisition*. Oxford University Press.

Eraut, M. (1994). *Developing professional knowledge and competence.* Routledge.

Faber, P., & León-Araúz, P. (2016). Specialized knowledge representation and the parameterization of context. *Frontiers in Psychology, 7,* 196. https://doi.org/10.3389/fpsyg.2016.00196

Farouk, M. (2019). Measuring sentences similarity: A survey. *Indian Journal of Science and Technology, 12*(25), 1–11. https://arxiv.org/pdf/1910.03940.pdf

Fellbaum, C. (1998). *WordNet: An electronic lexical database.* MIT Press.

Feng, F., Yang, Y., Cer, D., Arivazhagan, N., & Wang, W. (2022). Language-agnostic BERT sentence embedding. In *Proceedings of the 60th annual meeting of the Association for Computational Linguistics* (vol. 1, pp. 878–891). Association for Computational Linguistics. https://aclanthology.org/2022.acl-long.62.pdf

Firth, J. R. (1957). A synopsis of linguistic theory. In *Studies in linguistic analysis.* Blackwell (for the Philological Society). Reprinted in F. R. Palmer (Ed.). (1968). *Selected papers of J. R. Firth, 1952–59* (pp. 168–205). Longmans.

Flowchart Symbols and Notation. (n.d.). *Lucidchart.* Retrieved August 19, 2022, from www.lucidchart.com/pages/flowchart-symbols-meaning-explained

Folaron, D. (2006). A discipline coming of age in the digital age. In K. Dunne (Ed.), *Perspectives on localization* (pp. 195–219). John Benjamins.

Freitag, M., Foster, G., Grangier, D., Ratnakar, V., Tan, Q., & Macherey, W. (2021). Experts, errors, and context: A large-scale study of human evaluation for machine translation. *Transactions of the Association for Computational Linguistics, 9,* 1460–1474. https://aclanthology.org/2021.tacl-1.87

Friedman, N., & Halpern, J. Y. (2013). *A qualitative Markov assumption and its implications for belief change.* https://arxiv.org/abs/1302.3578

Garcia, I. (2014). Computer-aided translation. In C. Sin-wai (Ed.), *The Routledge encyclopedia of translation technology* [eBook edition]. Routledge. www.routledgehandbooks.com/doi/10.4324/9781315749129.ch3#bodymatter1_book-part3_sec2

Gardner, H. (2003). *Frames of mind. The theory of multiple intelligences* (2nd ed.). Basic Books.

Gentzler, E. (2014). Translation studies: Pre-discipline, discipline, interdiscipline, and post-discipline. *International Journal of Society, Culture & Language, 2*(2), 13–24. www.ijscl.net/article_5620_fdde5469d71359e7bb41dcee95329e13.pdf

Ghanooni, A. R. (2012). A review of the history of translation studies. *Theory and Practice in Language Studies, 2*(1), 77–85. www.academypublication.com/issues/past/tpls/vol02/01/11.pdf

Gile, D. (2009). *Basic concepts and models for interpreter and translator training* (2nd ed.). John Benjamins.

Gillies, A. (2013). *Conference interpreting: A student's practice book.* Routledge.

Goldberg, Y. (2017). Neural network methods for natural language processing. *Synthesis Lectures on Human Language Technologies, 10*(1), 1–309. https://doi.org/10.2200/S00762ED1V01Y201703HLT037

Goodfellow, I., Courville, A., & Bengio, Y. (2016). *Deep learning.* MIT Press.

Google Developers. (n.d.-a). *Bucketing. Machine learning.* Retrieved from https://developers.google.com/machine-learning/data-prep/transform/bucketing

Google Developers. (n.d.-b). Evaluating models | AutoML translation documentation. *Google Cloud.* Retrieved July 4, 2022, from https://cloud.google.com/translate/automl/docs/evaluate

Google Developers. (n.d.-c). *Machine learning glossary. Machine learning.* Retrieved from https://developers.google.com/machine-learning/glossary

Griffiths, P. (2006). *An introduction to English semantics and pragmatics*. Edinburg University Press.

Gu, J., Wang, Y., Cho, Y., & Li, V. (2019). Improved zero-shot neural machine translation via ignoring spurious correlations. In *Proceedings of the 57th annual meeting of the Association for Computational Linguistics* (pp. 1258–1268). Association for Computational Linguistics. https://aclanthology.org/P19-1121.pdf

Hampton, J. (1989). Women, fire, and dangerous things. [Review of the book *Women, fire, and dangerous things*, by G. Lakoff]. *Mind & Language, 4*, 130–137. https://doi.org/10.1111/j.1468–0017.1989.tb00245.x

Hanneman, G., & Dinu, G. (2020). How should markup tags be translated? In *Proceedings of the fifth conference on machine translation* (pp. 1160–1173). Association for Computational Linguistics. https://aclanthology.org/2020.wmt-1.138/

Harris, D., & Harris, S. (2012). *Digital design and computer architecture*. Elsevier.

Harris, Z. (1954). Distributional structure. *Word, 10*(23), 146–162. https://doi.org/10.1080/00437956.1954.11659520

Hassan, H., Elaraby, M., & Tawfik, A. (2017). *Synthetic data for neural machine translation of spoken-dialects*. https://arxiv.org/abs/1707.00079

Henderson, H. (2007). *Artificial intelligence: Mirrors for the mind*. Chelsea House.

Hinton, G. E., McClelland, J., & Rumelhart, D. (1986). Distributed representations. In D. Rumelhart & J. McClelland (Eds.), *Parallel distributed processing* (vol. 1, pp. 77–109). MIT Press.

Hirschberg, J. (1998, July 29). "Every time I fire a linguist, my performance goes up", and other myths of the statistical natural language processing revolution [Invited talk]. In *15th national conference on artificial intelligence*, Madison, WI. www.aaai.org/Conferences/AAAI/1998/aaai98program.pdf

Holmes, J. S. (2004). The name and nature of translation studies. In L. Venuti (Ed.), *The translation studies reader* (2nd ed., pp. 180–192). Routledge. (Original work published 1972)

House, J. (2014). Translation quality assessment: Past and present. In J. House (Ed.), *Translation: A multidisciplinary approach* (pp. 241–264). Palgrave Macmillan. https://doi.org/10.1057/9781137025487_13

Hu, X., Liu, F., & Bu, C. (2020). Research advances on knowledge tracing models in educational big data. *Journal of Computer Research and Development, 57*(12), 2523–2546.

Hutchins, J. (1979). Linguistic models in machine translation. *UEA Papers in Linguistics, 9*, 29–52. https://aclanthology.org/www.mt-archive.info/70/UEAPIL-1979-Hutchins.pdf

Hutchins, J. (1999). Warren Weaver memorandum: 50th anniversary of machine translation. *MT News International, 22*(5–6), 15. https://aclanthology.org/1999.eamt-1.18.pdf

Hutchins, J. (2006). *The first public demonstration of machine translation: The Georgetown-IBM system, 7th January 1954*. https://docplayer.net/178185-The-first-public-demonstration-of-machine-translation-the-georgetown-ibm-system-7th-january-1954.html

Hutchins, W. J. (2000). *Early years in machine translation: Memoirs and biographies of pioneers*. John Benjamins.

Hutchins, W. J. (2004). The Georgetown-IBM experiment demonstrated in January 1954. In R. E. Frederking & K. B. Taylor (Eds.), *Machine translation: From real users to research* (pp. 102–114). Springer. https://doi.org/10.1007/978-3-540-30194-3_12

ISO. (2012). *ISO/TS 11669:2012(en): Translation projects – general guidance*. ISO Online Browsing Platform. Retrieved July 4, 2022, from www.iso.org/obp/ui/#iso:std:iso:ts:11669:ed-1:v1:en

ISO. (2015). *ISO 17100:2015(en): Translation services – requirements for translation services*. ISO Online Browsing Platform. Retrieved July 4, 2022, from www.iso.org/obp/ui/#iso:std:iso:17100:ed-1:v1:en

Jakobson, R. (2021). On linguistic aspects of translation. In L. Venuti (Ed.), *The translation studies reader* (4th ed., pp. 156–162). Routledge. (Original work published 1959)

James, G., Witten, D., Hastie, T., & Tibshirani, R. (2013). *An introduction to statistical learning with applications in R*. Springer.

Johnson, M., Schuster, M., Le, Q. V., Krikun, M., Wu, Y., Chen, Z., Thorat, N., Viégas, F., Wattenberg, M., Corrado, G., Hughes, M., & Dean, J. (2016). Google's multilingual neural machine translation system: Enabling zero-shot translation. *CoRR*, abs/1611.04558, 17 pages. https://doi.org/10.48550/arXiv.1611.04558

Jurafsky, D., & Martin, J. (2020). *Speech and language processing: An introduction to natural language processing, computational linguistics, and speech recognition* (3rd ed., draft). https://web.stanford.edu/~jurafsky/slp3/ed3book.pdf

Kashani, M., Joanis, E., Kuhn, R., Foster, G., & Popowich, F. (2007). Integration of an Arabic transliteration module into a statistical machine translation system. In *Proceedings of the second workshop on statistical machine translation* (pp. 17–24). Association for Computational Linguistics. https://dl.acm.org/doi/pdf/10.5555/1626355.1626358

KatanAI. (2015, July 28). What is translation error rate (TER)? *KantanAI* (A keywords studio). Retrieved July 4, 2022, from https://kantanmtblog.com/2015/07/28/what-is-translation-error-rate-ter/

KEOPS for evaluators. (n.d.). *GitHub*. Retrieved June 14, 2022, from https://github.com/paracrawl/keops/blob/master/evaluators.md

Kiraly, D. (2003). From instruction to collaborative construction: A passing fad or the promise of a paradigm shift in translator education. In B. J. Baer & G. S. Koby (Eds.), *Beyond the ivory tower: Rethinking translation pedagogy* (pp. 3–27). John Benjamins.

Kiraly, D. (2014). *A social constructivist approach to translator education: Empowerment from theory to practice*. Routledge.

Kiraly, D. (2015). *Toward authentic experiential learning in translator education*. V&R Academic.

Klavans, J., & Resnik, P. (1996). *The balancing act: Combining symbolic and statistical approaches to language*. MIT Press.

Koehn, P. (2005). Europarl: A parallel corpus for statistical machine translation. In *Proceedings of machine translation summit X: Papers* (pp. 79–86). https://aclanthology.org/2005.mtsummit-papers.11.pdf

Koehn, P., Och, F. J., & Marcu, D. (2003). Statistical phrase-based translation. In *Proceedings of HLT-NAACL 2003* (pp. 127–133). https://aclanthology.org/N03-1017

Kornai, A. (2008). *Mathematical linguistics*. Springer.

Kováříková, D. (2021). Machine learning in terminology extraction from Czech and English texts. *Linguistic Frontiers*, *4*(2), 23–30. https://doi.org/10.2478/lf-2021-0014

Kraiger, K., Ford, J., & Salas, E. (1993). Application of cognitive, skill-based, and affective theories of learning outcomes to new methods of training evaluation. *Journal of Applied Psychology*, *78*, 311–328.

Krallinger, M., Leitner, F., & Valencia, A. (2010). Analysis of biological processes and diseases using text mining approaches. *Methods in Molecular Biology*, *593*, 341–382. https://doi.org/10.1007/978-1-60327-194-3_16

Krashen, S. D. (1987). *Principles and practice in second language acquisition*. Prentice-Hall International.

Lakoff, G. (1987). *Women, fire, and dangerous things: What categories reveal about the mind*. University of Chicago Press.

Laurence, A. (n.d.). AntConc. *Laurence Anthony's Website*. www.laurenceanthony.net/software/antconc/

Lavie, A., & Agarwal, A. (2007). METEOR: An automatic metric for MT evaluation with high levels of correlation with human judgments. In *Proceedings of the second workshop on statistical machine translation* (pp. 228–231). Association for Computational Linguistics. https://aclanthology.org/W07-0734

Le, Q. V., & Schuster, M. (2016, September 27). A neural network for machine translation, at production scale. *Google AI Blog*. Retrieved August 6, 2022, from https://ai.googleblog.com/2016/09/a-neural-network-for-machine.html

LeCun, Y., Cortes, C., & Burges, C. J. C. (n.d.). *The MNIST database of handwritten digits*. Retrieved May 31, 2022, from http://yann.lecun.com/exdb/mnist/

Leech, G. (1981). *Semantics: The study of meaning*. Penguin.

Li, J., Luong, M. T., & Jurafsky, D. (2015). A hierarchical neural autoencoder for paragraphs and documents. *CoRR*, abs/1506.01057, 10 pages. https://doi.org/10.48550/arXiv.1506.01057

Liddy, E. D. (2001). Natural language processing. In *Encyclopedia of library and information science* (2nd ed.). Marcel Decker. https://surface.syr.edu/istpub/63/

LISA. (2003). *The localization industry primer* (2nd ed.). Author. www.immagic.com/eLibrary/ARCHIVES/GENERAL/LISA/L030625P.pdf

Lizzio, A., & Wilson, K. (2004). Action learning in higher education: An investigation of its potential to develop professional capability. *Studies in Higher Education, 29*, 469–488.

Localization-Related Formats. (2002, January 30). *W3C*. Retrieved July 2, 2022, from www.w3.org/2002/02/01-i18n-workshop/LocFormats

Locke, J. (1690). An essay concerning human understanding. In *Archive for the History of Human Thought*. McMaster University. https://historyofeconomicthought.mcmaster.ca/locke/Essay.htm

Lommel, A. R., Burchardt, A., & Uszkoreit, H. (2013). *Multidimensional quality metrics: A flexible system for assessing translation quality*. https://aclanthology.org/2013.tc-1.6.pdf

Love, N. (1983). Translational semantics: A discussion of the second edition of Geoffrey Leech's Semantics: The study of meaning. *Stellenbosch Papers in Linguistics, 11*, 115–136. https://doi.org/10.5774/11-0-106

Lyons, J. (1995). *Linguistic semantics: An introduction*. Cambridge University Press.

Malmkjær, K. (2011). Meaning and translation. In K. Malmkjær & K. Windle (Eds.), *The Oxford handbook of translation studies* (pp. 108–122). Oxford University Press.

Mampe, B., Friederici, A. D., Christophe, A., & Wermke, K. (2009). Newborns' cry melody is shaped by their native language. *Current Biology, 19*(23), 1994–1997. https://doi.org/10.1016/j.cub.2009.09.064

Mariana, V., Cox, T., & Melby, M. (2015). The multidimensional quality metrics (MQM) framework: A new framework for translation quality assessment. *Journal of Specialised Translation, 23*, 137–161. www.jostrans.org/issue23/art_melby.pdf

Marneffe, M., Manning, C., Nivre, J., & Zeman, D. (2021). Universal dependencies. *Computational Linguistics, 47*(2), 255–308.

Martínez-Freire, P. F. (1998). Mind, intelligence and spirit. In *Philosophy of mind. The twentieth world congress of philosophy*. www.bu.edu/wcp/Papers/Mind/MindMart.htm

Matusov, E., Leusch, G., Bender, O., & Ney, H. (2005). Evaluating machine translation output with automatic sentence segmentation. In *Proceedings of the second international workshop on spoken language translation*. https://aclanthology.org/2005.iwslt-1.19

McCarthy, J. (2007). *What is artificial intelligence*. http://jmc.stanford.edu/articles/whatisai/whatisai.pdf

McCarthy, J., Minsky, M. L., Rochester, N., & Shannon, C. E. (1955). A proposal for the Dartmouth summer research project on artificial intelligence, August 31, 1955. *AI Magazine, 27*(4), 12. https://doi.org/10.1609/aimag.v27i4.1904

McCulloch, W., & Pitts, W. (1943). A logical calculus of the ideas immanent in nervous activity. *Bulletin of Mathematical Biophysics, 5,* 115–133.

McLaughlan, B., & Bossarte, S. (2012). Computationally adjustable cognitive inertia. *Semantic Scholar.* Retrieved August 15, 2022, from www.semanticscholar.org/paper/Computationally-Adjustable-Cognitive-Inertia-McLaughlan-Bossarte/59e0b9deae1ed281459e30ed68c6ad3b43104d43

Microsoft Translator. (2018, September 24). Integrate end-to-end speech translation into your products with Microsoft Speech services. *Microsoft Translator Blog.* www.microsoft.com/en-us/translator/blog/2018/09/24/integrate-end-to-end-speech-translation-into-your-products-with-microsoft-speech-services/

Mikolov, T., Chen, K., Corrado, G., & Dean, J. (2013). *Efficient estimation of word representations in vector space.* https://arxiv.org/pdf/1301.3781.pdf

Mikolov, T., Karafiát, M., Burget, L., Černocký, J., & Khudanpur, S. (2010). Recurrent neural network based language model. *Interspeech.* www.fit.vutbr.cz/research/groups/speech/publi/2010/mikolov_interspeech2010_IS100722.pdf

Mikolov, T., Yih, W., & Zweig, G. (2013). Linguistic regularities in continuous space word representations. In *Proceedings of the 2013 conference of the North American chapter of the Association for Computational Linguistics: Human language technologies* (pp. 746–751). Association for Computational Linguistics. https://aclanthology.org/N13-1090.pdf

Miller, G. A., & Beebe-Center, J. G. (1956). Some psychological methods for evaluating the quality of translations. *Mechanical Translation, 3,* 73–80.

Mitkov, R. (2003). *The Oxford handbook of computational linguistics.* Oxford University Press.

Muegge, U. (2020). Why you should care about terminology management – even if you never translate a single term. *ATA Chronicle, 49*(2), 22–25. www.ata-chronicle.online/featured/why-you-should-care-about-terminology-management-even-if-you-never-translate-a-single-term/

Mulkar-Mehta, R., Hobbs, J. R., & Hovy, E. H. (2011). Applications and discovery of granularity structures in natural language discourse. In *AAAI spring symposium: Logical formalizations of commonsense reasoning.* www.isi.edu/~hobbs/cs11-gran.pdf

Müller, V. C. (2020, April 30). Ethics of artificial intelligence and robotics. In E. N. Zalta (Ed.), *The Stanford encyclopedia of philosophy.* Stanford University Press. https://plato.stanford.edu/archives/sum2021/entries/ethics-ai/

Munday, J., Pinto, S. R., & Blakesley, J. (2022). *Introducing translation studies: Theories and applications* (5th ed.). Routledge.

Munkova, D., Hájek, P., Munk, M., & Skalka, J. (2020). Evaluation of machine translation quality through the metrics of error rate and accuracy. *Procedia Computer Science, 171,* 1327–1336. https://doi.org/10.1016/j.procs.2020.04.142

National Information Standards Organization. (2004). *Understanding metadata.* NISO Press. www.lter.uaf.edu/metadata_files/UnderstandingMetadata.pdf

Newmark, P. (1988). *A textbook of translation.* Prentice Hall.

Ng, A. (2021, July 29). Artificial intelligence in industry. *Bosch Global.* www.bosch.com/stories/artificial-intelligence-in-industry/

Nida, E. A., & Taber, C. R. (1969). *The theory and practice of translation: With special reference to Bible translating.* Brill.

Nilson, N. (2009). Preface. In *The quest for artificial intelligence* (pp. xiii–xvi). Cambridge University Press. https://doi.org/10.1017/CBO9780511819346.001

Nirenburg, S., & Wilks, Y. (2000). Machine translation. In M. V. Zelkowitz (Ed.), *Advances in computers* (pp. 159–188). Elsevier. https://doi.org/10.1016/S0065-2458(00)80018-2

Noble, S. U. (2018). *Algorithms of oppression: How search engines reinforce racism*. NYU Press.

Norman, D. A., & Bobrow, D. G. (1979). Descriptions: An intermediate stage in memory retrieval. *Cognitive Psychology*, *11*(1), 107–123. https://doi.org/10.1016/0010-0285(79)90006-9

Oakley, B. (2014). *A mind for numbers: How to excel at math and science (even if you flunked algebra)*. Penguin.

OASIS. (2008). *XLIFF version 1.2. OASIS standard*. Retrieved December 16, 2022, from http://docs.oasis-open.org/xliff/v1.2/os/xliff-core.html

Okrent, A. (2019, June 12). Artificial languages. *Oxford Bibliographies*. www.oxfordbibliographies.com/view/document/obo-9780199772810/obo-9780199772810-0164.xml

Ortiz-Martínez, D., Leiva, L. A., Alabau, V. García-Varea, I., & Casacuberta, F. (2011). An interactive machine translation system with online learning. In *Proceedings of the ACL-HLT 2011 system demonstrations* (pp. 68–73). Association for Computational Linguistics. https://aclanthology.org/P11-4012.pdf

Ožbot, M. (2015). Translation studies – interdisciplinary, multidisciplinary or transdisciplinary? *Meta*, *60*(2), 360. https://id.erudit.org/iderudit/1032911ar

Pantiru, S., Jolley, S., & Barley, R. (2012). Strengths and limitations of a learner-centered approach to teaching research methods. *Student Engagement and Experience Journal*, *1*(3). https://journals.shu.ac.uk/index.php/seej/article/view/58/Pantiru

Papineni, K., Roukos, S., Ward, T., & Zhu, W. (2002). BLEU: A method for automatic evaluation of machine translation. In *Proceedings of the 40th annual meeting on Association for Computational Linguistics* (pp. 311–318). Association for Computational Linguistics. https://doi.org/10.3115/1073083.1073135

Paulik, M., Rao, S., Lane, I., Vogel, S., & Schultz, T. (2008). Sentence segmentation and punctuation recovery for spoken language translation. In *IEEE international conference on acoustics, speech and signal processing*. https://isl.anthropomatik.kit.edu/downloads/Sentence_Segmentation_and_Punctuation_Recovery_for_SLT.pdf

Pine, K. H., & Liboiron, M. (2015). The politics of measurement and action. In *CHI'15: Proceedings of the 33rd annual ACM conference on human factors in computing systems* (pp. 3147–3156). Association for Computing Machinery. https://doi.org/10.1145/2702123.2702298

Pinnis, M., Vasiļjevs, A., Kalnins, R., Rozis, R., Skadiņš, R., & Šics, V. (2018). Tilde MT platform for developing client specific MT solutions. In *Proceedings of the eleventh international conference on language resources and evaluation (LREC 2018)*. European Language Resources Association (ELRA). https://aclanthology.org/L18-1214.pdf

Pöchhacker, F. (2010). Interpreting studies. In Y. Gambier & L. Doorslaer (Eds.), *Handbook of translation studies* (vol. 1, pp. 158–172). John Benjamins.

Poncelas, A., Shterionov, D., Way, A., Wenniger, G. M., & Passban, P. (2018). Investigating back translation in neural machine translation. *CoRR*, abs/1804.06189, 10 pages. https://doi.org/10.48550/arXiv.1804.06189

Porter, M. (2006). The Porter stemming algorithm. *Tartarus*. Retrieve August 7, 2022, from https://tartarus.org/martin/PorterStemmer/

Psotka, J., Massey, L. D., & Mutter, S. A. (Eds.). (1988). *Intelligent tutoring systems: Lessons learned*. Lawrence Erlbaum Associates.

Pustejovsky, J., & Stubbs, A. (2012). *Natural language annotation for machine learning*. O'Reilly.

Pym, A. (2014). *Exploring translation theories*. Routledge.

Qi, P., Zhang, Y., Zhang, Y., Bolton, J., & Manning, C. D. (2020). Stanza: A Python natural language processing toolkit for many human languages. In *Proceedings of the 58th annual meeting of the Association for Computational Linguistics: System demonstrations* (pp. 101–108). Association for Computational Linguistics. https://aclanthology.org/2020.acl-demos.14

QuEst++. (2022, July 4). *GitHub*. Retrieved July 4, 2022, from https://github.com/ghpaetzold/questplusplus

Raya, R. M. (2005). XML in localisation: Reuse translations with TM and TMX. *Maxprograms*. www.maxprograms.com/articles/tmx.html#:~:text=Translation%20memory%20(TM)%20is%20a,aided%20translation%20(CAT)%20tools

Rich, J., Colon, A., Mines, D., & Jivers, K. (2014). Creating learner-centered assessment strategies for promoting greater student retention and class participation. *Frontiers in Psychology*, *5*(595). https://doi.org/10.3389/fpsyg.2014.00595

Robertson, S. (n.d.). NLP From scratch: Translation with a sequence to sequence network and attention – PyTorch Tutorials 1.12.0+cu102 documentation. *PyTorch*. Retrieved August 9, 2022, from https://pytorch.org/tutorials/intermediate/seq2seq_translation_tutorial.html

Rosenblatt, F. (1958). The perceptron: A probabilistic model for information storage and organization in the brain. *Psychological Review*, *65*(6), 386–408.

Rosetta Stone. (2022, July 17). *Wikipedia*. https://en.wikipedia.org/w/index.php?title=Rosetta_Stone&oldid=1098692277

Rowda, J. (2016, November 1). Inside eBay's translation machine. *Slator*. https://slator.com/features/inside-ebay-translation-machine/

Rowda, J. (2017, March 19). Polysemy in statistical machine translation – tips for linguists. *Medium*. https://medium.com/@rowda/polysemy-in-statistical-machine-translation-tips-for-linguists-f755680c6e9

Sahlgren, M. (2008). The distributional hypothesis. *Rivista di Linguistica*, *20*(1), 33–53.

Sahu, D. K., & Sukhwani, M. (2015). Sequence to sequence learning for optical character recognition. *CoRR*, abs/1511.04176, 9 pages. https://doi.org/10.48550/arXiv.1511.04176

Sambasivan, N., Kapania, S., Highfill, H., Akrong, P., & Aroyo, L. (2021). "Everyone wants to do the model work, not the data work": Data cascades in high-stakes AI. In *CHI'21: Proceedings of the 2021 CHI conference on human factors in computing systems* (pp. 1–15). Association for Computing Machinery. https://doi.org/10.1145/3411764.3445518

Samuel, A. L. (1959). Some studies in machine learning using the game of checkers. *IBM Journal of Research and Development*, *3*(3), 210–229.

Sánchez, J. L. B. (2018, August 8). Evaluation of MT quality/productivity at eBay – AMTA 2018 [PowerPoint Slides]. *Slideshare*. www.slideshare.net/tercio28/evaluation-of-mt-qualityproductivty-at-ebay-amta-2018

Saussure, F. D. (1966). *Course in general linguistics* (C. Bally, A. Sechehaye & A. Riedlinger, Eds., W. Baskin, Trans.). McGraw-Hill. (Original work published 1916).

Schäfer, R., Barbaresi, A., & Bildhauer, F. (2014). Focused web corpus crawling. In *Proceedings of the 9th web as corpus workshop (WaC-9)* (pp. 9–15). Association for Computational Linguistics. https://aclanthology.org/W14-0402/

Schnepp, J. C., Wolfe, R., & McDonald, J. (2010). Synthetic corpora: A synergy of linguistics and computer animation. In *Visual communications and technology education faculty publications* (vol. 15). Bowling Green State University. https://scholarworks.bgsu.edu/vcte_pub/15

Schrimpf, M., Blank, I. A., Tuckute, G., Kauf, C., Hosseini, E. A., Kanwisher, N., Tenenbaum, J. B., & Fedorenko, E. (2021). The neural architecture of language: Integrative modeling converges on predictive processing. *Proceedings of the National Academy of*

Sciences of the United States of America, *118*(45), e2105646118. https://doi.org/10.1073/pnas.2105646118

Schwartz, M. (2019). Lecture 6: Entropy [Lecture notes]. *Harvard*. Retrieved July 5, 2022, from https://scholar.harvard.edu/files/schwartz/files/6-entropy.pdf

Searle, J. (1980). Minds, brains and programs. *The Behavioral and Brain Sciences*, *3*, 417–457.

Seleskovitch, D. (1975). *Langues et memoire*. Lettres Modernes.

Seleskovitch, D., & Lederer, M. (1989). *Pédagogie raisonnée de l'interprétation*. Didier Erudition.

Sennrich, R. (2010). Bleualign: A MT-based sentence alignment tool. *GitHub*. Retrieved July 4, 2022, from https://github.com/rsennrich/Bleualign

Sennrich, R., & Volk, M. (2010). MT-based sentence alignment for OCR-generated parallel texts. In *Proceedings of the 9th conference of the association for machine translation in the Americas: Research papers*. Association for Machine Translation in the Americas. https://aclanthology.org/2010.amta-papers.14.pdf

Shannon, C. E., & Weaver, W. (1964). *The mathematical theory of communication*. University of Illinois Press.

Simon, H. A. (1995). Artificial intelligence: An empirical science. *Artificial Intelligence*, *77*(1), 95–127.

Simon-Vandenbergen, A. M., & Aijmer, K. (2007). *The semantic field of modal certainty: A corpus-based study of English adverbs*. Mouton de Gruyter.

Smilkov, D. (2016, December 7). Open sourcing the Embedding Projector: A tool for visualizing high dimensional data. *Google AI Blog*. Retrieved July 29, 2022, from https://ai.googleblog.com/2016/12/open-sourcing-embedding-projector-tool.html

Smith, N. A. (2019). Contextual word representations: A contextual introduction. *CoRR*, abs/1902.06006, 15 pages. https://doi.org/10.48550/arXiv.1902.06006

Snover, M., Dorr, B., Schwartz, R., Micciulla, L., & Makhoul, J. (2006). A study of translation edit rate with targeted human annotation. In *Proceedings of the 7th Conference of the Association for Machine Translation in the Americas: Technical Papers* (pp. 223–231). Association for Machine Translation in the Americas. https://aclanthology.org/2006.amta-papers.25/

Socher, R., Bauer, J., Manning, C. D., & Ng, A. N. (2013). Parsing with compositional vector grammars. In *Proceedings of the 51st annual meeting of the association for computational linguistics (Volume 1: Long papers)* (pp. 455–465). Association for Computational Linguistics. https://aclanthology.org/P13-1045/

Specia, L., Paetzold, G. H., & Scarton, C. (2015). Multi-level translation quality prediction with QuEst++. In *Proceedings of ACL-IJCNLP 2015 system demonstrations* (pp. 115–120). Association for Computational Linguistics and The Asian Federation of Natural Language Processing. https://aclanthology.org/P15-4020

Specia, L., Shah, K., Souza, J. G. C., & Cohn, T. (2013). QuEst – A translation quality estimation framework. In *Proceedings of the 51st annual meeting of the Association for Computational Linguistics: System demonstrations* (pp. 79–84). Association for Computational Linguistics. https://aclanthology.org/P13-4014

Specia, L., & Soricut, R. (2013). Quality estimation for machine translation: Preface. *Machine Translation*, *27*(3/4), 167–170. www.jstor.org/stable/42628813

Specia, L., Turchi, M., Cancedda, N., Cristianini, N., & Dymetman, M. (2009). Estimating the sentence-level quality of machine translation systems. In *Proceedings of the 13th annual conference of the European Association for Machine Translation* (pp. 28–35). European Association for Machine Translation. https://aclanthology.org/2009.eamt-1.5.pdf

Sperber, D., & Wilson, D. (1995). *Relevance: Communication and cognition* (2nd ed.). Basil Blackwell.

Stein, B. E., Stanford, T. R., & Rowland, B. A. (2009). The neural basis of multisensory integration in the midbrain: Its organization and maturation. *Hearing Research, 258*(1–2), 4–15. https://doi.org/10.1016/j.heares.2009.03.012

Stenetorp, P., Pyysalo, S., Topić, G., Ohta, T., Ananiadou, S., & Tsujii, J. (2012). BRAT: A web-based tool for NLP-assisted text annotation. In *Proceedings of the demonstrations at the 13th conference of the European chapter of the Association for Computational Linguistics* (pp. 102–107). Association for Computational Linguistics. https://aclanthology.org/E12-2021.pdf

Sulubacak, U., Caglayan, O., Grönroos, SA., Rouhe, A., Elliott, D., Specia, L., & Tiedemann, J. (2020). Multimodal machine translation through visuals and speech. *Machine Translation, 34*, 97–147. https://doi.org/10.1007/s10590-020-09250-0

SYSTRAN. (2016). *Pure neural machine translation – SYSTRAN White Paper.* www.systransoft.com/download/white-papers/systran-white-paper-PNMT-12-2016_2.pdf

Tan, C. (2018, February 15). Human-centered machine learning: A machine-in-the-loop approach. *Medium.* https://medium.com/@ChenhaoTan/human-centered-machine-learning-a-machine-in-the-loop-approach-ed024db34fe7

Tawalbeh, T. I., & AlAsmari, A. A. (2015). Instructors' perceptions and barriers of learner-centered instruction in English at the university level. *Higher Education Studies, 5*(2), 38–51. http://dx.doi.org/10.5539/hes.v5n2p38

Tensorflow. (2022, January 6). Visualizing data using the Embedding Projector in TensorBoard. *TensorFlow.* Retrieved July 29, 2022, from www.tensorflow.org/tensorboard/tensorboard_projector_plugin

Tiedemann, J. (2012). Parallel data, tools and interfaces in OPUS. In *Proceedings of the eighth international conference on Language Resources and Evaluation (LREC'12)* (pp. 2214–2218). European Language Resources Association. www.lrec-conf.org/proceedings/lrec2012/pdf/463_Paper.pdf

Tinsley, J. (2017, December 7). A report from the front line of NMT. *Multilingual.* https://multilingual.com/articles/a-report-from-the-front-line-of-nmt/

TMX Implementation Notes. (n.d.). *TTT.* Retrieved August 13, 2022, from www.ttt.org/oscarStandards/tmx/tmxnotes.htm

Tomozeiu, D., Koskinen, K., & D'Arcangelo, A. (2016). Teaching intercultural competence in translator training. *The Interpreter and Translator Trainer, 10*, 1–17.10.1080/1750399X.2016.1236557

Toury, G. (1995). *Descriptive translation studies and beyond.* John Benjamins.

Tuan, Y., El-Kishky, A., Renduchintala, A., Chaudhary, V., Guzmán, F., & Specia, L. (2021). Quality estimation without human-labeled data. In *Proceedings of the 16th conference of the European chapter of the Association for Computational Linguistics* (pp. 619–625). Association for Computational Linguistics. https://aclanthology.org/2021.eacl-main.50.pdf

Turing, A. M. (1950). Computing machinery and intelligence. *Mind, 59*(236), 433–460. https://doi.org/10.1093/mind/LIX.236.433

Universal dependencies. (n.d.). Retrieved June 14, 2022, from https://universaldependencies.org/

U.N. General Assembly. (2021). *Nature knows no borders: Transboundary cooperation – a key factor for biodiversity conservation, restoration and sustainable use* (75th session, A/RES/75/271). United Nations Digital Library. https://digitallibrary.un.org/record/3921758?ln=en

Valery, G., & Sene, J. (2020). Detection and localization of embedded subtitles in a video stream. In *Computational science and its applications – ICCSA 2020, 20th international conference* (pp. 119–128). Springer. https://dl.acm.org/doi/10.1007/978-3-030-58817-5_10#

Vapnik, V. (2000). *The nature of statistical learning theory*. Springer.

Vaswani, A., Shazeer, N., Parmar, N., Uszkoreit, J., Jones, L., Gomez, A. N., Kaiser, Ł., & Polosukhin, I. (2017). *Attention is all you need*. https://arxiv.org/abs/1706.03762

Vaswani, A., Shazeer, N., Parmar, N., Uszkoreit, J., Jones, L., Gomez, A. N., Kaiser, Ł., & Polosukhin, I. (2022, July 2). Position-wise feed-forward layer explained. *Papers with Code*. https://paperswithcode.com/method/position-wise-feed-forward-layer

Vauquois, B. (1968). A survey of formal grammars and algorithms for recognition and transformation in mechanical translation. In A. J. H. Morrel (Ed.), *IFIP congress (2)* (pp. 1114–1122). International Federation for Information Processing.

Vehicle E System Diagnostic Standards Committee. (2016, August 17). *Translation quality metric (STABILIZED Aug 2016) J2450_201608*. SAE International. Retrieved July 4, 2022, from https://www.sae.org/standards/content/j2450_201608/

Vinay, J. P., & Darbelnet, J. (1995). *Comparative stylistics of French and English: A methodology for translation*. John Benjamins.

W3C. (2020, March 21). *Main page: Synthetic media community group*. Retrieved July 18, 2022, from www.w3.org/community/synthetic-media/wiki/Main_Page

Wang, P. (2019). A relevancy approach to cultural competence in translation curricula. In D. B. Sawyer, F. Austermühl, & V. E. Raído (Eds.), *The evolving curriculum in interpreter and translator education: Stakeholder perspectives and voices* (pp. 271–299). John Benjamins.

Wang, P. (2021). On the role of machine learning in a human learning process. In *Teaching culturally and linguistically diverse international students in open and/or online learning environments: A research symposium* [Conference presentation]. University of Windsor. https://scholar.uwindsor.ca/cgi/viewcontent.cgi?article=1019&context=itos21

Webb, M. E., Fluck, A., Magenheim, J., Malyn-Smith, J., Waters, J., Deschenes, M., & Zagami, J. (2021). Machine learning for human learners: Opportunities, issues, tensions and threats. *Educational Technology Research and Development, 69*, 2109–2130. https://doi.org/10.1007/s11423-020-09858-2

Web Page Word Counter. (n.d.). *Word counter: Every word counts*. Retrieved July 18, 2022, from https://wordcounter.net/website-word-count

Weng, L. (2022, July 3). Multi-head attention explained. *Papers with Code*. https://paperswithcode.com/method/multi-head-attention

Williams, J., & Chesterman, A. (2002). *The map: A beginner's guide to doing research in translation studies*. Routledge.

Williams, T. A. (n.d.). Statistics. *Britannica*. Retrieved June 14, 2022, from www.britannica.com/science/statistics

Wilson, D., & Sperber, D. (1994). Outline of relevance theory. *Links & Letters, 1*, 85–106. https://raco.cat/index.php/LinksLetters/article/view/49815

Woolf, B. P. (2009). *Building intelligent interactive tutors: Student-centered strategies for revolutionizing e-learning*. Elsevier.

Word2vec. (2013, July 29). *Google Code archive*. https://code.google.com/archive/p/word2vec/

Word2vec Embeddings. (2022, May 6). *Gensim: Topic modeling for humans*. Retrieved June 13, 2022, from https://radimrehurek.com/gensim/models/word2vec.html

Wu, Y., Schuster, M., Chen, Z., Le, Q. V., Norouzi, M., Macherey, W., Krikun, M., Cao, Y., Gao, Q., Macherey, K., Klingner, J., Shah, A., Johnson, M., Liu, X., Kaiser, Ł., Gouws, S., Kato, Y., Kudo, T., Kazawa, H., Stevens, K., ... Dean, J. (2016). *Google's neural machine translation system: Bridging the gap between human and machine translation*. https://arxiv.org/pdf/1609.08144.pdf

Xing, Z., Pei, J., & Keogh, E. (2010). A brief survey on sequence classification. *ACM SIGKDD Explorations Newsletter, 12*(1), 40–48. https://doi.org/10.1145/1882471.1882478

Xu, H., van Genabith, J., Xiong, D., Liu, Q., & Zhang, J. (2020). Learning source phrase representations for neural machine translation. In *Proceedings of the 58th annual meeting of the Association for Computational Linguistics* (pp. 386–396). https://aclanthology.org/2020.acl-main.37.pdf

Yee, K., Dauphin, Y., & Auli, M. (2019). Simple and effective noisy channel modeling for neural machine translation. In *Proceedings of the 2019 conference on empirical methods in natural language processing and the 9th international joint conference on natural language processing (EMNLP-IJCNLP)* (pp. 5696–5701). Association for Computational Linguistics. https://aclanthology.org/D19-1571

Yeong, Y., Tan, T., & Gan, K. H. (2019). A hybrid of sentence-level approach and fragment-level approach of parallel text extraction from comparable text. *Procedia Computer Science, 161*, 406–414. https://doi.org/10.1016/j.procs.2019.11.139

Zanettin, F. (2012). *Translation-driven corpora: Corpus resources for descriptive and applied translation studies*. Routledge.

Zanettin, F. (2013). Corpus methods for descriptive translation studies. *Procedia – Social and Behavioral Sciences, 95*, 20–32. https://doi.org/10.1016/j.sbspro.2013.10.618

Zydron, A. (2009). XTM for language service providers. *TranslationDirectory.com*. www.translationdirectory.com/articles/article2034.php

INDEX

For Product Safety Concerns and Information please contact our EU
representative GPSR@taylorandfrancis.com
Taylor & Francis Verlag GmbH, Kaufingerstraße 24, 80331 München, Germany

www.ingramcontent.com/pod-product-compliance
Ingram Content Group UK Ltd.
Pitfield, Milton Keynes, MK11 3LW, UK
UKHW021453080625
459435UK00012B/485